T0168990

Dining with the Victorians

Dining with the Victorians

A Delicious History

Emma Kay

AMBERLEY

About the Author

Emma Kay is a historian and writer. Her previous book, *Dining with the Georgians* (2014), is also available from Amberley. She has worked as a museum professional for over fifteen years in major institutions such as the National Maritime Museum, the British Museum and the University of Bath. She has a degree in History, postgraduate certificate in Roman Archaeology, MA in Heritage Interpretation and a diploma in Cultural Heritage Management. She is a private collector of antique and vintage kitchenalia and writes and speaks about the history of cooking and dining to a variety of audiences. Emma founded the Museum of Kitchenalia in 2012 (www.museumofkitchenalia.co.uk). She lives in the Cotswolds with her husband and young son.

First published 2015
This edition published 2018

Amberley Publishing
The Hill, Stroud
Gloucestershire, GL5 4EP

www.amberley-books.com

Copyright © Emma Kay, 2015, 2018

The right of Emma Kay to be identified as the Author of this work has been asserted in accordance with the Copyrights, Designs and Patents Act 1988.

ISBN 978 1 4456 7721 7 (paperback)
ISBN 978 1 4456 4655 8 (ebook)

British Library Cataloguing in Publication Data. A catalogue record for this book is available from the British Library.

Typesetting and Origination by Amberley Publishing
Printed in the UK.

CONTENTS

ACKNOWLEDGEMENTS

Firstly I would like to say a big thank you to Antony Worrall Thompson and Simon Jenkins, two very talented men in the field of culinary excellence, who were gracious enough to endorse my last book. I consider myself very lucky that the wonderful Amberley Publishing invited me to write a second book, following on from *Dining with the Georgians*. To be honest I didn't think I had it in me, having a three-year-old still at home almost full-time and embarking on a big house move. But somehow despite all the odds I achieved it. Writing about cooking and food in the eighteenth century was challenging in terms of the resources available and I believe I unearthed a great deal of new research in this area.

When writing about Victorian history there is an abundance of information out there, almost too much, which made this book challenging in other ways.

I took heed of readers' suggestions following my first book, one of which was the desire for more recipes, so I have attempted to include a few interesting ones to accompany the themes of each chapter. As before, my amazing husband, who I am so thankful for, has created some wonderful images using my private collection of kitchenalia and I hope to be out and about in the next year promoting both my independent museum and my books that have been the inspiration from it.

This year marks the tenth anniversary of my mother's death and she has frequently been on my mind throughout the writing of this book. Not only did she manage to bring up three children, paint amazing works of art and photograph for leading magazines, all from home, but she also managed to produce the most incredible food, the memory of which continues to inspire some of my own dishes.

There remains in this country a strange underlying and unfounded criticism of women who choose to stay at home to bring up their children, while also working from home, but believe me it is the hardest thing in the world to do. I salute all those women and men out there who do it and are not recognised for their achievement.

Emma Kay
2015

PREFACE

I hope that the one thing both *Dining with the Georgians* and *Dining with the Victorians* have achieved is to highlight some of the wonderfully talented men and women who are, or were, working in the field of culinary arts in many forms, who have been denied recognition. Both the past and the present have influenced this book. It was important to me to draw attention to the fact that actually very little has changed in our current British society. Just as back then, we now have celebrity chefs, a mass-consumer market for literature on cooking, endless expos and large-scale food exhibitions, an obsession with French and Continental cuisine and a retail industry flooded with new food products and kitchenware designed to cook and prepare food. We also have an abundance of choice where restaurants, tea shops, cafes, public houses and independent artisan craftsmen are concerned. Britain is still even sharing the same debates about health and diet – in schools and on our shelves. All of this has been available to us for centuries, sometimes in different guises but always with the same purpose: to provide the public with good food. Food that is both high-end and affordable, food that inspires and food that delights. Long may it continue to do so.

INTRODUCTION

The pleasure of eating is one familiar to us all. What, how and why we consume what we do in Britain today has largely been shaped by our history, a fact that we all take for granted. My last book, *Dining with the Georgians*, explored the way Britain as a nation ate, drank, cooked and dined at a time when the country was ripe for change, innovation and a broadening of the cultural avant-garde. *Dining with the Victorians* considers the next stage of this culinary transformation in the context of class, society and the overall modernisation of Britain.

The golden age of the European Enlightenment transformed Britain's cultural and intellectual outlook. The Victorians were the first to truly implement these ideals of reason, rationality and individualism through industrial evolution and philanthropic social empathy. This is perhaps best illustrated by the great visionaries, artists and writers of the time. While the Brontë sisters and George Eliot provided both a romantic and realistic insight into the minds of contemporary female consciousness, Dickens exposed the underbelly of urban society, while Thomas Hardy revealed the harshness of Britain's declining rural communities, all while Oscar Wilde playfully exposed the more ridiculous nature of British aristocracy. Scientists such as Darwin changed the very fabric of human understanding, while William Morris legitimised the notions of a social utopia from a middle-class perspective. He, like the Pre-Raphaelite artists and poets of the age, reclaimed old English folklore, myths and legends and in many ways transformed Britain's aesthetic approach to design and architectural style. This was an age rich in transformation across every discipline of life.

From an everyday perspective following the famines and crop failures of the mid-nineteenth century, England's commercial and industrial progress changed the country forever. People flocked to the towns and cities, generating extreme overcrowding and public health systems on the threshold of crisis, with the wage of an urban labourer significantly higher than that of his rural neighbour. There were radical changes for the countryside as well. The chemistry of agriculture determined revolutionary new information in relation to how plants behaved in different types of soils, providing the necessary means with which to balance these differences. As a consequence, Britain's agricultural productivity improved considerably by the 1870s. Somewhat ironically though, free trade and the increasing reliability on cheaper imports from abroad eventually made the country's crop-growing and animal-rearing responsibilities less demanding.

Alongside cheaper imports Britain also adopted new ways of storing foodstuffs, such as drying, preserving and canning.

Robert Roberts lived as a child in turn-of-the-century Salford. A typical industrial city composed of individual communities, or 'villages', with their own different standards and social stratas. Roberts described the food situation in the city slums as basic. By 1904 luxury goods were still only available at middle-class grocery stores. Luxury foods afforded by the working classes were purchased solely for the benefit of the male head of the household, who needed protein-rich foods to work in physically demanding environments. These would be bought from corner shops and consisted of items such as corned beef, boiled mutton, cheese, bacon, eggs, saveloys, tripe, pig's trotters, sausage, cow heels, herrings, bloaters and kippers. Often 'parings', or a handful of tripe bits, provided a substitute to any of these items in times of financial difficulty. Similarly a dish called 'brewis' consisting of a strip of bread, covered in dripping and mixed up in boiling water made an excellent substitute meal for the labouring poor. Everything was cooked in a frying pan, which only added to the unhealthy nature of their diets. Roberts explained that the very poor never got into debt, as no one allowed them credit, so no money simply equated to no food.

Robert's 'village' neighbourhood consisted of a network of around thirty streets and alleyways, within which some 3,000 people resided. To the west of this district lived the middle classes, as Roberts emphasises, 'We knew them not.' This area, as many typically were at the time, was dominated by food and drink related businesses, including fifteen beerhouses, a hotel (which would have housed a cafe, grill or restaurant of some kind), two off-licences, nine grocery stores, three greengrocers, two tripe shops, two cook shops, one fish-and-chop shop and an array of colourful street-food hawkers.[1]

Much of the food that was bought and eaten by the poor and not so poor, including Robert's own family, was heavily adulterated. Bread contained alum, beer contained copperas (a poisonous, often fatal copper sulphate), capsicum was added to mustard, oatmeal was mixed with less superior barley-meal and even general refuse, and milk was frequently diluted with filthy water.

It was the German chemist Friedrich Accum who would alert the people of the world about the dangers of adulterating food. Accum was really a pioneer of the Georgian age, but his research would have the most profound impact on Victorian society. Living and working in Britain in the early part of the nineteenth century, Accum published the highly controversial and contentious *A Treatise on Adulterations of Food and Culinary Poisons* in 1820. He exposed the individual businesses who were adding other substances to their products to make them cheaper to produce. Almost every town bakery was using alum and the breweries were adding all number of chemicals to enhance wine and beer. Even cheesemakers came under scrutiny for using red lead to give Gloucestershire cheese its trademark colour, while cream was thickened with arrowroot and flour. Unsurprisingly, Accum became a wanted man. He had interfered with the big corporations and blatantly made allegations against tradesmen and manufacturers across the country. It is understood Accum was subsequently framed for a petty crime that he did not commit and, fearing the worst, fled England for his native Germany. By 1850 the *Lancet* had picked up where Accum had started his campaign and once again those accused of adulterating their products were exposed in a series of new revealing publications.

The satirical periodical, Punch picked the story up in 1851 writing:

Our contemporary the *Lancet* has conferred a great boon on the public by establishing a new order of constabulary, which may be called the Scientific Detective Police. The function of these detectives is to investigate and expose the fraudulent adulteration of articles of food practised by a set of scoundrels under the names of grocers and other tradesmen. In his researches into this rascality, the Lancet's policeman is assisted by a microscope, which, in throwing light on the fraud in question, exerts a power far superior to that of the common bull's eye. By the help of this instrument, an immense quantity of villainous stuff has been discovered in coffee, arrowroot, and other substances sold for nutriment, and some of them, 'particularly recommended to invalids'.

The Lancet seconds the exertions of its intelligent officer by spiritedly publishing the addresses of the rogues at whose swindling establishments the samples of rubbish were purchased. If any of the knaves thus pilloried in the Lancet, abetted by a disreputable attorney and a dishonest barrister, endeavour to avenge themselves through the technicalities of the law, Punch hopes they will meet with twelve true men in the jury-box who will scout both them and their legal accomplices out of court'.[2]

Punch's early consumer support is refreshing during an age where profit-making nearly always out-rivalled the underdog. As Friedrich Accum died in 1838, he would sadly not have witnessed the contribution his early valiant and enlightening research eventually made ensuring that proper regulations surrounding the manufacture of food and drink were implemented in Britain. By 1860, although flawed in its implementation, the first Food and Drink Act ensured the quality of food was analysed and monitored and by 1872 every county and borough in England had an analyst responsible for maintaining standards across all manufacturing.

While the Victorians continued to legislate, improve and innovate for a better society all within the confines of a strong work ethic, they also played hard. This was the era of the rise of leisure and recreation, from holiday clubs to music halls and museums. The population of the United Kingdom in 1899 was around 40,188,927, while the total population of the British Empire had reached 385,280,140.[3] This large and influential authority needed to continue to evolve and develop.

While many of the great bastions of Victorian leisure and entertainment still stand today as a homage to this era's potency, including the museums of South Kensington, theatres, pavilions, parks, music halls, spas and baths, and even department stores and supermarket chains nationwide, there are many leisure facilities that were either converted – their original use long expired, or destroyed during wartime. Many simply fell into decline and have been largely wiped out of popular social history. The Cyclorama of Niagara was one such building. Built in York Street, Westminster in 1888, it essentially housed a giant reproduction of Niagara Falls painted by the French artist Felix Philippoteaux. With a canvas four hundred feet long and fifty feet high the public flocked to see it at a shilling a head.[4] Over the course of a year some 750,000 visitors marvelled at this reproduction of one of the great wonders of the world. The Victorians, as with everything during this period, capitalised on the exhibit by building not only an accompanying American bazaar but an authentic themed American candy store, 'museum' restaurant, cafe and smoking lounge. Grills, restaurants, cafes and tea rooms could be found integrated into every aspect of Victorian leisure activity.[5]

Work days were shorter, seaside holidays were de rigueur, as were trips to the zoo, and cheap efficient new travel networks guaranteed a stress-free relaxing time for the hard workers of Britain. Some of the very lucky destitute city slum dwellers were enveloped by charities and given sojourns in rural environments to better their health, minds and bodies generally.

The Children's Country Holiday Fund, founded in 1884, was one such charity that sent some 20,000 young people out into the country annually. In addition, many factory owners paid for their workers to take brief excursions, which led to the traditional 'wakes week' and 'trades fortnight' holidays that continued in industrial regions right up until the middle of the twentieth century. Others simply saved money. One account taken from a participant in the *Old People's Reminiscences,* Lancashire Record Office, remembers himself being around thirteen years of age and working as a weaver. His family went on holiday to the north-west coast and stayed in lodgings costing half a crown a night. The accommodation was cheap as food was not included. Instead, the week before the family travelled was spent baking breads and 'fancy cakes', making enough food for seven days. This was all then carefully packed in a large oblong tin box and taken on the train.[6]

Britain was a confident land of opportunity and power, whose drive to influence and govern every other nation in its grip afforded it a false sense of imperious conceit.

The nineteenth century is perhaps best known for its divisions of rich and poor, the age of both austerity and philanthropy. Nowhere is this more noticeable than with the way in which food and diet contrasted across society. One resident of Walworth, London in 1886, a Mrs Ball, who had six children at home and a husband whose income was sporadic, would survive on a weekly diet of four pence worth of lean beef, onion and carrots, which she bulked out with 'Norfolk dumplings', that could supposedly serve around nine to ten people.[7]

During the early part of Queen Victoria's reign wages fell for the poorer rural classes, while the new aspiring middle classes were flourishing in the burgeoning cities. Farmhands and factory workers alike floundered the most, and food staples were both expensive and difficult to access.

We tend to associate London the most with the Victorian era of street urchins, mud larks, prostitutes and sellers of rotting meat and vegetables shrouded in an all purveying filth of industrial pollution, the stench of the Thames filling the lungs of the already diseased and weak poorer populations. We also harbour a stereotypical view of the north at this time, with its mills, bleak, dark moors, granite skylines, and hard labour in harsh, cold environments. Engels' description of an area of Bradford in 1844 does nothing to dispel these notions:

On week-days the town is enveloped in a grey cloud of coal smoke, but on a fine Sunday it offers a superb picture, when viewed from the surrounding heights. Yet within reigns the same filth and discomfort as in Leeds. The older portions of the town are built upon steep hillsides, and are narrow and irregular. In the lanes, alleys, and courts lie filth and debris in heaps; the houses are ruinous, dirty, and miserable, and in the immediate vicinity of the river and the valley bottom I found many a one, whose ground-floor, half-buried in the hillside, was totally abandoned. In general, the portions of the valley bottom in which working-men's cottages have crowded between the tall factories, are among the worst built and dirtiest districts of the whole town. In the newer portions of this, as of every other factory town, the cottages are more regular, being built in rows, but they share here, too, all the evils incident to the customary method of providing working-men's dwellings, evils of which we shall have occasions to speak more particularly in discussing Manchester.[8]

One can only imagine the delights of Manchester, hinted at here, over 150 years ago.

In stark contrast, for the wealthier, a typical Victorian urban house was either a compact, neat and stylish neoclassic terrace, or a newly built semi-detached property positioned in the suburbs. The dining room was often Gothic in style, with dark woods and wall hangings, family portraits, a long sideboard for serving dinners and a long heavy dining table with round or straight-back chairs. *The Gentleman's House: Or How to plan English Residences,* stipulates that a small dining room should never be less than sixteen feet wide. The width of the table should be between four and six feet, with twenty-four to thirty inches in length needing to be allocated as sitting spaces for each person. The sideboard should be positioned at one end of the room, at the back of the master's chair. In addition, caution must be taken to ensure the sideboard should never be flanked by windows, as this could make the servants more visible and also encourage a glare on any ceramics being displayed. A dining room door should be near to the sideboard and the route between dining room and kitchen must be short; unlike the Georgians, who preferred a good distance between the two to discourage the smell of food from permeating the activity of dining. Above all the servants' route must never collide with the route that family or guests use.[9]

In more well-to-do residences dinner would be announced to the family in advance, usually by the footman who would ring a bell, once about fifteen minutes before serving, and then again just prior to the arrival of the food. After the entrees, typically soup and/or fish, another bell would alert the kitchen staff that the first course, generally consisting of joints of meat, needed to be sent up, and so on course after course, with further bells rung after dinner to announce coffee, cakes and other sweet and savoury bread products.[10] With all that exposure to excessive bell ringing going on meal after meal, it's a wonder that more Victorians didn't suffer from tinnitus.

According to the Census returns of 1891, migrants resident in the UK totalled 219,523, almost double the number recorded in 1881.[11]

Victorian Britain was indeed a melting pot of different cultures. The great naval fraternity of the century before left Britain's town and city ports thriving with pockets of new communities struggling to earn a living, while maintaining their own cultural identities and contributing to British society in a way that has since shaped the multi-diverse diet of an entire nation.

The French continued to dominate British kitchens – both domestic and commercial, while Italian ice cream vendors and confectioners maintained their empires and secured their places in society. The Germans inspired our bakeries and made the traditional sausage and bacon breakfast. This was the new culinary alternative to the cold meats, bread and cheese of the century before.

Just as easily as those entered and remained in Britain, so too did they leave. In the nineteenth century convicts could find themselves assigned to an employer while serving their term under a 'ticket of leave'. These employers were legally bound to provide them with certain clothing and food rations including meat, flour, salt and sometimes tea and sugar.[12]

Domestic travel and tourism with the growth in network rail systems and the age of the great liner travel opened up new opportunities for the wealthier classes to experience both European and wider world choices.

Then of course there was the Empire, which took whole families overseas to work and live in far-reaching nations such as India, Africa, China, Australia and New Zealand. The culinary influences were two-way, and just as Britain brought back new foods and recipes, Anglo-English cuisine is still visible across the globe today from roast beef, to fish and chips, rissoles, soup and hybrid dishes like kedgeree.

Wider travel, greater freedom of expression and a fascination for keeping diaries meant that people wrote prolifically in the nineteenth century in the form of letters, journals, social commentary and social observations. There were also countless guides, handbooks and manuals instructing on the benefits of dining – frugally, for health, to improve morals and behaviour and so on. Much can be gleaned from this literature about what people ate and where they ate it.

We learn from the letters of Thomas Carlyle that in Annandale, Scotland, in 1848 there were no potato harvests that year and as a consequence 'Indian meal' – a grain-based food, usually only consumed in the direst of circumstances – was used as a substitute. Britain was relying more and more on foreign imports to counteract the European famine years of the mid-1840s and early 1850s, most notably impacting on Ireland.

Carlyle mentions that the Indian meal he ate had a bitter taste with the quality of sawdust and was best prepared by making it into a 'porridge', tying it in a linen cloth and then boiling it for several hours. Despite its cheapness and availability at around one penny for a pound, the poorer labouring population of Scotland would not eat it and Indian meal became more of a substitute for the middling classes.[13]

The problem with making Indian meal popular was largely a consequence of ignorance over how to cook it. If not cooked thoroughly, the maize-like meal could cause terrible internal intestinal pain, and after years of trial and error, by the 1860s it became one of the main staple diets across some of the larger counties in Ireland.

In his English Notebooks, Nathaniel Hawthorne recollects a visit to Coventry, which architecturally is extremely valuable in building up a picture of this town, lost almost in its entirety during the Second World War. Hawthorne notes that his party visits the Red Lion for 'a luncheon of cold lamb and cold pigeon-pie. This is the best way of dining at English hotels, – to call the meal a luncheon, in which case you will get as good or better a variety than if it were a dinner, and at less than half the cost'. During a visit to Newby Bridge Hawthorne again describes the Inn where he stayed as 'an old-fashioned inn, where the landlord and his people have a simple and friendly way of dealing with their guests, and yet provide them with all sorts of facilities for being comfortable? They load our supper and breakfast tables with trout, cold beef, ham, toast, and muffins; and give us three fair courses for dinner, and excellent wine, the cost of all which remains to be seen'.[14]

Writing as an adult and recalling her life as it transcended the Victorian and Edwardian periods, Pat Barr is among many biographers of the 1950s and 1960s who left their legacies in print, recalling reminiscences of childhood, working in domestic service or factories. All of these provide an excellent insight into first-hand late nineteenth- and early twentieth-century social history. Growing up in the village of Davenham in rural Cheshire, Pat described that: 'The shops supplied almost all our wants. The public bakehouses baked for the people who made their own bread, the butcher killed his own meat and also killed the pigs for the cottagers, for almost every cottage had a sty and kept pigs. The shoe-shop sold, made and mended boots and shoes ... Davenham was fortunate in having so many craftsmen of one kind and another.'[15]

Barr's recollection of the local bake house is elaborated on by a Mrs Layton from Bethnal Green, London, who wrote that the baker at the corner of her street conducted the best of their business on a Sunday – the day when most people were able to get some sort of meat together for their Sunday dinner. Layton confirms that no one in her neighbourhood had a stove, so meat, potatoes and some pudding were put into one dish, taken to the bake house for cooking and then collected after church. It was reputed that the baker would steal a small amount from each dish to provide for his own family's dinner and people frequently complained about him. Layton also recalls how one Christmas there was a family in the neighbourhood that had no dinner to take to the bake house and instead were reduced to sitting down to a less than festive feast of a single piece of bread and one pound of sprats.[16]

Even the very poor communities in Britain today would struggle not to find something a little more fulfilling than sprats and a piece of bread for their Christmas dinner. In a society that relies increasingly on credit and the availability of twenty-four hour, seven-day-a-week shopping, even the very unfortunate, who are provided with state benefits could thankfully not contemplate the woes of the depravation that prevailed throughout nineteenth-century cities, towns and villages. Few people are likely to die of starvation in Britain today, whereas less than a hundred and fifty years ago it was a reality for many.

While the words 'restaurant' and 'menu' had crept into dining culture during the Victorian period, it was still more typical to use language such as 'Restroom' and 'Bill of fare'. 'Grill rooms' replaced the Georgian 'chop house'.

Different types of eating houses opened to suit different tastes. There were restaurants for women only, temperance bars and cafes just serving tea, coffee and cocoa, and vegetarian restaurants were becoming extremely popular. The novelist George Bernard

Shaw was a vegetarian and listed the restaurants that catered specifically to meat-free diets in London in his diaries. These included The Porridge Bowl in Holborn, Orange Grove in St Martin's Lane, the Pine Apple in Oxford Circus, Central Restaurant in Farringdon Street, The Wheatsheaf in Rathbone Place and many others.

The nineteenth century was also one epitomised by the institution; whether school, workhouse, prison, or hospital, the food that made its way into these places and influenced public diet – mostly for the worse – all plays a significant role in Britain's culinary heritage.

Prior to the 1834 Poor Law Amendment Act diets in institutions were perhaps somewhat surprisingly more favourable, as Commissioners highlighted the need for greater economy. Expenditure on poverty needed to be reduced. There followed a series of ridiculous public arguments linking overfeeding to disease, as a means of justifying drastic cuts in food rations. A London workhouse in 1832, prior to the changes, demonstrates a reasonably good and varied diet for its inmates:

Sunday	7 oz boiled beef/mutton, with vegetables. 1 pint broth, 13 oz bread and 2 pints of beer
Monday	1 pint milk pottage, 3 oz butter, 3 oz cheese, 13 oz bread, 2 pints of beer
Tuesday	7 oz boiled beef/mutton with vegetables, 1 pint broth, 13 oz bread and 2 pints of beer
Wednesday	1 pint Pease soup, 13 oz bread, 2 pints of beer
Thursday	7 oz boiled beef/mutton with vegetables, 1 pint broth, 13oz bread and 2 pints of beer
Friday	3 oz butter, 3oz cheeses, 1 pint rice milk, 13 oz bread, and 2 pints of beer
Saturday	1 pint milk, pottage, 12 oz suet pudding,13 oz bread and 2 pints of beer

Six years after the amended act, Charles Dickens illustrated in *Oliver Twist* the extent to which meals had been radically limited across workhouses.

> The room, in which the boys were fed, was a large stone hall, with a copper at one end: out of which the master ... ladled the gruel at mealtimes. Of this festive composition each boy had one porringer, and no more – except on occasions of great public rejoicing, when he had two ounces and a quarter of bread besides. The bowls never wanted washing. The boys polished them with their spoons till they shone again; and when they had performed this operation (which never took very long, the spoons being nearly as large as the bowls), they would sit staring at the copper, with such eager eyes, as if they could have devoured the very bricks of which it was composed; employing themselves, meanwhile, in sucking their fingers most assiduously, with the view of catching up any stray splashes of gruel that might have been cast thereon. Boys have generally excellent appetites. Oliver Twist and his companions suffered the tortures of slow starvation for three months.[17]

A somewhat rosier picture of an institutional mealtime for young boys is presented in Thomas Hughes' autobiographical account of his experiences spent at public school in Rugby. Served at a quarter past one, Tom sits down to his first lunch, which he describes while observing the boys and the activities of the dining room:

> ...loitering over the fire at the pastry cook's dainty mortals bringing with them pickles and sauce bottles to help them with their dinners. And a great big bearded man whom Tom took for a master began calling over the names while the great joints were being rapidly carved on a third table in the corner by the old verger and the housekeeper. Tom's turn came last and meanwhile he was all eyes looking first with awe at the great man who sat close to him and

was helped first and who read a hard looking book all the time he was eating and when he got up and walked off to the fire at the small boys round him some of whom were reading and the rest talking in whispers to one another or stealing one another's bread or shooting pellets or digging their forks through the tablecloth. However notwithstanding his curiosity he managed to make a capital dinner by the time the big man called Stand up and said grace.[18]

By 1891 school was both compulsory and free for all children aged five to thirteen, but grant-in-aid was provided to some schools as early as 1833 and fees were still being issued for compulsory education from 1880. Most children of the middle classes attended school at least up to the age of ten from the 1840s, with boys generally receiving the best learning provision at grammar or boarding schools.

Many working class districts established the Ragged School system, which were charitable organisations offering free education to the poorest, most destitute children.

While offering a crucial service to the wider public, many families abused the Ragged School system, as they viewed it as a place where children could be fed and maintained, thus relieving them of their childcare responsibilities. Even the parents who could afford to send their children to the fee-paying schools were substituting their income by submitting them into the Ragged Schools and abusing the state system.[19]

Alongside charitable pioneers like William Booth, who set up Farthing breakfasts for hungry children either going to school or work in the morning, the Destitute Children's Dinner Society successfully opened fifty-eight dining rooms across London by 1870, providing hot meals in the winter. Apparently, the dinner was an Irish stew made with beef and mutton, potatoes, barley or rice and onions. In addition, each child received a piece of bread with their meal. In other parts of the country, Sir Henry Peek, a wealthy baronet and tea importer, established school meals for children across parts of Devon, as did the Reverend W. Moore Ede in Tyneside. Peek's school dinner experiment at a cost of one penny a meal proved to be particularly successful. His objective was to demonstrate the correlation between education and food and by many accounts the children were healthier, both visibly and physically, for the benefit of just one hot midday meal.[20]

There was a general understanding as the nineteenth century progressed that the correlation between poverty and food, in particular knowledge relating to healthy diets and economical cooking techniques, was one that was intensifying the ongoing issue of the poor.

As with the century before there was a huge commercial market for cookery books and recipe writing that focussed both on the economies of cooking, training the novice and advising the experienced cook. As a national training syllabus was rolled out throughout Britain, both in schools and for the wider female public, the art and science of cooking was present everywhere, from the media to book shops, training schools and educational institutions. Well-meaning guides for the poor (regardless of whether they could read them), technical manuals, richly illustrated publications demonstrating high-end French cuisine, and handbooks for 'plain' domestic cooks and housekeepers were available for all levels of skill and understanding.

By 1900 the London School Board secured a many as 168 cookery centres, run by trained teachers who had learnt their trade from attending the national training colleges that had been established some twenty years earlier. The School Board cookery centres operated collaboratively with schools to teach female pupils aged between approximately ten and fourteen.

Initially these classes were met with considerable resentment by some parents in labouring families. Many felt the lessons unnecessary, as their daughters could learn the skills at home, and detrimental to the family generally by taking an often important member of the family away from her roles and responsibilities at home and work.[21]

The National Training School for Cookery was founded in 1874 and at around the same time the Glasgow School of Cookery, which merged with the West End School of Cookery in Glasgow, opened. They represented the UK's major teacher training colleges at the time, with the overall objective to instruct cookery across schools in Britain. Certificates, diplomas and teaching licences were issued following whichever course students undertook. The minimum requirements to teach were twenty hours a week over six months. Many training schools followed in their wake, but the *Handbook of the National Training School for Cookery* outlines the definitive lesson plans, tips on food preparation and kitchen utensils required. Chapter Three discusses the re-cooking of meat, with the fifth lesson providing the framework for a basic Shepherd's Pie:

Ingredients
Scraps of cold meat. One small onion. Pepper and salt. One and a half pound of potatoes. One ounce of butter. One-half a gill of milk.

Time required
About an hour and a half.

To make 'Shepherd's Pie'

1. Take one and a half pound of potatoes, wash them and boil them as described (see 'Vegetables,' Lesson No.1).

N. B. – This quantity of potato will cover a quart pie-dish.
N. B. – Any remains of cold potatoes should be used, instead of boiling fresh ones.

2. Put one ounce of butter and half a gill of milk into a saucepan, and put it on the fire to boil.

3. Put the boiled potatoes into another saucepan, and mash them up with a fork or spoon.

4. When the milk boils, pour it into the mashed potatoes and stir them into a smooth paste.

5. Put the saucepan on the fire, and let the potatoes just boil. Be careful they do not burn.

6. Take any scarps of cold meat, cut them in small pieces, and put them in a pie dish in layers.

7. If there is not much fat with the meat, mix with it a few slices of pork-fat.

8. Take one small onion, peel it, and chop it up as finely as possible on a board.

9. Sprinkle each layer of meat with plenty of pepper and salt, and a little of the chopped onion.

10. Fill the dish half full of cold water.

N. B. – If there is any cold gravy, it would, of course, be better than the water.

N. B. – The pie-dish should be quite full of meat, and rather heaped in the centre, so as to raise the crust of potato.

11. Take the mashed potato and put it over the top of the meat, smoothing it over neatly with a knife.

12. Take a fork, and mark all over the top of the potato.

N. B. – If liked, the mashed potato might be mixed with half its weight of flour into dough, to make a more substantial crust; it must then be rolled out with a rolling-pin like pastry.

13. Put the pie dish into the oven, or into a tin oven in front of the fire, for half an hour, to brown the crust of potato and warm the meat through.

What is most captivating about this handbook and the recipes within, is the notion that these are the very recipes Britain's great-grandmothers, grandmothers, and all other female relatives before would have learnt from. This is essentially what and how modernising Britain learnt to cook and how mainstream society was instructed in cooking. Many of the recipes contained in the National Training School for Cookery handbook are ones that are familiar today because they are what generations learnt in the kitchen from their fore-mothers. This is what defines it as an extremely valuable and important historical work. Other notable recipes on the list of those considered most important to master in the kitchen include rice pudding, bread pudding, treacle sponge pudding, suet pudding, Yorkshire puddings, dumplings, vanilla ice cream, rock cakes, ginger nuts, scones, tea cakes, shortbread, Mulligatawny soup, Irish stew, sausage rolls, rissoles and many more. To me, these are the recipes remembered from childhood, the type of quintessentially national British dishes that have sustained themselves over the centuries.[22]

For much of the Victorian age food, cooking and dining remained as it had the century before, with the exception that it was more prolific, commercialised, and later, mass-produced.

By the beginning of the twentieth century Britain was recovering from its impoverished, diseased and dispassionate past. There were systems in place to educate and inform the public about food, diet and cooking – both theoretical and practical. Science and technology was changing the way people cooked and ate and the division between rural and urban was widening considerably, as a consequence of developments in transport networks, new industry and modernisation. Much like today the demand and market for kitchen utensils, recipe books and luxury products was significant. Breakfast, lunch(eon) and dinner were the three meals of the day, rather than the snack breakfast, dinner and supper of the late Georgian through to the early Victorian era. Afternoon tea was also taken with greater frequency. Women were beginning to take more control of their own households and domestic staff were diminishing. Despite poverty still being entrenched in society, the ignorance that went with it was improving. In general women were changing, empowering themselves. They no longer hid in the shadows or at home. They dined out, took tea un-chaperoned, educated themselves, started jobs and built careers. One of the few areas in government that women had any influence was with the national curriculum and syllabus for cooking and domestic science. The great food exhibitions, demonstrations, cookery schools, culinary innovation and lectures of the late Victorian era were retained and became more competitive. Public dining was as important socially as dinner parties at home. The restaurant of the late Victorian era remained traditionally French. Auguste Escoffier like so many before him in Britain, including Ude, Francatelli, Kitchiner and Soyer to name a few, became the celebrity chef of the ensuing century who took advantage of the fashion for public dining, post-theatre suppers and the demand for the grand opulence of the modern dining room.

So much of our own culinary culture today reflects that of the Victorians. Dining out is as popular a pastime as ever, with our leisure time governed tremendously by what cafe we might visit as part of the day's activities. Rather than referring to the press, guides or published reviews as so many of the middle and higher classes did in the nineteenth century to establish which were the most fashionable dishes to try, or the smartest, most talked about restaurant, we look to their twenty-first century equivalents. Social media and websites like TripAdvisor can inform us immediately as to whether somewhere is worth visiting; what the food tastes like, what range of wines they have, whether they are child friendly (not something the Victorians concerned themselves with),whether the staff are rude or the location salubrious. Britain is obsessed with its food culture and celebrity chef status, on television and radio, through recipe books and numerous nationwide courses promising to make us all artisan bakers and traditional cheese makers in our spare time. It spends millions each year on staging large-scale food expositions to gain even more millions back in revenue and spin-off merchandise. I myself am guilty of these things. But they are not new trends. They have been with us for centuries. Keep reading and you will find out why.

As mentioned in the preface to this book, it has been my intention while writing Dining with the Victorians to include a selection of recipes that reflect the themes of each chapter.

Irish stew was what would have been termed a 'family favourite' in the nineteenth century, for both its heartiness and economy. It is included in the original Handbook of the National Training School for Cookery as a staple recipe to be learnt by all. Irish stew was also one of the dishes The Destitute Children's Dinner Society served up to its most needy and vulnerable children.

The following recipe is taken from The Magazine of Domestic Economy, 1837, citing it as an excellent dish described as homely and one that suits the palates of everyone.

Recipes

Irish Stew

Any kind of cold meat will make Irish stew, but mutton, either roast or boiled, and any joint (especially the saddle) will be most desirable. Cut it in slices, then pepper salt and flour it. Peel an onion, put it with the bones (and any gravy that may be left in the house) into a saucepan with a pint of water, and a little salt; set it on the fire to stew for about an hour .When the potatoes are ready for dinner – for who dines without potatoes? – mash or crush about half of them; which add to the water and onion then put in the meat, and let the whole stew very gently for five or ten minutes, and it will be ready for table. Those who prefer the additions of anchovies, mushrooms, ketchups, spices, frying the meat first in butter &c &c. can so prepare it; we give the simple plan, as more wholesome, and in accordance with our own taste. When children are to partake of the dish it is obvious which of the two methods is preferable.[23]

Norfolk Dumplings

The writer of the book containing the following recipe considered any type of pudding that was 'hasty', which tended to be quickly prepared flour-based puddings – to be 'unsuitable for many stomachs'. Norfolk puddings were a favourite among the poor, as they would have been quick, economical and filling which is why Mrs Ball living in London in 1886 cooked them for her family. They would also have contained very little nutritional value.

Make half a pint of milk, two eggs well beaten and a little salt into a thick batter with flour, drop them into boiling water and let them boil two or three minutes. Drain them and serve them up with a lump of fresh butter stirred among them. Note this is another of those hasty dishes which we cannot approve.[24]

I

REGENCY TO REGINA

One of the best descriptions of Britain's transition from Georgian excess, expansion and industrialisation to the great Victorian infrastructures and reforms, is neatly outlined in an extract from Virginia Woolf's *Orlando*. Written in 1928 it offers a slightly satirical comparison between the cultural shift from eighteenth to nineteenth-century cultures:

The hardy country gentleman, who had sat down gladly to a meal of ale and beef in a room designed, perhaps, by the brothers Adam, with classic dignity, now felt chilly. Rugs appeared; beards were grown; trousers were fastened tight under the instep. The chill which he felt in his legs the country gentleman son transferred to his house; furniture was muffled; walls and tables were covered; nothing was left bare. Then a change of diet became essential. The muffin was invented and the crumpet. Coffee supplanted the after-dinner port, and, as coffee led to a drawing-room in which to drink it, and a drawing-room to glass cases, and glass cases to artificial flowers, and artificial flowers to mantelpieces, and mantelpieces to pianofortes, and pianofortes to drawing-room ballads, and drawing-room ballads (skipping a stage or two) to innumerable

little dogs, mats, and china ornaments, the home – which had
become extremely important – was completely altered.[1]

The earnest Victorians characterised their grandparents as immoral,
corrupt and greedy, although we understand now the enormous
wealth of knowledge and innovation the Georgians contributed,
despite the economic and political turmoil of this era.

The food riots that dominated the eighteenth century were far
less frequent in the nineteenth. The germ theory and sanitation
reform seeds that were planted in the Georgian age had come to
fruition by the mid-nineteenth century, stimulating a fall in the
death rate and a significant rise in life expectancy at birth.

Just as the eighteenth-century national diet was dependant on
geographical location, with more fresh produce and greater choice
of food available in the towns and cities, the early Victorians
also suffered a similar pattern of the choice and availability of
provisions, despite the burgeoning industrial networks. More
starchy bread, potatoes, meat and milk products were consumed
rurally. However food prices decreased and wages rose, largely
due to England's thriving import market, including cheap wheat
from the Atlantic, frozen beef and mutton from Australia, pork
from the USA, beef from Argentina and lamb from New Zealand.

It is interesting to compare this to the age that we now live
in, where the desire to harken back to an old England is driving
so many out of the cities and into the countryside. Never more
was the desire to start a small enclosure, rear animals and grow
your own produce so appealing. Yet, in the nineteenth century as
towns and cities continued to grow through mechanisation and
industrialisation, agriculture began its slow but consistent decline.
Britain began importing its raw materials on a large scale. In 1850,
agriculture amounted to over 20 per cent of the total national
income. This had declined to just 6.5 per cent by the time Queen
Victoria died.[2]

Rural life was proving just as hard in the nineteenth century as it had in the century before, in comparison to the conveniences afforded to town and city living. Eating was seasonal, with fruits still preserved year-round, relentless baking butter and cheese-making remained labour-intensive as these accounts from rural servants confirm. The women would 'bake forty "standing pies" together once or twice a week; these were made of meat in winter, fat mutton being commonly used, and fruit in summer. Eight stone of flour and one stone of bacon would be used, and a sheep killed every week'.

As for the hard physical dairy work:

> I have heard of a girl ... who had to help in the milking of nearly twenty cows daily. The cows would assemble on the back 'causer' in a ring; they would not be tied, for without the least trouble each would go to its accustomed place. It was reckoned rather a feat to milk these cows in an hour, but Jane was 'a rare strapping lass' ... Then came the dairy work, 'siling' the milk, churning and what-not.[3]

Even for those living in the new towns and cities, many upper-working-class families had a garden attached to the house, often owned and leased out by the church. As a consequence everyone kept pigs, chickens or ducks. All three if you were lucky. Sometimes dairymen would keep sheds on this land for milking cows, although few people were able to afford milk in large quantities.[4] The smell, one imagines, must have been horrendous, let alone the sanitation and exposure to disease, particularly smallpox. This practice contrasts with the social researcher Sir Frederick Morton Eden's observations a hundred years before, stating,

> It is not to be expected that milk should ever form a considerable part of the diet of labourers in the South of England, until the practise of keeping cows becomes more general among cottagers than it is

at present ... In the vicinity of large towns the value of grass land is much too high to enable labourers to rent it to advantage.[5]

Nonetheless the dark agricultural ways of living in the eighteenth century were in stark contrast to modern-built environments of the Victorian age, with some twenty-three-plus new cities emerging in Britain by the end of the era. However, as with the Georgian transition from medieval crudity, the evolution of the modern society as we know it now still relied on the old ways of working with and utilising nature, as well as defending traditions and maintaining superstitious beliefs.

Many Victorians had an inexplicable obsession with mysticism from the occult, life after death, magic and a firm irrational belief that if they did not adhere to carrying out simple tasks or acts of daily life in a certain way that the consequences could be fatal. We have all seen those dodgy early images of Victorian séances with 'ectoplasm' oozing from participants apparently communicating with the dead and bloodthirstily read the accounts of grave-robbing and anatomy murders conducted to better understand the human body. Despite significant breakthroughs in medicine and scientific understanding, the Victorian reliance on herbal poultices and blood-letting with leeches, among other eccentric practices, enhances their appeal as a society still transcending from a once primitive world.

In relation to food and cooking these superstitions were plentiful. Butter-making was still linked to old folklore advocating its healing properties, particularly where scalds and burns were concerned. In fact, grandmothers and even mothers of our own generation have been heard to champion the benefits of slathering a burn immediately in butter. In some counties such as Lincolnshire salt was also thrown into the fire as a portent for producing a good batch prior to the churning, while Lancashire considered the insertion of a hot iron into the cream as a means of expelling the witch believed to reside within.[6] Eggs had all manner of superstitions attached to them. One – of which I am guilty of myself; and is considered Irish in origin – is to ensure the shell is crushed after eating it boiled and my favourite utterly irrational one includes avoiding bringing eggs into or taking eggs out of the house after dark, both of which can prompt bad luck. And who hasn't at some time thrown or been tempted to throw salt over their left shoulder to ward off the evil spirits residing on the left-hand side of the body. There were also countless superstitions involving both the cooking and preparation of meat. The Victorians adhered to the notion that if meat shrank when being boiled it was unlucky, whereas if it swelled this indicated prosperity. Similarly meat was used to shrink warts. It needed to be rubbed on the area and then hidden to decay, thus allowing the wart to also shrink and dry up in correspondence to the meat.[7]

Women's biological functions were a fascination for the Victorians. Combined with superstition, as a woman you could often find yourself the target of many unfortunate incidents should you happen to be on your period. It was recommended that women employed in kitchens not to be given the responsibility of curing meat with salt while menstruating, as it was thought to affect the salt's ability to preserve.[8]

Other cooking superstitions included avoiding turning a lump of coal on the fire when poking it, as death or poverty was likely to ensue if you did. Neither should wood be burnt from an old tree, which naturally resulted in instant death.[9]

The moon and lunar activity was still considered central to daily activities. As late as 1938 in Herefordshire women were encouraged to sit astride a gate and welcome the new moon with the words. 'A fine moon. God bless her.' And it would never do to slaughter a pig for the pot in the wane of the moon, as the meat would spoil in cooking.[10]

In Yorkshire at the turn of the twentieth century, many women still baked their own bread at home. Those wondering why a cross is sometimes indented in the dough before baking can rest assured that this was to ensure the witch within could be 'let out', a practice which continued into the mid-twentieth century. And perhaps still does in some parts of Yorkshire. In Scotland, bread bakers maintained that the yeast must be added within an hour of sunrise or the bread would not be light enough.[11]

For all their strange, quirky and endearing irrationality, superstitions can also be dangerous in their ignorance and influence to wrongly label people or incite mass hysteria. The Salem Witch Trials is perhaps one of the best known examples of this.

Food has always traditionally played a role in contributing to sinister practices if need be. This was certainly the case in a crime recorded in Lincolnshire in 1867. Mrs Smith, a farmer's wife, reported a five pound note missing from her work box and in the presence of her cook, Sarah Digby, announced to a neighbour that she planned to visit a 'wise woman' in Peterborough who it was heard told could reveal the faces of criminals in a looking-glass. That night Mrs Smith fell ill following a bowl of broth cooked by Digby. She was then given some tea later that same evening and instructed by her cook to stir it well. The tea made her sickness worse and a doctor was called who diagnosed poisoning. On examining the tea cup it was discovered enough 'Blade's Vermin Powder' had been added to kill up to six adults. So it was lucky indeed that Mrs Smith neglected to follow the instructions of her cook to stir it up. Obviously it emerged that the young cook, having stolen her employer's five pound note, had believed that the visit to the 'wise woman' would reveal her identity and she therefore set out to kill her mistress before her crime was exposed.[12]

Perhaps one of the most curious, less-documented and certainly macabre superstitions which continued to survive into the nineteenth century in places like the east of England in particular, was the practice of sin-eating. This involved paying someone to literally eat food over the coffins of dead people. When a person died, the local sin-eater was given notice to perform this ritual, pawning his own soul to free that of the departed. One testimony from 1852 notes:

> The food, bread, salt, cheese and drink, beer, milk, sometimes wine are either placed on the chest of the corpse or offered the sin-eater across the corpse. He eats and drinks the gift, chants, declares deceased to be without sin, gets paid and leaves – for the sin eater it is dangerous to remain where he is, because the other mourners are scared of him and might attack him. All the dead person's sins are supposed to be upon the sin-eater, which makes him a person to be feared.[13]

Superstitions also focussed indirectly on society as a whole. There were countless theories relating to how the issue of the poor should be managed. As with the century before, the press had a tremendous preoccupation for putting the situation to rights, with letters from the public, articles and advertisements all offering solutions many of which involved superstitious ideas. Some were more ridiculous than others, ranging from criticisms about substituting fish as the main staple diet for the poor, based on the notion that fish creates skin infections and eventually leprosy, to the idea that the poor should be fed solely on 'Savoury rice'. We're not talking the famed Bachelor's product here. The nineteenth-century recipe consisted of half a pound of rice being boiled in an ounce of pig's fat, which supposedly had the potential to provide people with all the nutrients they required in one dish.[14]

Although many aspects of the old world were retained in Victorian culture, they were of course great innovators in science, medicine, industry and technology. And the Georgian desire to gorge and feast on its own excesses made way for a new attitude towards food and dining in the nineteenth century which governed the way they ate both publically and at home. Contrary to the fifteen-plus courses prepared during Georgian meal times, Queen

Victoria – perhaps inspired by her one time chief cook Charles Francatelli – made famous the two- or three-course meal served in the *à la russe* style, with courses served in sequence one at a time. This was in contrast to the old French style of eating made popular by the Georgians which involved bringing all the food out at once. This had previously encouraged beautifully displayed tables with many dishes, centre-pieces and elaborate decorative meals. Although stunning, with more attention often being made to the appearance of the food than the quality, this method was highly impractical; not only in terms of the space it required, but due to the fact that the food was likely to go cold so quickly.

Breakfast for the middle classes became the most important meal of the day. It was also one by which class could also be identified. Something as unassuming today as the way in which toast was cooked became a measure of how adept the mistress of the house was at her responsibilities. Mrs Beeton describes what to expect as a typical breakfast in her *Book of Household Management*. It was usual for a selection of cold meats to be displayed on the sideboard, accompanied by the following hot dishes:

> Broiled fish, such as mackerel, whiting, herrings, dried haddocks, &c; mutton chops and rump steaks, broiled sheep's kidneys, kidney *a la maître d'hôtel*, sausages, plain rashers of bacon, bacon and poached eggs, ham and poached eggs, omelets [*sic*], plain boiled eggs, *oeufs-au-plat*, poached eggs on toasted muffins, toast, marmalade, butter &c &c.[15]

Beeton also recommends a selection of fresh fruits in summer and the presence of a vase of flowers on the table daily. The working classes strove to consume as much as possible during the morning to set themselves up for the hard, labour-intensive day ahead. Street food was one of the most common sources of breakfast with a boiled egg costing one penny or a ham sandwich two pence.[16]

Similarly, as recommended in the *Handbook for the Breakfast Table*, 1873: 'Men of business should leave their homes in the morning physically fortified against the fatigues of an anxious day'. Failing which they would suffer 'a malady of incurable character'.

The Victorian era was also when the Sunday lunch really came into its own. For many of the labouring classes, Sunday was the one day they would eat meat; usually a small joint of beef, pork or mutton accompanied by two types of green vegetable and potatoes. Invariably this would be followed by some form of fruit pie or pudding or jam roly-poly. Whatever meat was left over would be eaten cold with pickles or vinegar. If they were lucky enough to afford meat on any other day of the week, the poorer classes would indulge in offal, anything from liver to heart. Only the very poor and destitute would choose to eat soup, broth or boiled meat with any regularity, as the labouring classes felt it had too many associations with poverty, often labelling it as 'slops'. The Victorians were big fish consumers with estimates of the UK overall consumption of fresh, salted and other fish products exceeding £6,000,000 annually. Billingsgate Market sold on average some £193,000 worth of shellfish alone each year, including oysters, periwinkles, mussels, shrimps, cockles, whelks, lobsters and crabs.[17] Healthy, protein-rich and still relatively cheap, fish would have enhanced Victorian diets significantly. An interesting article appears in an 1893 edition of the *Manchester Courier* and *Lancashire General Advertiser*, condemning meat as one of the main contributors to bad temper, something the writer points out is missing in Japan with their simple diet of fish and rice.

This is an interesting early observation of diet and mental health, particularly as the writer continues to note the importance of diet and exercise for both menstruating and pregnant women. This analogy is a familiar one with the media today and our obsession with the link between food, behaviour and general well-being.

Economy of the kitchen and a waste-not-want-not philosophy became popular, in stark contrast to the throw-away culture of the Georgian age. The luxury goods that would often conveniently slip through port authorities for the benefit of the bellies of the rich, like chocolate in its solid form, became less of a commodity in Victorian Britain, despite its popularity in the preceding era, with scarcely eight tons a year being imported annually for the purposes of drinking or being consumed as confection.[18] Typically cocoa in its raw capacity was manipulated in the kitchen for the purposes of consumption in a variety of forms and was imported from the West Indies, Brazil and Guayaquil for domestic use, as well as to be sold on for the wider export market.

Alcohol, another luxury item, received different attitudes by the middle of the nineteenth century. There was a more pervading awareness of the dangers of too much hard alcohol and the temperance movement was embraced wholeheartedly by many sectors of society. Just as there had been in the Georgian age, there were strict regulations where licensing was concerned. Licensing reforms were changeable and by the 1890s roughly adhered to the definition that a refreshment room was a class of eating establishment where people could eat inside after ten o'clock at night. Many railway stations had this type of licence, or fish and chip shops. A publican's licence allowed the selling of beer and wine to be consumed with food, whereas an off-licence permitted the retail of wine and beer and a hotel licence was for accommodation only and not for the selling of alcohol. Licences were only granted for five years at a time.[19]

The mid-nineteenth century also witnessed the emergence of the first consumer protection-related legislation, in particular the Sale of Food and Drugs Act, 1875. Fraudulent trade was common practice in Britain and one of the key examples of this activity is best exemplified by the sale of margarine, a new concept of the nineteenth century that many retailers masqueraded as butter.

Consumers believed the mixed margarine to be butter and butter producers were being undermined by this rival product.

As a consequence the Margarine Act was implemented in 1887 whereby all margarine manufacturers had to register with local authorities, who also had the powers to request samples for testing as and when they felt necessary. Much of this new legislation was on the back of research published by the *Lancet* throughout the 1850s, providing scientific information relating to the extent of food adulteration and its consequences on public health. This research was widely reported in the media at the time, leading to the formation of a new committee specifically responsible for monitoring national issues of food adulteration. Following the establishment of this select committee, a vast number of traders and manufacturers were taken to court to investigate the extent to which edible consumer goods were being adulterated, and there were considerable numbers of prosecutions made as a consequence. There were obvious complications with testing all types of food effectively, as an article that appeared in the *Nottingham Evening Post* of 1892 alludes to. The story reflects on an incident in Luton, Bedfordshire, where complaints were abundant with regard to a hawker touting eggs, claiming them to be freshly laid, when they were in fact 'foreign' and, more often than not, rotten and unfit for human consumption. As the sampling laws dictated that samples be divided into three parts, with one to be returned to the seller, this made eggs almost impossible to split. It led to a re-assessment of aspects of the Food and Drugs Act. Nonetheless the legislation was in the main successful, with a difference in levels of adulterated purchased food samples reducing from just over 9 per cent in 1899 to around 5.5 per cent by 1938.[20]

The chemist Frederick Accum was instrumental in generating awareness about the dangers of adulteration in the century before; his research was widely published and well received until he spoke out publically about the illegal tactics of big businesses, leading to his expulsion back to Germany. George III did however pass a law forbidding the use of a number of poisons, exposed by Accum for their fatal toxicity. George III was a modest eater for a Georgian, which may have been a contribution of his ongoing unusual and complicated illness. Towards the end of his life he refused to eat meat of any kind. Even after years of royal banquets and formal dinners the king is said to have insisted on having just one 'plain joint' prepared for him, which was usually mutton. He ate breakfast early and he never consumed alcohol before midday, all of which made him quite unusual for the time.[21]

In contrast the *Hartlepool Mail* of 1886 provides an inside account from a French journalist writing about Queen Victoria's dining habits. It was reported that fifteen minutes before the dinner hour, the guests were arranged in a semi-circle while a band played 'The Roast Beef of Old England', as the Queen entered. She shook hands with all the ladies and saluted the gentlemen in the group. The Queens family members always sat to her left, guests only to the right. She always wore gloves, unless it was a state meal. No one was allowed to address the Queen directly. Any conversation directed at the Queen was discussed among other guests, to be heard and filtered by the Queen herself. And once the Queen finished her course, so too did her guests, whether they had finished or not. There would have been around six courses, each one consisting of about eight dishes. It was observed that the Queen ate vast quantities and fast; unlike George III who ate very little at rapid speeds, leaving those who dined with him very hungry and wanting. Aware of his unusual eating habits he would often announce to his co-diners to carry on without him and thus disregard the customary way of finishing their meal as the king finished his.[22]

Christmas Day 1895 for Queen Victoria and her family was spent at Osborne House and the dinner consisted of six courses, along with a separate hot and cold buffet. The menu included,

Clear Rice Soup
Mock Turtle Soup

Turbot with Butter sauce
Fried fillets of Sole

Lobster Croquettes

Turkey with Chipolatas
Loin of Pork

Asparagus with Sauce

Mince pies
Plum Pudding
Chocolate Éclairs

Buffet
Baron of Beef, Boar's Head, Game Pie, Brawn, Hot Roast Beef[23]

Quite frankly you'd think the main menu itself would be enough, but the buffet reflected the English aspect of the meal. Although French cuisine was considered far superior in the eighteenth and nineteenth centuries, ensuring English dishes or English produce were always integrated into a menu was something that was essential in British society. Made of boiled calf's head, Mock-Turtle soup was incredibly popular as it had been the century before. The lobster would have been wrapped in pig's membrane, then battered and deep-fried.

Greater attention was afforded to food preparation in the Victorian period. There was more of an emphasis on the need for society generally to embrace the wider understanding of the basic principles of cooking. This would eventually lead to new legislation and extensive training programmes to be rolled out across the country. This extract from Dickens' Journal, *Household Words, Volume 1,* bemoaning the problems of English cooking, is testament to this national attitude at the time.

Medical statistics tell us that of all diseases with which the English are afflicted, those arising directly or indirectly from impaired digestive organs are the most prevalent. We are falsely accused in consequence of over-eating; but the true cause of our ailments is bad cooking. A Frenchman or a German devours much more at one of his own inexhaustible *tables- d'hôte* than an Englishman consumes at his dining-table—and with impunity; for the foreigner's food being properly prepared is easily digested. 'The true difference,' says a pleasant military writer in Blackwood's Magazine, ' between English and foreign cookery is just this: in preparing butcher's meat for the table, the aim of foreign cookery is to make it tender, of English to make it hard. And both systems equally affect their object, in spite of difficulties on each side. The butcher's meat, which you buy abroad, is tough, coarse-grained, and stringy; yet foreign cookery sends this meat to table tender. The butcher's meat which you buy in England is tender enough when it comes home; but domestic cookery sends it up hard. Don't tell me the hardness is in the meat itself. Nothing of the kind; it's altogether an achievement of the English cuisine. I appeal to a leg of mutton, I appeal to a beef-steak, as they usually come to table; the beef half- broiled, the mutton half-roasted. Judge for yourself. The underdone portion of each is tender; the portion that's dressed is hard. Argal, the hardness is due to the dressing, not to the meat: it is a triumph of domestic cookery.

Several other important changes emerged in the transition between Georgian and Victorian society and the role of cooking. During the eighteenth century, the kitchen maid was considered the most lowly and underpaid of all the servants. Nonetheless their role was critical to the household, and if, as was the case with the eighteenth century's most famous of kitchen maids, the poet Mary Leapor, any prepared food was spoilt or burnt in its preparation, the punishment was instant dismissal. Both the eighteenth and nineteenth-century kitchen maids were expected to keep the kitchen and food preparation and storage areas spotlessly clean. While the large houses of the Georgian period would have employed a wealth of kitchen staff, including a clerk of the kitchen, confectioners, patissiers and esteemed French cooks, many Victorians moved away from the extravagances of the previous century and female cooks began to replace the dominant male presence that epitomised the eighteenth century.

Having spent many hours cleaning each morning the Victorian kitchen maid prepared the breakfasts, then under the direction of the cook, made dinner for the servants, then for the family, followed by all the necessary cleaning up before setting up supper for the other servants. Her role was one of aspiring cook and therefore it would be imperative for the nineteenth-century kitchen maid to apply herself fully to all the tasks at hand, learn from the teachings of her existing cook and study as much available literature on the subject as possible. Samuel and Sarah Adams' *The Complete Servant* advocated the use of the manual 'Directions to the Cook', a comprehensive learning resource on this subject. If the kitchen maid was lucky enough to elevate her position to cook, they could expect to receive in the region of twelve to fourteen guineas.[24]

The overpaid, high ranking and extravagant temperamental French cooks of the century before that were demanded in all the best of households began leaving private domestic service to go and work in the new fashionable hotel and club restaurants that were opening daily in the towns and cities of Victorian Britain. Subsequently the kitchen and scullery maids of the last generation were trained in the rigorous tradition of fine dining and best kitchen practice by their male French superiors. They may also have inherited some of their authoritative superiority, as many cooks in good Victorian households were confident, strong-willed and prone to putting any staff beneath them to task. Only expected to undertake the 'proper' cooking, the cook needed waiting on, had her own room and generally supervised and developed menus while the plain cooking, cleaning, preparation and any other menial kitchen duties were carried out by the kitchen and scullery maids. Her staff were even expected to bring her a cup of tea in bed each morning.[25]

The transport networks and industrial and scientific technology that had become a possibility for the future advancement of British society in the Georgian age had bloomed by 1848. With the success of the new railway systems, standards for people generally began to improve. Mass production and new food products as a direct consequence of advanced technology in preserving meant that people were growing less food at home. They were enjoying a range of choice, including better quality fresh meat, fish and vegetables. Cheaper imports from the foreign market enabled communities of all classes to become less dependent on the land or nature. A crop or cattle disaster could be substituted with cheap American goods. Technology in flour-milling towards the end of the nineteenth century meant that the often inedible bread provided to the poor, became more palatable and accessible.

By the middle of the 1800s the tin canning revolution, following its invention almost one hundred years before, together with Schweppes' early experiments with bottling, had succeeded. Among other domestic benefits, canning and bottling provided the means to sustain troops out in the field and sailors at sea.

Queen Victoria's accession to the throne in 1837 heralded a number of large-scale national patriotic events, many of which were formal dinners or banquets in honour of the lady herself.

The Grand Banquet held at London's Guildhall in November that year, representing Victoria's first official visit into the city, saw a lined procession of loyal followers from Buckingham Palace to the Guildhall, generating considerable public excitement and media attention. Houses were decorated and flags festooned the streets. The scale and magnitude of the banquet was tremendous; attended by the Mayor of London, Archbishop of Canterbury, Dukes, Duchesses, Earls and Viscounts and countless other dignitaries, the schedule for the dinner itself consisted of La Table Royale, Buffet, Second Service followed by another Buffet. Some of the dishes served were as follows:

La Table Royale
Potages
Plats de Poisson – including Turbot and fried whiting
Releves – boiled chicken, veal and beef
Entrees – lamb sweetbreads, turkey, pheasant stuffed with truffles, sole, Italian casserole and decorative vegetables

Buffet
Turkey soup, pheasant, fried smelts, beef, ham, lamb, venison, truffles, pâtés, croquettes, roast turkey

Second Service
Roast meats (various)
Releves – vanilla soufflé
Pastries
Desserts – creamed pineapple, champagne jelly, peaches, nougat, maraschino cherry jelly, gateaux, creamed peaches

Buffet (number 2)
Roast chicken, roast duck, apple pie, cherry pie, parmesan fondue, trifle, mince pies and plum pudding

This typical mix of French cuisine merged with classic English dishes, and a smattering of Italian, were very typical of higher and middle-class dining during the nineteenth century, as was the extravagance inherited from the era before. The amount of food consumed at Queen Victoria's visit to the City of London inaugural dinner was staggering – 220 tureens of turtle, fifty boiled turkeys, fifty chickens, forty capons, sixty pigeon pies, forty-five hams, forty tongues, ten sirloins of beef, forty-five shell fish dishes, fifty salads, forty tarts, eighty roast turkeys, ten hares, eighty pheasants, forty partridges, one hundred pineapples, eighty pear dishes, eighty dishes of dried fruit and so on. The guests enjoyed Champagne, Hock, Claret, Burgundy, Madeira, Port and Sherry to wash it all down with.[26]

Many issues of the late Georgian age filtered through into the Victorian era; the great divide between wealth and poverty, starvation and excess, urban over-crowding and rural decline. The mid-1800s were also steeped in strange logic and false beliefs almost as powerful as those of the Middle Ages. The Victorians were probably marginally kinder and more aware of the importance of their own spirit and the humane need for compassion than the Georgians were. They were able to take forward many of the ideas and concepts borne out of the century before, essentially re-inventing themselves and evolving into a burgeoning sophisticated, civilised and humane society. More analytical in their approach to alcohol, diet, health and well-being, the Victorians were a strange confused mix of austerity, avarice and aspiration which was certainly reflected in their attitudes towards food and dining.

Recipes

Jules Gouffé's *Royal Cookery Book* 1869, was originally printed for the French market, but was quickly translated into English due to its popularity. In his publication Gouffe provided a recipe for Vanilla Soufflé, which would have been very similar to the one served at the Guildhall Banquet for her majesty Queen Victoria.

Vanilla Soufflé

Put in a 2 quart stewpan:

6 oz of flour
4 oz of sugar
2 tablespoons of vanilla sugar
1 small pinch of salt

Mix these well with 1 pint of cold milk; put on the fire till boiling and stir with a wooden spoon till smooth; then take out the fire; Break 6 eggs; put the whites in the whipping bowl, and add the 6 yolks to the batter; Whip the whites very firm, and mix with the batter stirring very lightly; pour the whole in a buttered dish, and put in the oven – twenty to twenty five minutes should be sufficient to cook it. When done sprinkle with pounded sugar; and serve. This soufflé-like omelette soufflé must be served as soon as it is taken out of the oven.[27]

The Georgian period heralded the popularised cooking manual. It was the age of the mass consumerist culture for recipe books and food literature. The eighteenth century also produced some of the most well-known cooks in culinary history and signified Britain's long obsession with cooking and relationship with food.

This was an age of public dining, not as refined as the restaurants of the Victorian era, but in terms of its high-profile dining clubs, eating houses, cook shops, taverns and Inns and street food vendors. The nineteenth century catered for every class.

As the French style of cooking dominated British culture, the streets were swarming with Alamode Houses, a popular larded beef stew, marinated and slow-cooked in wine. This recipe for Beef Alamode was published in the Housewife's Manual section of the *Ladies Literary Cabinet*, *1819*.

Beef Alamode

Take some of the veiny piece, or a part of the thick flank, or rather a small round, commonly called the mouse-buttock, of the finest ox-beef, but let it be about five inches thick. Cut some thick slices of fat bacon, into proper lengths, for lardings of about three quarters of an inch thick; dip them first into vinegar, and then into a mixed powder of finely beaten mace, long pepper, nutmeg, a clover or two, and double the united weight of salt. With a small knife or larding pin, cut holes in the beef, to receive the bacon thus prepared; place the lardings tolerably thick and even; rub the beef over with the remainder of the seasoning; put it into a pot or deep pan, just sufficiently large to contain it; and add a gill of vinegar, a couple of large onions, some sweet herbs, a few chives, a little lemon peel, some truffles and morels, and half a pint of white wine. It should be very closely covered up, and have a wet cloth round the edge, to prevent the steam from evaporating. It must be dressed over a stove, or very slow fire; and will require full six hours to do it properly. When half done, it should be taken off, turned, and again closed up as before.[28]

The Victorian era undoubtedly produced some of the most iconic dishes in culinary history that we still cook and eat today. What could be more iconic than the Victoria sponge sandwich? In the nineteenth century the cake that we know today did not resemble the 'Victoria Sandwiches' from where it emerged, a sweet treat that Queen Victoria enjoyed with her tea.

This recipe of Mrs Beeton's illustrates its probable origins. The fact that Victoria Sandwiches were also popularly served with whipped cream – as Beeton follows this recipe with one explaining how to whip cream with sugar, sherry and lemons – suggests why it finally morphed into a cake with jam and cream.

Victoria Sandwiches

Ingredients – 4 eggs, their weight in pounded sugar, butter, and flour 1/4 saltspoonful of salt, a layer of any kind of jam or marmalade.

Mode – Beat the butter to a cream; dredge in the flour and pounded sugar; stir these ingredients well together, and add the eggs, which should be previously thoroughly whisked. When the mixture has been well beaten for about 10 minutes, butter a Yorkshire pudding tin pour in the batter, and bake it in a moderate oven for 20 minutes. Let it cool, spread one half of the cake with a layer of nice preserve, place over it the other half of the cake, press the pieces slightly together and then cut it into long finger pieces; pile them in crossbars on a glass dish and serve

Time: 20 minutes.

Average cost is 3*d*.

Sufficient for 5 or 6 persons Seasonable at any time.[29]

2

THE POOR, PHILANTHROPY AND PLENITUDE

For many Victorians the division between rich and poor was as wide as it had been in the century before. However, this was the era of reform and for millions of people, by the beginning of the twentieth century, many of the old embedded issues of poverty and hunger would begin to ease.

The Poor Law Amendment Act of 1834 witnessed the introduction of the workhouse system and represents one of the singularly most important pieces of social legislation in the nineteenth century. It offered welfare for the poor and sought solutions to manage the most impoverished.

Despite central government's proactive and successful attempts to sanitise the towns and cities of Britain and provide schools for children, by the end of the nineteenth century disease was reduced and life expectancy raised. But the issue of real poverty still remained, which impacted on how much food both adults and children were receiving, as well as how much nutritional value that food actually had. Surveys conducted by both Charles Booth for London and Seebohm Rowntree for York determined that, while a quarter of London's population were living below the poverty line, nearly half of York's population were in the same situation. The vast majority of people simply could not afford to eat.

There are numerous accounts of workhouse food documented from the period. An article in the Grantham Journal of 1895 relays a surprise inspection at a Workhouse in Pontefract that discovered inmates being fed with 'potatoes he would not have given to his pigs' and eating butter 'fit for nothing save greasing cart-wheels and calculated to poison anybody'.[1]

Similarly the extent of the poverty trap in Sunderland in the north of England is illustrated by a story dating to 1884. Acting on her own suspicions a lady who kept a pig decided to keep watch one night and determine whether anything happened. Sure enough, at dusk a man and woman approached the sty and reached into the animal's trough to scoop out the kitchen scraps and bread that had been thrown out. Having followed the couple, the lady discovered their five children eagerly devouring the food taken from the trough.[2]

According to Sir Henry Thompson's 1891 book *Food and Feeding*, the Victorian labouring classes survived on bread, cheese and the occasional portion of bacon and potatoes, meat being a rarity.

Charity and the state provided a degree of welfare for the poor with food coupons and milk for babies. But these were often traded and bartered in lieu of cash or other items. The Charity Organisation Society was founded in 1869 and involved a type of early social work through investigative home visits and interviews with the poor. Food coupons were issued by the society and would be distributed among other places to schools via the School Board and given to teachers to allocate to the most needy of children. Food coupons were also retailed at a variety of places for the sum of one old penny. Lists of where they were on sale were commonly announced in the local press in advance. Many argued that the sale of coupons made their purpose ineffectual, as those in most need would be unlikely to have a penny to purchase one in the first place. One of the reasons why there was a charge placed on food vouchers was a deliberate attempt to ensure that neither were the poor patronised or allowed to rely on charity, for fear of creating a culture of dependency where handouts were concerned. This is an argument that still very strongly resonates in British political discourse today. Some schools like the King and Queen Street Board School in Walworth, London, in 1886 stopped providing the penny dinners as they determined that the very poor children were not benefitting as they didn't have a penny to pay for the meal. When questioned, the head teacher, Mr Pond noted that out of the 507 boys attending the school who were questioned on the subject one day, only 138 of them had any lunch at all, with 13 of these lunches consisting of dried bread and 125 bread and butter.[3] None of the girls were questioned, for whatever reason is unexplained, other than that boys and their opinions were frequently elevated in every way against those of their female peers. Penny dinners were balanced and varied from day to day. One description of those offered at the Gifford Street Board School relays that sometimes stew was served on Tuesdays and Fridays (the same dish re-heated), but often the pattern would remain: soup on Tuesday (with meat), suet pudding on a Wednesday, treacle, bread and bacon on Thursday and soup again on Friday.[4] The preparation and serving of the penny dinners largely relied on volunteer support and the kitchens, which could not always be integrated into the school itself, would often be located nearby, as with Gifford Hall meal services, which utilised an Evangelical church and mission opposite the school. The Charity Organisation Society also opened a number of public soup kitchens, serving daily provisions.

The following data taken from the accounts of St Marylebone Workhouse in 1846 reveals a surprisingly well-proportioned diet across all inmates from able-bodied adults to children, the aged and infirm, infants and nursing mothers. Infants from nine months to two years were given an ounce of cooked mutton three times a week, as well as rice pudding twice a week and six ounces of bread every day. One would hope that the cooked meat and bread was generally geared towards the older toddlers. Although more was being understood about childcare and child rearing by the Victorian age, they were still largely adhering to old-fashioned practices. Wet nurses were commonly hired by those gentrified women who did not wish to breastfeed. This was often an illicit and dangerous practice in itself; not just because many poorer women would give birth regularly, allow their children to die and profit from giving their milk to others, but also from the fact that disease, particularly sexually transmitted disease, was rife during the nineteenth century and could be spread easily from the breast to the child.

Interestingly the diets of able-bodied adults and those adults classified as 'insane' varied considerably in the workhouse setting. While the 'insane' male inmates were provided with sixteen ounces of bread each on a daily basis, their 'able-bodied' colleagues were given just twelve. The former group of men and women also received meat dishes four times a week in larger quantities than the latter who received it just three times a week. Those with diagnosed mental health issues also benefited from twice as many potatoes, but missed out on the extra beer rations, which was no doubt a sensible approach depending on their potential for instability. According to the records children in the workhouse aged seven to fourteen were in receipt of the greatest weekly treat – a supplement of suet pudding – and they had more treacle rations than their younger counterparts, in addition to butter three times a week, which was also only fed to the aged and infirm, who themselves were served regular drinks of hot tea throughout the week.[5]

Although an official report conducted by the Poor Law Commissioners in 1846 demonstrates a high level of good provision, the actual results documented by Marylebone remain sceptical in the light of so many conflicting accounts of workhouse conditions and the food they provided during the nineteenth century. In Charles Shaw's well-known diary of his early life in Victorian Staffordshire, he describes the bread at the time to have been made of sawdust 'blotched with lumps of plaster of Paris'. Shaw spent time in a workhouse in Stoke-on-Trent where he was given this same bread to eat, along with a substance that he just describes as 'greasy water' and a couple of lumps of something that 'would have made a tiger's teeth ache to break the fibres of!' In fact, so repugnant was the food that Shaw would occasionally pass it on to others to eat, despite his raging hunger. Supper, unlike the listed butter and treacle served in the Marylebone workhouse, consisted of a substance known as 'skilly', which Shaw describes as 'culinary-making nausea'. The skilly served to the children in Staffordshire was basic meal boiled in water, the water resembling that 'boiled in old clothes, which had been worn upon sweating bodies for three-score years and ten.' With no salt or sugar added, Shaw determines his supper to be 'the vilest compound I ever tasted, unutterably insipid'.[6]

There were alternative solutions to poverty that didn't depend on welfare or handouts as Titus Salt's communal living and working factory, Saltaire, illustrates. With its cottages, almshouses, church, shops, laundry houses and so on, it was the epitome of Victorian entrepreneurial and philanthropic endeavour. The self-supporting public dining hall for the commune residents advertised the daily Bill of Fare on the front door. One of the most popular dishes was the soup and bread. And at just one penny a portion, the diner was getting a bargain of a meal, considering the average price for soup could be around nine pence. Other items on offer included a plate of corned beef, meat and potato pie, or mutton for just two pence. With a fruit, currant or rice pudding for only one penny, a whole three-course meal could be consumed for less than six pence.[7]

It could be argued that another solution to the issue of the poor was with the burgeoning industrial revolution. Mills and factories were thriving and offered many the chance to escape the hardships of the workhouse and even the opportunity to develop, if lucky enough to find a well-run establishment. The new industrial working society experienced different mealtimes at work, with meals and tea-breaks providing an excuse to socialise both on and off-site with arrangements varying from employer to employer. In some trades the workers were expected to bring their own packed lunches and snacks to work, or could send out for food. In other industries on-site facilities were made available for employees where a cook was brought in to prepare and serve up meals. Research of the time denotes that female employees were more likely to want to eat on the premises than go out. This was not necessarily by choice, but rather motivated by inferior pay.[8]

Undeniably there was the more sinister side of poverty, with the despair, anxiety and hopelessness of the situation meant many living in appalling conditions were driven to crime. This issue was also perpetuated by the overall belief that criminal activity in society was attributed to the failings of the persons connected, that only the weak and lazy stole, the sick and crazed murdered and raped, that the depraved nature of your character was what drove you to commit offences. There was very little correlation between crime and poverty until the end of the era, as society began to accept the findings of reformers like Henry Mayhew, Charles Booth and psychologists like Maudsley who made the connection between environment and behaviour, with the theory that often the poor and vulnerable were groomed for crime from a very young age.

Britain's prisons were overrun with inmates guilty of anything from minor offences like petty thieving to more serious criminal activity like murder. Those in charge of the criminal justice systems did not always share these contemporary philosophies. Edward Du Cane was the Surveyor-General of prisons from the mid- to latter part of the nineteenth century. The main focus of his work centred on colonial convict and military prisons but he was also tasked with reorganising borough and county prisons throughout England during the 1870s. His theories on punishment and confinement were harsh with prisoners conditioned into reforming based on a points system of good behaviour. Du Cane's rules were so severe that it was said even if a prisoner blew his nose at the wrong time of the day he would be remorselessly punished for it. He also introduced the parole system still maintained today, whereby those released from prison are continuously monitored and recalled if caught re-offending. As well as administering torture and solitary confinement, Du Cane determined that diet was fundamental to a prisoner's rehabilitation. In the early weeks of a prisoner's term Du Cane prescribed 'scientific starvation', a belief that abstinence from food was not only healthy but also taught other criminals a lesson. If a prisoner was seen to be too well fed, this might encourage others to offend, in an attempt to gain more food. One report on the prison system in 1872 revealed that inmates go 'to bed hungry and [get] up hungry, in fact he is always hungry; and this lasts for not weeks, not months, but for years'. There was very little meat, if any and no vegetables. Prisoners were given stale hard bread, inedible suet pudding and gruel. If well behaved, a prisoner would sometimes be rewarded with a cup of hot chocolate, but it was said this was often swimming in a film of grease.

Despite Du Cane's activities the issue of prison diets was one closely scrutinised by government, with new committees established and investigations and reports submitted regularly. This had a great deal to do with the issue of illness and death in prisons from malnutrition and the ongoing problem of scurvy.[9]

By the 1840s it was determined that slops and gruel were detrimental to the health of prisoners and greater steps were taken to ensure that more solid foods were made available. A new 'principle' was adopted and is summarised here as a consequence of a nationwide inspection conducted in 1842:

'The principle' which we are of opinion ought to be acted on is framing a scale of prison diet, and that which we have endeavoured to carry into effect as far as possible in the annexed scale, is that quantity of food should be given in all cases which is sufficient and not more than sufficient, to maintain health and strength, at the least possible cost; and that, while due care should be exercised to prevent extravagance or luxury in a prison, the diet ought not to be made an instrument of punishment ... We are of the opinion that there ought to be three meals each day in prison, and that at least two of the three should be hot.[10]

Du Cane clearly operated within these recommendations, but with the absolute minimum of distribution and quality of foods proposed. He also most certainly used food as an instrument of punishment in contradiction to overall government guidelines.

What families chose to eat was not dissimilar from class to class, with the exception of the very poor. They just ate greater or lesser quantities. For example the annual family expenditure for a wealthy household for a couple of residents and around three domestic staff looked like this in 1824:

Meat	£65
Fish and poultry	£25
Bread	£18
Butter and cheese	£25
Milk	£7
Vegetables and fruit	£20
Tea and sugar	£15
Table ale	£25

In comparison the annual food expenditure for a middle class family, in this case four adults and one child included:

Bread	5s
Meat	9s
Cheese, butter, ham	4/6
Milk and cream	2/-
Vegetables and fruit	4/
Fish	5/-
Groceries	11/-
Beer	9/-

Finally for a craftsman, such as carpenter or stained-glass worker, they would have the following commitments where annual food budgets for their family were concerned.

Bread	4/-
Meat	3/-
Cheese, butter, ham	1/3 (Including eggs)
Milk and cream	6d (milk only)
Vegetables and fruit	1/-
Fish	-
Groceries	1/6
Beer	1/3

What these figures suggest, is that although comfortable, many lower middle class and middle class families were in some ways still just keeping the wolves from the door. Despite earning considerably less, many artisan craftsmen ate almost as well as the wealthier professionals, although in this example the latter had no fish in their diet and considerably fewer vegetables.[11]

In stark contrast to Britain's poor, starving and dying masses in the slum dwellings of the towns and cities, many wealthy Victorians still ate like the Georgians, although in greater moderation and with a combined holistic attitude towards mixing and combining French and English dishes for dinner. Many of the eighteenth-century nobility had insisted on French cuisine cooked by the finest French cooks and pastry chefs. Nonetheless the fashion for French dining remained popular. As a rule for dinner there should have been a minimum of five dishes, ideally more; including one of fish, one meat, one game, one poultry and a selection of truffles (the fungal kind). It was expected that there should be a sweet dessert course of puddings, pies, tarts, or all three.

The most significant change was the meal of breakfast. The cold meats, cheese and beer of the eighteenth century began to make way for the multi-course approach of porridge, fish, bacon, eggs, toast and marmalade. The hour of dinner also changed from 5 p.m. to 7 p.m., which made the late meal of 'supper' less and less relevant. It was replaced by luncheon – a corruption of 'nuncheon', an old Anglo-Saxon phrase that has many regional derivatives – essentially a snack taken at noon by farm labourers or well-to-do ladies who liked some afternoon repose, accompanied by something like cold meats and a drink. It was the Victorian era that really saw an increase in the fashion for taking tea, coffee and cakes, either to bridge the gap between breakfast or luncheon and dinner, or as a late-night alternative to the old supper time of about 9 p.m. The Duchess of Bedford the century before had popularised this trend, complaining daily of a 'slump' in her energy levels during the day, which was rectified by a tray of tea, bread and butter and cakes at around 4 p.m.[12]

An aperitif served just before dinner was also becoming more commonplace during the nineteenth century, while a large glug of olive oil was ingested by young men about to embark on an evening of rich food, entertainment and plenty of alcohol, in an attempt to stay sober for longer.[13]

Many plain cooks of the Victorian era were women, but the most fashionable families still employed highly skilled French male cooks, at extortionate rates. The next best alternative was an English cook who had trained in France. While a top male cook could earn in excess of around £100 a year or more (equivalent to about £80,000 in today's money), a good female cook would earn half this. Board and lodging would of course be an additional benefit. By comparison a provincial female cook working for a middle-class family might expect to earn in the region of £15 annually, or £12,000 in today's currency. Commission could also come from the sale of stale food, pigswill and other leftovers.[14]

One of the most documented female cooks of her time thanks to her journals is Avis Crocombe. Her greatest achievement was securing the position of head cook at Audley End House in Essex where she worked for five years before leaving to marry. According to her journal Crocombe used the recipes of Eliza Acton which she copied verbatim from Acton's *Modern Cookery for Private Families*.[15]

Interestingly the large house kitchens of Victorian Britain did not always follow suit with innovation and modernisation. Given the extent of variety of new technology available to cooks during this time, including the closed range and smoking jacks. One account of the kitchens at Nuthall Temple, Nottinghamshire as late as 1912 is described thus:

> The huge kitchen with its centre table and surrounding ones all round, shelves of copper pans and moulds, a large window looking out onto two courtyards with outbuildings for the game shoot and home killed sheep ... the coal range in the far end of the kitchen had two large ovens on each side and had chimney fittings of brass, spits for baking bread and cooking large meat joints in front. The scullery was below ground level with a shallow round sink and a hole in the back to the outside, facing the lawns ... Two large oak metal-banded tubs, one for washing up all kitchenware and the other for rinsing, nothing to help with grease which I collected and saved for the man.[16]

Fitting out a large country house kitchen was immensely expensive, and it wasn't uncommon for Victorians to install wooden sinks or barrels in an attempt to minimise breakages. However high-ranking cooks would expect their kitchens to be fully equipped and contain at least some of the latest gadgets. Clearly there was also some misguided loyalty and snobbery by some moving in higher circles with regard to kitchen stove innovation, as noted here by Anne Cobbett in her Manual of Domestic Management.

> The fire place of a kitchen is a matter of great importance .I have not it is certain been so circumstanced as to witness the operations of many of the newly invented steam kitchens and cooking apparatuses, which the last twenty years have produced but those which I have seen have failed to give me satisfaction. To say the truth the inventors of cast iron kitchens seem to me to have had every other object in view but that of promoting good cooking. It is certainly desirable and proper that every possible saving should be made in the consumption of coals, but I am sure it is not possible to have cooking in perfection without a proper degree of heat,and as far as my observation has gone meat cannot be well roasted unless it be before a good fire.[17]

One of the first kitchens to install a modern gas cooker, of the kind lambasted by Cobbett, was the elite Reform Club, where many a well-renowned cook worked. Most of the furbishing of the Reform Club kitchens was implemented by Alexis Soyer, while he was engaged as head cook during the late 1830s and early 1840s. So inspirational and innovative were the kitchens that conducted tours were operated around them, and sectional views of the kitchen plans were mocked up, copied and sold to the general public at a guinea for a coloured print and half a guinea for a black and white version. A total of 1,400 copies were sold.[18]

The Victorians were always theorising on diet and exercise; much as with media speculation today, their opinions of what was nutritious, healthy, bad or good for you frequently contradicted one another. As a consequence, it is interesting to note that vitamin deficiencies and issues of inadequate diet were not just the downfall of the poor during the nineteenth century. The *Family Oracle of Health* published a beauty regime for all ladies that was shocking in its recommendations:

Breakfast itself – not later than eight o'clock – ought, in rigid training, to consist of plain biscuit (not bread), broiled beef steaks, mutton chops, under-done, without any fat, and half a pint of bottled ale – the genuine Scots ale is the best. Our fair readers will not demur to this, when they are told that this was the regular breakfast of Queen Elizabeth, and Lady Jane Grey. But should it be found too strong fare at the commencement, we permit, instead of the ale, one small breakfast cup – not more – of good strong black tea or of coffee – weak tea or coffee is always bad for the nerves as well as the complexion ... dinner at two, the same as breakfast; no vegetables, boiled meat, nor made-dishes being permitted, much less fruits, sweet things or pastry. Those who are very delicate may begin with a bit of broiled chicken or turkey, but the steaks and chops must always be the chief part of your food. A mealey potatoe, or a little boiled rice, may now and then be permitted, but no other vegetable ... supper at seven or eight as most convenient, at which we allow you tea or coffee, if you have had none at breakfast; if you have, you must take your half pint of mild ale, and a bit of cold fowl, or cold roast mutton or beef, but no fat. Butter, cream, milk, cheese and fish are prohibited. You may take an egg occasionally with a biscuit.[19]

This diet is worryingly unbalanced. To exclude green vegetables and dairy products in this way would have surely contributed to vitamin deficiencies. Likewise lack of any fruit or vegetables would have led to scurvy. It also surmises that just because the wealthier classes could afford more choice, they were often ignorant in their food combinations, potentially leaving them as unhealthy as their poorer neighbours.

Pineapples became synonymous with wealth during the nineteenth century. Favoured by the upper classes, they were served and displayed at dinner to indicate prosperity.

In order to cultivate this fruit in cold, northern European temperatures Victorian gardeners invented 'pineapple pits', which were essentially three trenches covered in glass, slightly below ground level. The external walls of the trenches were bolstered with horse manure to generate heat. In order to maintain the 'pineapple pit', gardeners had to spend some considerable time regularly feeding the trench with manure and maintaining warm temperatures. It is understood that the last surviving pit is located at the Lost Gardens of Heligan, Mevagissey, Cornwall. As of 2013 there were a total of eight pineapples fruiting in the lovingly restored pits.[20]

Exotic fruits such as pineapples, melons, apricots and peaches were not sent to the kitchen from the garden, rather they were handed to the butler or housekeeper for safety.

Interestingly an 1890s survey of forty-two middle-class families revealed that they spent more on charitable donations than they did on rent, clothing, staff wages or any other item except food.[21]

In terms of public food aid for the wider poor during the Victorian period in London, it is possible to determine that there were three areas of provision – breakfast for children, soup kitchens and 'Dinner tables', with the latter two usually only open for a few days during the week. There were also a number of 'casual kitchens' which were only open during very severe weather conditions.

Food items and soup were also given away free of charge by a number of private residences and shopkeepers, but it is difficult to determine the figures for this as there were no official statistics recorded. In terms of soup kitchens and dinner tables, in 1887 West London had forty-nine open on average about three to four days a week, each one serving at least several hundred people over a two month period. North London had around thirty-nine opening about three days a week, serving over 400 people per day when they were open from January to February. There were only about twenty in central London, but these appear to have been open for longer hours – on average six days a week. Somewhat surprisingly, as one of the poorest areas, there were only twenty-nine soup kitchens established in East London, with many only open one to two days a week. One provider in Bethnal Green was open six days a week and fed around 1,180 people on the days when it was open, again in January and February. The district with the largest number of public catering facilities for the poor was South London, with sixty-nine soup kitchens and dinner tables, of which Deptford and Woolwich had the largest turnover of meals served in a two month period, totalling 6,186 between them. These were London's Dockland areas and therefore likely to have had significant migrant communities living there, trying to sustain work and provide for their families. Most of the official soup kitchens and dinner tables would have been for adults only. There were seven specific main-meal providers for children in the city during 1887, including the South London Dinners Fund, the Central Council for Self-Supporting Dinners, the Destitute Children's Dinner Society, Free Dinners at Southwark, Jews' Schools Westminster, Mrs Pennington's Dinners and the London Cottage Mission. Combined they served up nearly 4,000 meals to children on a weekly basis.[22]

By the 1890s The Salvation Army Farthing breakfasts made provision for a cheap meal for school children in the winter months across its seventeen centres in London. At only a farthing for hot drinks, and more often than not bread and jam, these centres provided important sustenance to thousands of children having to go to school and learn on empty stomachs. In fact, in the winter of 1892, 17,503 children were in receipt of these basic but life-preserving breakfasts.

Its founder William Booth, together with his eldest son, ran soup kitchens, where hot drinks could be sought at any time of the night and a three-course meal could be purchased for next to nothing. In order to achieve this Booth's son, Bramwell, had the task of getting up at three o'clock every morning and pushing a wheel barrow the four mile journey it took him to get to Covent Garden Market in order to collect all the unwanted vegetables and stew bones needed to make soup. It was this diligent work, together with the Salvation Army shelters for discharged prisoners and other disadvantaged members of society, which sat under the umbrella of Booth's broader national initiative titled 'Darkest England'. A significant aspect of this initiative was the establishment of a colony in Essex, which utilised over 3,000 acres of farm land to educate and house a communal training ground for those seeking employment and offered the ability to learn new skills. Participants on the scheme operated a market garden and orchard and learnt basic construction skills, such as brickmaking. *The Edinburgh Evening News* even reported on the existence of a fully operational boot factory there. Aside from the colony, in 1893 it was reported that in the same year 1,670 women had passed through the Salvation Army rescue homes, of which 800 had found employment (predominantly in service), while 320 returned to their families. Nothing is mentioned about the remaining 550, and it must only be assumed that they continued to be lost somewhere in the great poverty cycle.[23]

One of the areas most affected by food poverty in the Victorian period was Ireland. The Quaker Renaissance of the nineteenth century established soup kitchens in Waterford, Enniscorthy, Limerick, Clonmel and Youghal among other towns in 1846. The Quaker movement in these areas set up committees, working with other 'members of the Society' out of both Dublin and London, to create a shared resource with which to raise funds across a wider geographical area. They also sourced alternative means to produce food. One way in which they achieved this was to re-establish fishing communities who had pawned their equipment in order to feed their families. The Quakers reinstated their nets and tackle enabling them to support their communities again. They also raised the funds to grow new crops, bought up land and began harvesting small yields of turnips. Funds were raised to build a considerably sized model farm in Galway employing over 200 people where green crops were grown in abundance and a variety of cattle, sheep and pigs were reared. The farm exceeded expectations and survived long after the famine.[24]

Some of the greatest heroes of the nineteenth century were missionaries, with various religious societies distributing personnel out, not only to countries within the Empire, but further afield to assist the poor, needy, sick and destitute in less advantaged nations. The role of the missionary was not just confined to the continent. There were many city missionaries in the nineteenth century who were disseminated across Britain to assist with domestic issues of deprivation and hopelessness.

In 1866 George Campin was sent to Canterbury, Kent, to act as a city missionary. The local paper described him as a man with 'a rare combination of excellencies'. He kept accounts of his daily activities detailing life on the streets, the people and their concerns. He organised and coordinated help when it was needed from his team of like-minded parishioners, from supplying blankets and clothing to food and comfort. He even went so far as to resolve domestic disputes and arrange marriages where they were necessary in the eyes of God. He described the conditions of one woman in 1872 as:

Ill with rheumatics and in a destitute and starving state. She said that her husband was a soldier and was in India ... She said that she was dying for want and she had neither food nor fire in the house ... she said that she had not had any help from anyone and she had pledged everything she could for food even to the flannel she wore and now did not know what she should do for she had nothing more to pledge. For all she had left was on her back. And that did not appear to me to be more than one very thin garment ... I presented her case to the Relief Association. The case was investigated and relief was given at once.[25]

There was also a more cynical attitude towards missionaries or 'soupers' as they were termed, for seducing people into religion in return for food. But one wonders what would have become of so many people in the Victorian age living in these conditions, with no one to turn to other than the kindness of strangers and charity. It is inconceivable to imagine their plight and their absolute hunger.

The biggest proponent of the city mission was David Nasmith who established missions across Glasgow, Paris and New York, before founding the London City Mission in 1835. The *London City Mission Magazine* was a regular periodical outlining the work of the organisation. In 1868 a report published on the Old Kent Road District of London illustrates a sad picture of destitution:

This district is made up of a number of small streets in a corner of the parish of St George the Martyr Southwark.

The district is in and belongs to the ecclesiastical district of St Mary Magdalene, Clarence Street, Old Kent road. The Incumbent of the district is the Rev AW Snape M A who is the superintendent of the Missionary. The Mission district with its numerous small streets, is entirely occupied by poor and miserable people; but the missionary does some special visitation in other small streets of poor people lying to the south and east of this district; these streets being part of the St Mary's Church district, although occupied by a more respectable class of working people. In the district the houses are poor, miserable hovels, small, damp and badly drained; not fit to live in. Some of them have only two rooms. On my first acquaintance with it, the drains did not act, and the yards were filled with filth. When it rained, the slops from the houses, the refuse of the food, rotting vegetables, putrid remains of fish and the excrements of the people, were swimming about the yards and the streets. Heaps of this kind of rubbish used to lie about the streets under the burning sun of summer; and to finish the horrid picture, the closets were all open.Women and men might be seen sitting in them as you walked about or sat in the houses in rags, and sometimes it could hardly be called a clothing. Some of the women had never had a bit of flannel on them since they were born, many of them had no whole garment of any sort. As to a pair of new shoes or stockings, they had never had such things on their feet; a bonnet they did not pretend to wear.[25]

This raw imagery of poverty, combined with the ugly remnants of rotting food immediately makes me think that for some desperate opportunists there would be meals to be found here, which does not bear contemplating, despite knowing it was probably a reality.

Non-working families suffered terribly in Victorian Britain, often dying of starvation, malnutrition in lonely, cold and miserable conditions. Even full-time employed workers, like cotton weavers, who were paid less than a penny an hour, failed to maintain a consistently healthy diet. Casual seasonal workers often went days without food.

The phenomenal growth of charitable institutions and individuals helped contribute towards spreading national and government awareness of the fundamental issues of poverty and the consequences of simply not having enough food, as well as the right kinds of food.

For the middle and higher classes of society, dining had never been so good. Luxuries from abroad continued to provide the very latest in consumer-able and desirable food items, while sophisticated transport networks meant not having to wait weeks for certain products and the promise of a slightly longer shelf life. Public dining and entertaining in the most opulent surroundings was avant-garde, as unchaperoned women freely luncheoned and took tea in their clubs, or while shopping and visiting galleries and museums.

The gap between rich and poor was still significantly wide, but social reform and early welfare prevailing into the early twentieth century would slowly begin the shift away from the hardships and social deficiencies of Victorian Britain.

Recipes

Herring was often known as the 'poor man's friend' and it was important at a time when fresh produce was still vulnerable to quick decay to make a number of checks before selecting which ones to buy. If too full of roe it would be too oily and lacking in salt and if soft and stringy it would have been past its best. A good herring needed to be firm to the touch, slightly sweet smelling, with a reddish tinge to the skin. Soyer offers a number of options when cooking herring. He recommended the fish be cooked on a gridiron after a few incisions across its back, dried with a cloth, rubbed in flour and cooked for five minutes. It could also be dressed in mustard and butter, or parsley and lemon, or even fennel and onions.[26]

The following is believed to be the basic soup recipe that the Quakers served in their famine relief soup kitchens set up in Ireland in the mid-1800s. As other supplies became available they were added to the pot.

Quaker Soup

75 lbs of beef

35 lbs of dried peas

21 lbs each of oatmeal and barley

1.5 lbs pepper

14 lbs salt[27]

Just as the Georgians felt that much of the solution to feeding the poor en masse could be found in a good economical and nutritious soup, so too did the Victorians. There are countless published recipes in the media from the time offering variations on the best soup recipe, one that would yield the most volume and the greatest sustenance. One letter published in the *Portsmouth Evening News* on 14 December 1882 retaliates against an anonymously published letter from the week before, criticising the standard of soup served at the Borough of Portsmouth Soup Kitchen. He challenges the criticism by publishing the following recipe and requesting an alternative that can provide the same results for the budget provided.

For a 90 gallon copper, two bushels of split peas, 40 pounds of meat (shin of beef), carrots, onions, and celery. The meat and vegetables are put into the copper in cold water the previous evening, and allowed to stew about an hour and a half, when the peas are added, and the whole boiled for two and a half hours more. The fire is then let out, and the soup left in the copper all night. In the morning the fire is again lighted and the soup boiled for three hours more, when it is ready for use.

Quite frankly my allegiances probably sit with whoever criticised the dish in the first place, as after that amount of boilage I wouldn't want to guess at how much nutritional value would be remaining in the soup once served.

Savarin cake was named after Jean Anthelme Brillat-Savarin, the polymath and gastronome of the eighteenth and early nineteenth centuries. It was a type of rum baba. A favourite at any 1970s British dinner party, it was also adorned at the tables of the very finest houses during the Victorian period.

Clarke, who was Lady Superintendent of the National Training School of Cookery for some forty-five years, included this recipe for the yeasty spongy delight in her book *High-Class Cookery Recipes*, the elitist version follow-up to the popular *Recipes for Plain Cooking*, published the year before:

Savarin

Ingredients

One pound of Vienna Flour.

Half an ounce of German Yeast.

Quarter of a teaspoonful of Castor Sugar.

Two gills of Milk.

Five Eggs.

Three quarters of a pound of butter.

Warm one gill of milk, mix the yeast and sugar together, and stir the warm milk to them. Sift the flour into a basin, make a well in the middle, and pour in the milk with the yeast and sugar in it; just mix a little flour with it, and put it in a warm place to rise. When this sponge has risen to twice its original size, add the other gill of milk and two eggs; beat it well with the hand, adding by degrees the other three eggs and the butter beaten to a cream. Work all this well together, and put it into a mould to rise; when it has risen, bake it in a moderate oven for forty-five minutes. Turn it out, and when cold pour a good rum syrup over it.[28]

3

CHILDHOOD AND THE VICTORIAN FAMILY

Despite her secret loathing of childbirth and the restrictions of married life, a fact that is now discernible from more modern historical interpretation, Queen Victoria understood the importance of advocating public support for the family. This was particularly relevant at a time when the family unit was being challenged by the availability of new transport systems and factories, with commuting and more time spent away from the home needed. Greater numbers of women were also working, with one third of the total Victorian workforce being female, although most of these heralded from the labouring classes.

Women also became more child-focussed, although this varied hugely from mother to mother, but generally the day-to-day care of children by their mothers during the Victorian age became less delegated to nursemaids and more proactive on the part of the mothers themselves. They began reading to children, listening to them recite texts and involving themselves in the tasks of bathing and dressing etc.[1]

Motherhood for many became a special time in the nineteenth century. Children who went into positions of service to assist with contributing to the family finances were granted leave to travel home back to their main parish church or 'mother church' during Lent. This period of family reunion encouraged children to bring flowers home with them to give to their mothers. Later, this trend extended into the custom of larger gifts, in particular a Simnel cake. Mid-Lent Sunday, or Mothering Sunday, marked a break in the austerities of Lent and therefore the eating of the cake also provided much needed refreshment.[2] Although an earlier than Victorian custom, it retained some of its popularity in different communities across the country, particularly in Lancashire and the north of England. This was also a tradition very much still celebrated in the market town of Bury in the nineteenth century. Midlent or Mothering Sunday was also acknowledged in Newchurch and Haslingden where they also prepared 'fag pies' made with bacon and mulled ale.[3] Today the Simnel cake is more widely associated with Easter.

Writers such as Charles Dickens also helped change perceptions around children, particularly with characters such as David Copperfield and Oliver, both victims of society.

The realities were that many Victorian families lived in cramped tenement conditions. As the main providers, fathers were largely absent from the home and preferred to spend any spare leisure time in the pub. Often considerable in size, due to the lack of birth control, children in the nineteenth century were frequently part of a large family unit, receiving little attention from either parent, and inevitably neglected and cared for by other siblings.

There were a number of key dates in Victorian era that heralded the onset of child emancipation and child welfare. This process had started towards the end of the Georgian era alongside the revision of the Poor Laws. The Commission of Enquiry of 1832 saw inspectors visiting industrial sites and factories around the country to gain information about child labour conditions. The findings were shocking, with serious injuries and fatalities being commonplace, as well as harsh working hours and long days without breaks or refreshment. This was followed by a further enquiry in 1842 investigating children working in coal mines and in 1867 into the working conditions of children in agricultural labour, all of which proved to be depressing reading.

Work place food in particular was something that inspectors monitored throughout these enquiries which was unwholesome or often non-existent. This account in particular illustrates the common practices of the time:

The boy, on being brought before the magistrates, was unable either to sit or stand, and was placed on the floor of the office, laid on his side on a small cradle bed ... It appeared from the evidence that the boy's arm had been broken by a blow with an iron rail, and the fracture had never been set, and that he had been kept at work for several weeks with his arm in the condition above described. It furthered appeared in evidence, and was admitted by (the boy's master) that he had been in the habit of beating the boy with a flat piece of wood, in which a nail was driven and projected about half an inch. The blows had been inflicted with such violence that they had penetrated the skin, and caused the wounds described ... The boy had been starved for want of food, and his body presented all the marks of emaciation. This brutal master had kept him at work as a waggoner until he was no longer of use, and then sent him home in a cart to his mother ... a poor widow residing in Church-lane, Rochdale.[4]

The reminiscences of James Holt, a Lancashire Cotton Mill worker, also describe how it was the role of child labourers to take their elders breakfast and dinner in the workplace. With breakfast served from around 8.00–8.30, many child workers like Holt had already been up for at least four hours, with a quick glug of coffee if they were lucky, followed by a two or more hours' walk to work where they toiled in often dreadful temperatures and dangerous environments. By thirteen years of age children like Holt were eligible for full-time employment.[5]

The census for 1871 reveals that over 32 per cent of boys and over 20 per cent of girls aged between ten and fourteen were employed. By 1876 work was prohibited if a child was under the age of ten and the Education Acts had begun to implement compulsory schooling for twelve to fourteen year olds.

Families and childhood must to a large extent be categorised by class in this chapter, as the lives, well-being and health of children during the Victorian age varied hugely according to the type of family unit they were brought up in. By the middle of the nineteenth century, around a quarter of families in Britain could be labelled as middle class, although profession wasn't always dependent on salary. While some professionals could secure salaries exceeding £1,000 annually, office clerks or factory managers may only have received a fraction of this. The desire for status however tended to surpass salary in terms of the ethos that many professional men and women would teach their children. This was aided by the necessity to employ at least one member of staff in the house, live in an area that was considered up-and-coming and acquire a suitable residence, while building influential networks in society. Keeping up appearances and associating with like-minded people in society was essential to maintaining middle-class family status.

I recall my own mother talking about the road she lived in as a child during the 1940s and 1950s. Even then it was still considered totally unacceptable to play with or enter the houses of those children whose families lived in the same street, but were thought to be of lower social standing, for fear of becoming infected by the immoral habits of others.

For children of working class backgrounds the way in which they were reared and evolved into adulthood was dependant on a number of factors as the reminiscences of Mrs H. Jones of Orrell in Lancashire outlines:

> Most of the houses were the two-bed roomed type; if you were lucky there would be a small parlour with a horse-hair suite ... and you might also have a cellar ... children often slept 4 in a bed, two at the top and two at the bottom. On freezing nights the beds were warmed with the oven shelf or a brick kept in the oven for the purpose ... Our staple food was bread and dripping, nearly every mother baked her own bread ... Broth was another popular meal; sheep's heads could be bought for one penny or two pence ... One could get bones free from the butcher – pot herbs free from the greengrocer – these with a little barley would make a dinner for the hungry children. Porridge too was cheap, always made with oatmeal and a little treacle added ... Saturday was an anxious day for many mothers, wondering if Dad would come home with his wages intact. Alas, many couldn't resist the pull of the strong beer and the company at the pub ... Their punishment came on Sunday. Instead of going off for a jaunt with a pal, they spent a day indoors ... Their Sunday suit was missing. It had found its way to the pawnshop.[6]

For many sadly even this was a fairly modest account of working-class life, in terms of its severity. As this alternative account from *Workhouse to Westminster. The Life Story of Will Crooks, MP*, reveals:

> We were so poor that we children never got a drop of tea for months together. It used to be bread and treacle for breakfast, for dinner, ... for tea, washed down with a cup of cold water. Sometimes there was a little variation in the form of dripping. At other times the variety was secured by there being neither treacle nor dripping.[7]

District Workhouse schools came about following the 1834 Poor

Law amendments. They proved largely unsuccessful, with a few exceptions including one located in the village of Quatt near Bridgnorth. With a total of 130 children the school provided both a home and an education. In return inmates grew their own produce and kept basic livestock enabling them to make all their own butter and milk. The outcomes demonstrated significant improvement in the children, mentally and physically and boosted their chances of seeking positions outside of the workhouse.[8]

If you were lucky to escape the workhouse, families, or even multiple families, would be cramped into one room tenement slums, with mothers constantly pregnant and bearing the heavy burdens of poverty and motherhood. Alcohol abuse was commonplace among many women; discipline was hard for children who experienced a tremendous out-pouring of physical and emotional abuse, coupled with the crippling afflictions of malnutrition and near starvation. For many children, becoming a provider at a very early age was paramount to the family being able to eat and survive. Much of the food in Victorian Britain was adulterated, particularly among the poor, contributing further to the population's wider health issues.

A report published in 1842 describes environments that the commissioning officer working on the report deems worse than those conditions for families some sixty years previously. He describes a series of cottages on the Isle of Sheppey rented at a cost of two shillings a week; each cottage had only one room containing a fireplace where the whole family cooked, slept and lived. Water was charged at a farthing a pint.[9]

The renowned cook, inventor and social reformer Alexis Soyer, who straddles both the Georgian and Victorian eras, visited a number of residences as part of his research into finding solutions to the widespread issue of poor diet and health in Britain. In one of his letters he mentions visiting several colliers' cottages. The first cottage he entered had a piece of meat recently roasted and left in a pan, he observed the meat to be very overdone and dried out. As it was left by the fire it continued to dry out even more. When he enquired about the food he was told that the meat was of little interest to the family who were trying to drain all of the fat out of it to make puddings. He estimated that the joint would have been in the region of five pounds prior to cooking, and a reduced three pounds after. At a cost of eight pence a pound for the meat, the family would have been better off spending just five pence for the cost of a piece of fat.[10] It was these sorts of findings that helped inform the way in which poorer families could be supported and educated in the future.

Children became highly skilled at securing food for the whole family in poorer communities as this account of a young Bristol girl relayed in Pamela Horn's *The Victorian Town Child* reveals. She would be sent to the local slaughterhouse to bring back bags of bones, recalling 'we'd go up ... with a big pillowcase and thru pence, and the man would fill 'n up with bones from the pigs ... Take them 'ome to my mother and granny and aunty. They'd share it between them and make stew'. The same little girl fetched slices of bread and butter and stood in the queue every morning at the pawnshop to trade items for cash, presumably to buy food. In London it was common to send children over to the cookshops and restaurants to beg for leftovers, or walk very long distances to get items at bargain prices.[11]

In contrast, rural families like the Prices of Monmouth would not have had the same choices available in the cities. Samuel Price, an agricultural labourer, was fifty-two years old and had to maintain his wife and nine children aged between eighteen months and seventeen, with a tenth child on the way. Samuel was paid eight shillings a week with beer. During the corn and hay harvests this wage increased to one shilling and six old pence a day. His annual salary amounted to around £21 and three shillings. Only one of his children worked, his fifteen-year-old boy who earned one shilling a week running errands. His wife earned an annual salary of twenty-five shillings baking bread. Their expenses went on bread at a cost of nine shillings a week, butter and cheese at six old pence a week, tea and sugar at four old pence a week, potatoes at six old pence a week. They had no meat in their diet and no money for beer. After food their greatest expense was the rent on their house. Their outgoings exceeded their income by over five pounds every year. This deficit was met by way of obtaining charity, relying on three pints of free milk from work a day, and eating as frugally as possible. The family were constantly in rent arrears, and like the aforementioned Bristol family, had to regularly sell many of their personal items to meet costs.[12]

There were other living arrangements that required adaptation for family life, such as army barracks. Knightsbridge Barracks, for example, had to undergo several refurbishments since the original site was built at the end of the eighteenth century. Until work was carried out in 1838 there were a number of small rooms designated to families of soldiers. These rooms were partitioned off and described as 'cubicle-like', poorly lit and with barely any ventilation. Cooking and washing facilities were located in an entirely different wing of the building. It seems that conditions remained bad right up until the 1870s when local neighbouring residents started to campaign to have the barracks shut down. This wasn't out a concern for the conditions families were living in, but rather they were voicing their concerns about properties in the area depreciating due to the slum like nature of the housing. Apparently the latrines and ablution rooms were thoroughly insanitary and the kitchens were devoid of ovens; in fact the only method of cooking provided was boiling. So the families of soldiers, some high-ranking at that, were subjected to very limited diets. The residents committee eventually got their way after years of fighting and in 1877 the whole building was demolished and the residents re-housed.[13]

For those families lucky enough to be earning over twenty-one shillings a week in the 1880s, they had a very different dietary experience to those earning less. With Charles Booth estimating that almost two in every five working people were living on a family income of less than twenty-one shillings a week, this was certainly not representative of the masses. Meals for these income earners were regular and included more meat, vegetables, bacon, eggs and fish. Those lucky to earn in excess of thirty shillings a week enjoyed formal and structured sit-down meals, where children were seen and not heard and ate from fine china using napkins.[14]

There were a great number of gypsy communities scattered across Britain during the nineteenth century. They bore no resemblance to the gypsies the media portray in our own modern-day society, rather these were true travelling migrants with ancient cultural beliefs and customs. They travelled as family units. In the main they earned their living from hawking, peddling, as street entertainers or fortune tellers. It is understood that there were large gypsy populations living in London in the eighteenth and nineteenth centuries particularly during the winter months. The biggest communities could be found at Lock's Fields, Walworth, Battersea and Wandsworth and by the 1850s their makeshift tents had been replaced with the distinctive ornate caravans that we are familiar with today. Their beliefs included the lack of any contact between cooking and food preparation and bodily or other forms of waste product. As a consequence they had no indoor plumbing or proper toilet facilities and many of the staunch or older generations of gypsy maintained the custom of not eating anything in animal form that had not died of natural causes. This meant that many survived on hedgehogs or badgers that got caught in traps. There were also suspicions related to cooking directly on the ground, and many families raised their cooking facilities (usually a crude cauldron) above the fire.[15]

Gypsies were subject to strict vagrancy laws and licences to work and life must have been harsh for these lowest of the low-status communities.

Court records refer to many petty crimes related to gypsies, but in the main they were often blamed maliciously or were witnesses in other criminal activity.

In fact the records of the Old Bailey illustrate the extent of the number of crimes generally committed out of hunger – desperate last acts to feed starving families.

James Mason, aged forty-two, stole and sold on books in an attempt to raise some money for what the police officer involved in the case described as 'his wife and children had not a bit of bread to eat till I gave them some.'[16]

Many families travelled to England during the nineteenth century and they frequently sought middle-class acceptance. One of the most significant of these groups was the Irish. Despite the obvious wave of famine driven migrants, records determine that there were substantial numbers of pre-famine Irish settlers. For example, at least 18 per cent of all the Irish families living in Bradford emigrated there prior to 1841.[17]

Some of the highest rates of pauperism and criminality throughout the latter part of the nineteenth century could be found in the more typically populated areas of Irish migrancy such as Liverpool, Coventry, London, Glasgow and Cardiff. There were many references to the conditions of the Irish living in England at this time, recorded by sociologists and reformers such as A. B. Reach and Henry Mayhew. *The Morning Chronicle* of the 9 October 1848 describes a 'nest of cottages' in the old Cripplegate Ward of London where a number of Irish families lived in 'the most wretchedly unwholesome and filthy condition' and 'each room was tenanted by a poor Irish family, and in one of them, besides the ordinary inmates, a donkey was kept. There was but one outhouse ... for the whole of these, and the cesspool belonging to it was overcharged and overflowing the court'. Thousands of Irish families were on the move during the famine years and their culture influenced communities worldwide, including foods traditionally eaten in Ireland – Irish stew, potato cakes, champ, coddle, soda bread and numerous cabbage-based dishes like colcannon and cabbage and bacon to name a few. Undoubtedly the early years of migration for many must have been harsh. If you were lucky enough to have money and status, finding lodgings and food would not have been problematic. After 1845 a lot of Irish migrants moved to England out of desperation. No food, no money and no dignity on arrival, half-naked and starving, these communities were frequently not welcomed, discriminated against and labelled as trouble. In Mayhew's *London Labour and the London Poor*, he recalls visiting one lodging-house where ten Irish family members were living in one room. There was no furniture except for one mattress pinned against the wall and a dirty piece of cloth hung across one corner to provide some modesty for the women and girls. There was a fire in the middle of the room that everyone congregated around, completely devoid of energy. When questioned, the men lamented at the lack of work, commenting on the abundance of food to be had in the city – 'plenty of taties, plenty of mate, plenty of porruk' – but none of it available to them for lack of funds. For those Irish families lucky enough to earn a living, Mayhew describes a typical Irish family breakfast of potatoes, coffee and bread, with lunch consisting of cheap fish and potatoes. Herring was a popular choice for dinner and there was a tendency to mash the fish into the potato to achieve a tastier flavour. Often the whole family would go out street-selling, eating breakfast beforehand, and then would reconvene at about four o'clock for their fish and potato dinner. While the English poor were unlikely to eat fish more than once a week, the Irish were happy to dine on it most days.[18]

As families generally were so considerable in size, it was also with some frequency that children were either killed at birth, sometimes sold, or just given away. This was the case of John and Bridget Rixon on the birth of their granddaughter. With seven children of their own to feed already they decided to leave the child in a basket on a doorstep of a wealthier neighbour. Their mistake was to contact a doctor, who was initially called to tend to the pregnancy and then informed that the baby had been sent to live temporarily with an old family friend.

Of the three accused, one was found not guilty, one guilty and one respited, which meant their sentence was postponed.[19]

Writing in 1817, Dr. J. B. Davis drew up a report that found there was virtually no medical attention at that time for mothers and their young children, with most hospitals excluding children under the age of two. Davis was a senior physician at the Universal Dispensary for Children, founded in 1816, and his studies revolutionised the way in which children were treated and seen by medical professionals. One study determined that over a fifteen-year period, 43 per cent of all children under the age of twelve died. Davis attributed this to improper feeding after weaning, as many were simply fed a diet of rotten potatoes and under-cooked vegetables, more out of ignorance than anything else. In the days of pre-sterilisation, many doctors did advocate the need to keep feeding bottles clean, but many deaths were simply a result of germs contaminating the bottle's teat, leading to the child's imminent death.[20] Of course one of the other major causes of death in children was the custom of allowing infants to drink harsh spirits, beer or take herbal remedies and opiates to keep them from crying and to keep them asleep. There was also the common practice of pre-chewing food before serving it to the child, thus potentially transferring a huge heap of germs from one mouth into another.

It was the chemist Justus von Liebig who pioneered the first patented infant formula around 1862, based on his theories on carbon, nitrogen and other nutrients. He advocated the need to completely replicate a mothers' milk in order to find a good enough substitute. His infant food consisted of wheat flour, cows' milk and malt flour cooked with bicarbonate of potash.

Liebig's solution was commercialised throughout England, under the name of 'Liebig's Registered Concentrated Milk Co. Ltd.' The product was marketed, distributed and sold at six old pence for a quarter of a pint. Sales were poor and a dried version containing pea powder followed, which also failed to capture the minds and purses of the public. This in part was due to the lack of confidence among the medical fraternity, with regard to the legitimacy of Liebig's product. What followed was a series of adulterated products similar to Liebig's entering the market but deficient in protein and fat, which caused a significant rise in infant illnesses. So severe were the effects of these milk solutions that they frequently caused rickets in a number of children and scurvy, as a consequence of their vitamin C deficiency. By 1870 the new trend for feeding infants was skimmed condensed milk. Initially, as with the former products and a consequence of the malt flour often present, children put on weight and looked healthier. But their overall vitality was poor. Skimmed condensed milk containers all carried a health warning after 1894. Nonetheless the cheap nature of these infant solutions had now attracted a new market of poorer mothers who, unable to afford any alternative continued to buy the condensed skimmed milk.

However by the 1870s, Louis Pasteur's Germ Theory and the spread of bacteria had become widely accepted throughout Europe. Communities were beginning to practice the concept of boiling water, scalding milk and most importantly sterilising all items of food and equipment used to feed babies.[21] Nonetheless for many of the poor, the issues surrounding proper methods of introducing the right food types to infants remained an ongoing problem. A survey conducted in Sheffield in 1900 revealed that over 60 per cent of the women in working-class districts were feeding their children completely unsuitable foods. Often this consisted of bread and jam.[22] In the absence of painkillers, mothers would use opiates to self-medicate. It was estimated on average each person living in England between 1830 and 1860 received in excess of 127 doses of opium annually. Opiate-based medicines were also available to children, many early deaths of children can be attributed to this and often if they weren't poisoned while they were young, there was a high possibility that they would grow up to be addicted to the drug.[23]

As the nineteenth century progressed improvements were being established with child welfare and safety at the heart of new legislation. The National Society for the Prevention of Cruelty to Children (NSPCC) was founded in 1884, Barnardos in 1866 and the Church of England Waifs and Strays Society (CEWSS – later the Children's Society) began in 1881.

In an age of increasing empathy, Isabella Beeton summarises how this impacted on the more privileged children at the time. 'We see elaborate care bestowed on a family of children, everything studied that can tend to their personal comfort – pure air, pure water, regular ablution, a dietary prescribed by art, and every precaution adopted that medical judgment and maternal love can dictate ...'[24]

In 1870 the first national Bill for Education was passed and hundreds of free schools for the poor were opened. As the era progressed school attendance was made compulsory throughout the nation.

The issue of school meals to provide poorer children walking long distances to and from school every day, and the need for some sustenance in school was tested over a period of six years. Some 110,221 eight-ounce dinners were provided to school children at a total cost of 107,406 pence. In addition female pupils often assisted with the cooking of these meals in support of their curriculum studies. Many articles published in the *Lancet* during this period supported the correlation between poor educational attainment with hunger and lack of nutrition. The wider arguments on school dinners are discussed in an article that appears in an 1883 edition of the *Shields Daily Gazette*. In particular the fact that some schools charged heftily for them, when they should been provided free of charge. The article mentions that some schools served meals sporadically and on a weekly basis, which while helping on some level, was not fulfilling the greater need and proposed urgent necessary measures by the newly established National School Board. The concept of daily free school meals would become a reality by 1906.

As with Liebig's infant milk, there were many creamy concoctions created during the Victorian period that were said to provide alternatives to breast milk and cod liver oil among others. One such potion was Angier's Petroleum Emulsion, said to promote appetite and correct stomach and bowel disorders, as well as miraculously treating rickets. It also came with a guarantee that the oil used in its production was obtained from 'particular wells', whatever that means! Oil which was impossible to substitute.[25] By the end of the 1890s there were calls for the Government's Food and Drugs Bill to include a clause condemning skimmed condensed milk as unfit for children. This was based on the fact that the type and volume of fat used in its manufacture was not suited to babies and young children, who needed a good supply of fat to aid development. This motion was reflective of a new approach to nurturing children's needs from an early age.

By the 1870s there was a holistic recognition by society to help in the overall development of children. Many organisations like the Universal Cookery and Food Association offered scholarships to give children the skills they needed to forge a career in cooking professionally, or simply to enable them to learn enough domestic skills in the kitchen to secure theirs and their family's future health.

The levels of affection among family members noticeably increased during the Victorian age. Whereas many marriages of the previous centuries had been about convenience or money, the emergence of the Romantic and Evangelical movements prompted a new-found sensitivity and public weeping and social expression became more acceptable. The Victorians were very pre-occupied with death, particularly as the death of babies represented one quarter of all deaths in Britain by 1900.[26]

The Housekeeper's Magazine and Family Economist, published in 1826, was a shining beacon for excellence in all family matters and advocated the need for regular meals as a means to 'promote the comfort and well-being of a family'. And those meals should be regular and set at specific times. In particular it recommended that an early breakfast contributed to family order and saved time in terms of preparing for the day ahead.

Isabella Beeton's *Book of Household Management* published in 1861 which was largely a mixture of plagiarised recipes and advice on the comprehensive daily workings of a household, provides an all year round selection of menus for 'plain family dinners' . For January she recommended the following for one week:

Plain Family Dinners for January

Sunday	1. Boiled turbot and oyster sauce, potatoes.
	2. Roast leg or griskin of pork, apple sauce, broccoli, potatoes.
	3. Cabinet pudding, and damson tart made with preserved damsons.
Monday	1. The remains of turbot warmed in oyster sauce, potatoes.
	2. Cold pork, stewed steak.
	3. Open jam tart, which should have been made with the pieces of paste left from the damson tart; baked arrowroot pudding.

Tuesday   1. Boiled neck of mutton, carrots, mashed turnips, suet dumplings, and caper sauce: the broth should be served first, and a little rice or pearl barley should be boiled with it along with the meat.
2. Rolled jam pudding.

Wednesday   1. Roast rolled ribs of beef, greens, potatoes, and horseradish sauce.
2. Bread-and-butter pudding, cheesecakes.

Thursday   1. Vegetable soup (the bones from the ribs of beef should be boiled down with this soup), cold beef, mashed potatoes.
2. Pheasants, gravy, bread sauce.
3. Macaroni.

Friday   1. Fried whitings or soles.
2. Boiled rabbit and onion sauce, minced beef, potatoes.
3. Currant dumplings.

Saturday   1. Rump-steak pudding or pie, greens, and potatoes.
2. Baked custard pudding and stewed apples.

It's clear to see that for an average family on an average wage, this is a lot of food, with even the leftovers sounding quite glamorous. Beeton stressed the need for all dinner times in every household, regardless of the size of the family, to retain the exact same amount of ceremony, care and attention as that of a formal dinner party with guests. In doing this the mistress of the house would undoubtedly become adept at dealing with any household culinary enterprise, through sheer practice and experience. Beeton also emphasised the importance attached to having exactly the right equipment in the kitchen to be able to cater for a middle class family. These items included:

Tea-kettle, Toasting-fork, Bread-grater, Pair of Brass Candlesticks, Teapot and Tray, Bottle-jack, Spoons, Candlesticks, Candle-box, Knives and Forks, 2 Sets of Skewers, Meat-chopper, Cinder-sifter, Coffee-pot, Colander, Block-tin Saucepans, Iron Saucepans, Steamer, Large Boiling-pot, 4 Iron Stewpans, Dripping-pan and Stand, Dustpan, Fish and Egg-slice, Fish-kettles, Flour-box, Flat-irons, Frying-pans, Gridiron, Mustard-pot, Salt-cellar, Pepper-box, Pair of Bellows, Jelly-moulds, Plate-basket, Cheese-toaster, Coal-shovel and a Wood Meat-screen.[27]

The Victorian era was the age of the housekeepers 'or general family guide'. Just as Benjamin Spock's iconic Baby and Child Care manual of the 1940s is still referred to today, the nineteenth century was flooded with popular books advising on how to treat a variety of family ailments. There were also general domestic guides that covered anything from the medicinal virtues of salt to how to make fabric waterproof.

It was also the age of mass consumerism and the media was flooded with advice in advertisements with what to feed your children with. Semolina and grape nuts were among the major products marketed in the 1800s as beneficial family foods.

In Brillat-Savarin's handbook of dining, he recommends that mother's should not allow their growing children to drink coffee on the basis that it both stunts growth and makes 'mummies of them'. Whether this was implying they would end up on show in the British Museum in a sarcophagus or something else is unclear.[28]

Between 1852 and 1880 the numbers of child patients admitted to Great Ormond Street Hospital London were shocking. A total of 3,106 in the district of Holborn and 2,664 in the district of St Pancras alone. The most common group of diseases that children were treated for during these same years included bone and muscle diseases with the highest number of cases at 2,803, followed by infectious fevers, diseases of the nervous and respiratory systems all around the 2,000-plus mark., the next highest group of diseases effecting children were tubercular, growth and nutritional deficiency and skin disorders. Sadly seventy-nine cases were venereal; undoubtedly a result of child-rearing by an infected mother, or from early child sexual activity. The age group of all these children were predominantly two to ten.[29] Most older children were taught to disregard ongoing ailments like itching, chilblains, sores and spots. Others who could afford it applied natural remedies such as liquorice powder to aid constipation, while quinine, hot rum and boiled onions was thought to cure a feverish cold and hot salt contained in a stocking and placed on the stomach removed tummy aches. And probably the most useless of all: pepper, vinegar and mustard rubbed into brown paper was the preferred remedy for toothache in the Victorian period. It was thought that by the latter part of the nineteenth century the average family had around six children, but often ten or twelve was the norm. Many babies died early or during childbirth and even those that survived were constantly under threat of the myriad of untreatable diseases. Death was ubiquitous, particularly among the poorer classes of society. The workhouse, together with the possibility of being torn apart as a family through homelessness, was always nagging away in the background for many. Immigrant families had the added concerns of discrimination and social isolation. Henry Mayhew reflected on the attitude of local street-sellers towards immigrants as

'thorough-bred costermongers' repudiate the numerous persons who sell only nuts or oranges in the streets, whether at a fixed stall, or any given locality, or who hawk them through the thoroughfares or parks. They repudiate also a number of Jews, who confine their street-trading to the sale of 'coker-nuts' on Sundays, vended from large barrows. Nor do they rank with themselves the individuals who sell tea and coffee in the streets, or such condiments as peas-soup, sweetmeats, spice-cakes, and the like; those articles not being purchased at the markets. I often heard all such classes called 'the illegitimates'.[30]

Those children lucky enough to be born into wealthier families enjoyed a range of activities and would go on bank holiday and day trips with their parents to the rapidly expanding seaside resorts of the north and south. Although typically families would prepare their own food for these trips, the tea rooms proved to be popular for light refreshments.

There are many disparities involved with categorising children, in that lives during the Victorian era would be very different according to your sex, what class or ethnicity you were born into, and even your generation. By the latter part of the nineteenth century compulsory schooling had been enforced for all and even those lucky enough to receive a private education would only benefit if male. Human labour was being replaced by new technology and innovation, as well as a desire by women to diversify. Those children growing up in the early nineteenth century would not have benefited as much from the social reforms that the late nineteenth century had adopted.

For poorer children their predominant memories would be based around feeling hungry and having to work from a very early age to help support the family unit. If entered into the workhouse, children would undoubtedly be separated from their other family members and be subjected to large quantities of adulterated and sometimes fatal food. It was a six to one, half a dozen to the other dilemma, as so often in large poorer families the father was either unemployed or absent most of the time, making the battle to secure food even harder.

Yet poorer children would definitely have had more contact time with their parent(s) than those of their wealthier peers, who from a young age would be expected to remain in the nursery, occasionally being removed to dine with the rest of the family and then restored to the children only spaces. It's not difficult to speculate that this association with dining and family reunion must have had an undeniably profound effect on a child's relationship with food into adulthood.

There were many ideals in the Victorian era about how family life should be and Queen Victoria and Prince Albert presented an image that middle- and upper-class members of society desired to emulate. As a consequence family was celebrated more publicly and with more tenderness and intimacy. W. P. Frith's painting Many Happy Returns of the Day (1854) provides an insight into this, with food placed at the centre of the celebrations, for the artist's own daughter Alice. The artist's dining room is a richly decorated and cheerful room in greens and reds and a number of bright paintings on the wall. Central to the table is a large cake covered in white royal icing, there are buns, cakes and bonbons and the hint of more sweet delights being delivered by the maid standing at the door. The young children are dressed in their finery and the women look on attentively.

This same dining room was a sacred space for the artist who ate his regular breakfast of fish, York ham and eggs, and toast and marmalade while writing his letters. His work would stop during the day for biscuits and a glass of sherry in this same dining room with the company of his children.[31]

Frith's picture and his dining room are symbolic of how many Victorian middle and higher-class families responded to and provided for their children and offers the viewer a brief glimpse into this world.

Recipes

As the need to safe-guard, nurture and help children develop became more of a national consensus by the 1880s, local government officials, medical practitioners, retailers and scholars and well-meaning journalists advocated the numerous ways in which alleviating child poverty, tackling issues of health and simply becoming more verbal about children generally could be achieved. These frequently included recipes to help benefit children. One fundamental concern for the Victorians was the ongoing problem of sanitation and clean water. Good parents feared their children becoming infected by the turgid water supplies, there were still mixed feelings about the safety of milk, and alcohol thankfully was now considered to be a very bad option. *The Sheffield Daily Telegraph* published a series of 'pleasant drinks for young children' including the following ideas:

Large tablespoon of pearl barley; mix with cold water, and steep until it is a thick mass. Then pour over it a quart of boiling water; put into a saucepan, and let it boil for ten minutes; add a lemon sliced, without the peel or pips; sufficient sugar to sweeten; boil ten ore minutes; put the drink in a jug to cool, and stir occasionally, to prevent a skin forming on the top.[32]

Treacle Water
Quarter pound of treacle; pour upon it a quart of cold water; add lemon juice to taste.

Mothering Sunday Simnel Cake
Six pounds of flour, four pounds of currants, two pounds of raisins, one pound and a quarter of butter, one pound and a half of sugar, one ounce of ground cinnamon, one nutmeg, half-pound of candied lemon, four ounces of almonds, twelve eggs, three-quarter ounce of

salts of tartar, rubbed well in the sugar before you put it into the flour, half-pound of barm. A slow oven prepared as they will rise the best.[33]

Mrs Beeton mentions Cabinet Pudding in her recommended list of weekly family dishes. This was a boiled pudding, most of which would typically require three to four hours of cooking. Reminiscent of a boiled trifle James Jennings's *Two thousand five hundred practical Recipes in Family Cookery* of 1837 provides a basic recipe requiring just one hour of boiling:

Cabinet Pudding
Soak six sponge cakes and two ounces of ratafias in a glass of sweet wine; then make a custard as for baking, butter a mould, and put dried cherries all over it; put in the cakes, and pour the custard on them; lay a buttered paper on the top, tie it down close, and steam it for an hour. Serve it with the following sauce: the yolks of two eggs well beaten a quarter of a pint of cream, some sugar, and a little white wine; make it hot but do not let it boil.

4

HIGH DAYS AND HOLIDAYS

There were a number of key individuals and companies during the nineteenth century that were instrumental in building the tourism industry as we know it today in Britain. Within that industry food and dining is integral to the historical narrative. After all, half the fun of leisure time is trying new or naughty foods.

From 1871 the introduction of bank holidays provided the less fortunate classes with a means to enjoy some quality leisure time, particularly for feast days and church events. The advent of the half-day Wednesday and general shorter working days and holiday clubs also meant that there was more opportunity for entertainment, travel and recreation. The food and drink trade capitalised on this new free time and provided Britain with greater cultural autonomy for all.

The German-born Karl Baedeker pioneered the first traveller friendly international travel guides, most of which were translated for the English market. They were unique in their style and attention to detail, incorporating maps, suggested routes and facilities as well as providing descriptions of the major attractions. In his third guide to Southern Italy, Sicily and the Lipari Islands. Written in 1867, Baedeker describes a steamboat tour and the food on board, which is included in the price of the ticket. He informs the reader that the food is of a good quality and of ample portions, he points out that this did not vary according to what class of travel you booked, with the exception that at 7 p.m. tea was served to first-class passengers only. Baedeker continues to describe the menu as a *dejeuner a la fourchette* (a fork lunch) served at 10 a.m. which included three or four courses, wine if you wanted it and a cup of coffee. Dinner was similar and served between 5 and 6 p.m.[1]

His handbook for travellers to Belgium and Holland recommends tourists visit the Bertrand Place de Meir, which he cites as one of the best restaurants in Belgium at the time, where diners can eat a la carte or take dinner for three francs. He also recommends eating oysters at the Croix Blanche and indulging in the many and varied ices to be had during summer in the cafes. Baedeker even suggests the best place to drink a good beer.[2]

There were two major advances during the nineteenth century that changed transportation. The first was by way of John McAdam, a Scottish engineer who invented an early process of surfacing roads, cementing a layer of granite and chips that alleviated the problem of dust and mud on the roads. McAdam was awarded £10,000 for his work and given the post of Surveyor General of the Metropolitan roads in 1827. Secondly was with the advent of railway. There were already some fifty lines spanning over 1,700 miles by 1845.[3]

There were a large number of railway companies operating in Britain by the mid-1800s – Great Western, London and North-Western, North Western and London and South Western, Midland, Lancaster and Carlisle, Eastern Counties, York Newcastle and Berwick, York and North Midland, Great Northern, Eastern Union, Lancashire and Yorkshire, Southern Eastern, Brighton and South Coast, Stockton and Darlington, Manchester, Sheff and Lincs, East Anglian, Caledonian, Scottish Central, North British,

Glasgow, Dumfries and Carlisle. First and second-class passengers would have afforded the luxury of rail dining cars when travelling to and from their leisure breaks. The service from Parkeston to Doncaster in 1891 served soup, fish, joint, poultry, sweets and desserts at a cost of 3s, 6d. This particular service offering breakfast, lunch and dinner also unusually catered to third-class passengers who were able to obtain light refreshments. Apparently it was the first of its kind to do so according to the *Cambridge Independent Press*, Saturday 4 July 1891.

The discount holiday deal was already in full swing by the 1880s with South Western Rail offering cheap excursions for travellers between London Waterloo and Windsor. One sunny summer Sunday in 1888 as many as a thousand passengers travelled to Henley from London on a special deal run by Great Western.[4] The earliest of these discounted travel opportunities that I could find was in 1858 with an Easter holiday special running from Cheltenham to London.[5] Of course, wherever there was travel, there needed to be refreshment.

There is a wonderfully detailed description of a new Pullman dining car established on the Great Northern Railway in 1879 published in the *Dundee Evening Telegraph* of the same year: 'At one end of the dining-car are two doors, one opening directly into the kitchen or cook's galley, the other the entrance into the dining-room.' We are informed that passengers can see into the steward's pantry where 'many cupboards have been made in a little space to hold stores, plates, glasses, decanters, &c.'. The cook then passes his dishes straight from the fire into the pantry. This particular dining car had six tables with ten chairs that revolved and were upholstered in velvet. The dining car also has a ladies' dressing-room, a lavatory for gentlemen and a smoking room. The style and opulence recorded here makes the modern day sandwich, bag of crisps and a drink purchased over a soulless counter in a crowded sweaty chamber, often next to a less than salubrious public toilet facility seem quite other worldly, like it never really existed, except in literature conjured up by the likes of Agatha Christie.

It is also important to mention that railway users were very likely to take their own packed provisions to eat en route. This was due to the fact that the refreshment points and dining cars were often extremely overcrowded and prone to queuing, and as the nineteenth century progressed, special refreshment baskets were made available on trains as an alternative to the more formal sit-down meal.

Molly Hughes' charming account of everyday life as a child living in Victorian London reflects on one of her favoured train journeys from London to Cornwall and in particular the connection they had to make on arriving at Swindon rail station. She describes the refreshment room there as 'the land of Canaan' with its joyful hot soup. The other most anticipated part of the family's long journey however was the packed lunch they kept in a basket on the luggage rack above them. Molly raptured over the fact that

Nothing compares with sandwiches, eggs, pasties, and turnovers, doled out one by one from napkins, when the supply is severely limited. Oranges in summer were unknown then, as well as all the foreign apples and other fruit to be had in London today. We had to slake our thirst with acid-drops and a tiny ration of lemonade. If by chance a fellow passenger remained we always managed to do some little barter of biscuits or sweets, because strange food is even more pleasant than one's own.

Molly also recalls the little boys who would run up and down the train platform at Didcot shouting out 'Banbury cakes, Banbury cakes!'[6]

Another station Molly might have been familiar with was Euston. At the refreshment rooms here passengers could enjoy breakfasts, lunches and dinners, with more informal buffet refreshments on offer in the main station hall. As well as the luncheon baskets that could be purchased to eat on board, hot lunches could be reserved in advance via telegram.[7]

The fast track snacks that we are all so familiar with today were very much in existence during the nineteenth century, including the newly available food vending machines, which quickly became regular features in rail stations and post offices, at first selling stationery and then edibles. There are reports of vandals breaking into sweet machines with some frequency. One regular offender kept raiding a 'Sweetmeat' coin-operated sweet machine on Aberdeen train station platform, until a decision was made to simply turn the machine to face the wall until the thief was found.

Sweetmeat and Nestlé were two of the biggest manufacturers of these types of machine.[8]

In 1891 a representative from one of the manufacturers of these new sweet machines was quoted as saying that throughout the city of London numerous thefts had been made, leaving the company facing considerable losses. The most creative method was to drop pieces of metal or coin-shaped objects into the slot, fooling the machine into dispersing its contents. One South London man, Arthur Coulson was fined twenty shillings when a witness reported him shoving a piece of iron into the machine's slot.[9] In fact the press is rife with stories relating to these sweet vending crimes throughout the Victorian period. With many streets rampant with scavengers, vagabonds and chancers it does rather question why they bothered to persevere with early vending.

With the rise of the holiday and increased leisure time, it was inevitable that young enterprising Victorians would find a way of capitalising on this new exciting trend. One of the first and most well known of these was Mr Thomas Cook. His pioneering brand of excursion promotion, travel agency and international tourism lives on today. Although British tourists had been travelling and exploring both Europe and the wider continents for many years, leading to the introduction of various new items of food and drink into the country; such as macaroni from the Grand Tours of the eighteenth century, to name but one.

Bearing in mind that the first Nile steamer excursions started as early as 1843, and that H. Gaze and son had already established themselves as a successful tour operator in the Holy Land by 1869 it is important to appreciate that Cook was not the first, however, what Cook did was provide comfortable, safe and specialised packages.

In 1872 Cook embarked on a round the World excursion, accompanying a group of his own paying tourists. He recorded the trip in a series of journals, remarking on the various forms of transportation, the different environments, cultural encounters and of course the food. Cook talks about his preference for American hotels and restaurants in terms of value and in relation to the 'simply enormous' portions of food, recounting:

> The American plan is to order about a dozen dishes of fish, meats, vegetables, pastry, &c, a small portion is eaten from each dish and the 'leavings' go no outsider can tell where. This service is repeated at least three times a day, besides which a supplement can be had in the shape of tea or coffee, cakes, fruit, &c., for supper. But the best feature of the American hotel tables is that relating to drinks. On every table large jugs of iced water are placed, and tea and coffee can be had with every meal; but though the bill of fare generally has a wine list printed on the back, there is no positive obligation to drink, and custom does not sanction the habit of taking wine and strong drinks with meals.[10]

Cook goes on to explain that alcohol is usually sold and drunk at a separate bar, often just the one drink prior to dining and never with food, as was (and is) so customary with the English.

What is particularly interesting about Cook's experiences of the American approach to eating and drinking, is so typical of today's American culture. My own experiences of eating in the States as a traveller have observed the exact same attitude to both portion sizes and towards alcohol. What does surprise me however is the idea of Americans always having tea available to drink. One of the hardest challenges about staying in America is with finding anywhere that serves tea, and even when it is available, it usually comes without milk, or in herbal form.

Integral to foreign travel and of course migration towards a new life was the passenger ship.

Although I personally have never experienced the delights myself, I have heard it said from many that one of the main daily occupations of modern-day cruise ship passengers is to consume as much of the round-the-clock food on offer as possible. Dickens relays his culinary experiences on a voyage to Canada in 1842, as much the same. Noting that people spent the vast majority of their time engaged with eating and cooking their own meals, exclaiming,

> The chief occupation on board seemed to be that of cooking and eating. The cooking apparatus for the steerage was on deck; each family, and each individual who had no family, was continually cooking for themselves. As the accommodation for cooking was not very ample for upwards of a hundred passengers, there was scarcely an hour of the day between sunrise and sunset, that was not witness to the progress of some culinary operations—men, women, and children were constantly appearing and disappearing at the hatchways with pots, saucepans, kettles, and other utensils; and it was not long ere some began to fear, having made but little account of the voracity of appetite engendered by convalescence after sea-sickness, that their stock of provisions would prove rather scanty for the voyage.

Dickens also notes that all the water on board for drinking and cooking with was treated with lime to preserve it, making it taste 'extremely unpalatable'.[11]

Each classification of traveller ate at different times and had their own menus. Most of the poorer immigrant travellers in steerage would be expected to bring their own food and were provided with a small inadequate cooking area. The higher echelon of passenger would have eaten food that was similar to that served in the best hotels.

A bill of fare for the P&O steam ship *Bangalore*, dated April 1871, informs us that there were entrées available such as mutton cutlets, sautéed kidneys, sausage rolls, fowl and mutton curry and desserts of rice pudding, apple tarts and selections of cheeses. A less extravagant menu of 11 November 1882 on board the S. S. *Assam* would have offered its passengers roast beef or roast mutton, brawn, ham, herrings and cheese salad. It should be remembered that on board ship in the 1800s food supplies would be limited due to the lack of refrigeration and live animals were carried as cargo for fresh meat. Any livestock would be housed at the opposite end of the passenger spaces, so as not to offend their senses.[12]

Built in 1901 the *Carpathia* possessed many of the modern conveniences of the Victorian age; the ship was fitted with three large refrigerated holds specifically designed to store cold food, particularly meats.[13] Prior to this most ships were equipped with special ice rooms.

Certainly for steerage passengers the experience was not quite as luxurious, as this account from a travelling German migrant travelling in the late eighteenth century suggests,

Howbeit, during the passage there doth arise in the vessels an awful misery, stink, smoke, horror, vomiting, sea-sickness of all kinds, fever, purgings, headaches, sweats, constipations of the bowels, sores, scurvy, cancers, thrush and the like, which do wholly arise from the stale and strongly salted food and meat, and from the exceeding badness and nastiness of the water, from which many do wretchedly decline and perish. Thereto come also the dearth of provision, hunger, thirst, cold, heat, damp, fear, want, janglings and lamentings, with other hardships, inasmuch as lice do often breed and proliferate, most of all upon the sick, so that a man may brush them off his body.[14]

By the beginning of the nineteenth century the British Passenger Act adopted minimum requirements for food on board ships, making the availability of biscuits, wheat flour, oatmeal, rice, tea, sugar and molasses essential. The captain also had the responsibility for ensuring that every passenger received three quarts of water each day. Although one passenger, after this act was enforced, advised that 'coffee is much preferable to tea, the water being so bad, as to render the tea rather insipid and tasteless.'[15]

In the latter half of the nineteenth century Children's Holiday camps was a scheme for poorer children living in the slums to go on seaside and country holidays. Originally tried and tested across Germany and Austria, children were sent away every summer for three weeks to improve their health and well-being. This was mimicked in England with schemes such as the 'Fresh Air Fund' enabling children from London's East End to benefit from time away spent in the countryside and be fed well. Often it was noted that these children put on weight and their mental health improved. But naturally they raised controversy as to how beneficial it was to spend large amounts of money letting children experience a life they could never achieve and then return to their dreadful circumstances.[16]

This idea spilled into the working club fund, predominantly started by the factory and mill workers of Lancashire and Yorkshire who all paid into a club fund each week which would pay for their annual works holiday. Some of these funds were quite considerable, with one family recorded as receiving over £70 for their holiday.[17] This would be in excess of £4,000 today.

The annual works holiday excursion was sometimes referred to as the 'gipsy' holiday. Perhaps due to the fact that the activity involved travelling. Numerous taverns and eating houses accommodated these big groups and openly advertised their availability, like the Forge Tavern, Birmingham who offered rowing, sailing, tea and dinner and travelling musicians, such as the Eastbourne Sax-Horn Band who were available to book and play at gipsy holiday picnics and private functions.

Another 'holiday' destination was that of the Hop Picking September sojourns to Kent. For many families residing in the East End of London, Sussex and East Anglia the five or six weeks spent picking hops to be dried and sold onto the breweries, despite being arduous work, provided both a change of cultural scenery as well as an opportunity to spend time outdoors in the stimulating air of the countryside. This was a tradition that existed for hundreds of years until modern industrial mechanisation replaced the loyal casual labourers in the 1960s. In her semi-biographical book *The Young Hop-Pickers,* Sarah Maria Fry writes about how one Kent farmer regularly selected Londoners to pick his hops, describing them as:

'a sad, ragged, untidy set, and during their stay, which seldom extended over more than four or five weeks, inhabited a number of little sheds, or huts, built for their accommodation'.

It was customary for pickers to bring with them their own bedding and cooking utensils and the farmer would often provide the group with a large sack of potatoes to last them the duration of their term of work.

The term picnic is a derivative of the French pique-nique, a meal that originally involved each person attending to contribute either financially or in real food terms. Picnics were very popular and often quite elaborate during the Victorian period. The diaries of Rev Francis Kilvert describes a group outing to Snodhill, where the group of men and women worked together to actually build a fire and boil potatoes on it in the ruins of the old castle. After waiting twenty minutes for them to cook; in which time flowers and leafy wreaths were made to adorn the giant table cloth spread beneath an oak tree, the potatoes were distributed among the group along with 'cold chicken, ham and tongue, pies of different sorts, salads, jam and gooseberry tarts, bread and cheese. Splendid strawberries from Clifford Priory brought by the Haigh Aliens. Cups of various kinds went round, claret and hock, champagne, cider and sherry, and people sprawled about in all attitudes and made a great noise'.[18]

The Picnic Society was established in London in the early part of the nineteenth century. The 200 or so members produced small plays to put on while they dined lavishly and gambled. Their motto was excess, together with a poem, Catullus's 'Carmina, Carmen, 13', which reflected the whole original ethos of picnicking and read,

> My Fabullus, my table.
> Like your name is fable,
> But may furnish a splendid repast.
> If you come, do not fail
> To bring bread, beef, an ale.
> Or, Egad! My dear friend, you will fast.

Originally picnic dinners took place in hired premises with no catering facilities, and the food and drink was provided by each member, a total of one dish and six bottles of wine. *The Times* newspaper best describes these meetings:

A picnic supper consists of a variety of dishes. The subscribers to the entertainment have a bill of fare presented to them, with a number against each dish. The lot, which he draws, obliges him to furnish the dish marked against it, which he either takes with him in his carriage, or sends by servant. The proper variety is preserved by the Maitre d'hôtel, who forms the bill of fare. As the cookery is furnished by so many people of fashion, each strives to excel. And thus a picnic supper not only gives rise to much pleasant mirth, but generally can boast of the refinement of the art.

The playwright and MP, Richard Sheridan spitefully tried to close the picnic parties down, as he found their amateur dramatics a threat to his own audiences at the Drury Lane Theatre, which he owned. The group was also derided by the caricaturist James Gillray and after much public baiting the picnickers decided to disband. It would be another three years later that the word picnic would appear in a children's story, with reference to an outdoor wedding dinner. From here on in it appears the term became synonymous with eating outdoors.[19]

Religion and festivals played a significant role in both urban and rural society during the Victorian period, with religious and some pagan customs still celebrated and commemorated across Britain often revolving around food and drink. Perhaps one tradition with the most longevity in Britain is Shrove Tuesday.

Shrove is a corruption of the word *Shrive*, an old Saxon word meaning confess. Originally Shrove Tuesday was Confession Tuesday. As a Roman Catholic country in the Middle Ages, people in parishes across England were obliged to confess their sins to their parish priest. Men and women would be encouraged to come forward by the ringing of the local church bell. This custom continued in some parishes into the nineteenth century. This bell was nick named the 'pancake bell', as people also dined on pancakes and fritters on *Shrive* Tuesday, prior to purging themselves for Lent. A quote from a poem of 1634 appears in William Hone's 1826 copy of *The Every-day Book:*

> Every stomach till it can hold no more
> Is fritter-filled, as well as heart can wish;
> And every man and maide doe take their tune,
> And lose their pancakes up for feare they burne;
> And all the kitchen doth with laughter sound;
> To see the pancakes fall upon the ground'

In Norwich in the 1800s it was still traditional to eat small buns rather than pancakes, called cocque'els, or scallop-shaped. An alternative definition of this tradition is that the buns were thrown at cockerels as part of a rather barbarous sport. They were continually eaten throughout Lent.[20] Moving into spring, Easter was a very popular holiday during the Victorian period. It was traditional on Good Friday to eat hot cross buns. Today they seem to be available in the shops as soon as the Christmas decorations are taken down. There are many superstitions around the crossed bun; if baked on Good Friday, they were said to never go stale and if shared, a friendship would bloom between those eating it. A crossed bun that survived one Good Friday to the next was thought to prevent whooping cough (that's if you didn't die from food poisoning first) The origins of the bun lie in pagan ritual, with the cross added by Christians to remove any pagan symbolism.

Another Easter tradition, pace egging was a practice that originated in Lancashire and involved children going from house to house to collect eggs, which were painted and decorated and then rolled down the nearest hill, a tradition which has survived into the twenty-first century.

During the 1940s it became fashionable to widen the turkey season and, although still rather unorthodox, some households slowly began replacing their traditional lamb joint with a turkey at Easter.

Certainly this tradition was also out of favour in 1883, when a royal mandate against eating lamb was decreed by Queen Victoria. The price of lamb in the market fell from fourteen pence to just nine pence which impacted hugely on sheep farmers just before Easter, one of their busiest times of the year. Those receiving the benefit from the mandate were the butchers, who were able to buy meat cheaply from the farmers.

The rationale for the royal mandate wasn't clear, other than at the time there was a great national shortage of lamb. It was said that in Northumberland alone there were some 100,000 fewer sheep in 1883 than there were in 1879. This was a common occurrence throughout the country and could largely be attributed to disease. Thus the Queen's declaration that *'no lamb shall be served in the Royal Household during the present season'*, an action based on the assumption that consumers should demand less considering the unavailability of lamb, was somewhat counter-intuitive to the problem, that only served to cripple the farmers financially even more.

More of a northern England custom, Carlin – or sometimes Carling – Sunday was marked on the fourth Sunday in Lent. Carlin peas, a type of hard black pea, were soaked overnight, with any faulty ones that floated removed. They were then strained and dried in a towel, fried in butter and seasoned with salt and pepper. Cooking them to perfection was apparently a bit of an art form as they needed to remain crispy, but also soft enough to eat. Across Cumberland and Northumberland they were distributed freshly fried by tradesmen to their customers, the saltier the better. The origin of this dish is contentious. The most popular theory is that when Newcastle was besieged by Scotland and facing starvation a ship load of dried peas managed to work its way up the Tyne on the fourth Sunday of Lent. This saved the citizens of

Newcastle and ended the siege. As late as the 1930s some people still recognised the custom and distributed the peas to friends and relatives living abroad and across England to keep the tradition going.[21]

Traditional May Day celebrations are still marked round Britain today at village fetes, special events and carnivals. In the nineteenth century, it was perhaps commemorated with the most vigour in Cornwall. In Penzance on May Eve young men and women would congregate in the public houses to drink until the clock struck twelve and then they trouped round the town with violins, drums and other instruments before visiting neighbouring farmhouses to drink junket. This was a mixture of raw milk, rennet, sugar and a little cream. The junket was accompanied by a heavy fruit cake, followed by rum and milk and dancing back round the town into the next day. The festivities continued into the first Sunday after May Day, when groups of two or three families local to Penzance carried flour and other ingredients to a place called Rose-hill and other nearby villages to make the same heavy fruit cake eaten on May Eve. A small payment was made to have the cakes baked, after which it was consumed with tea, milk and rum. There was sour milk or curd cut into diamond shapes dipped in sugar and cream for the children.[22]

As autumn drew its curtains over the land it was traditional for all villages in England in the nineteenth century to prepare a feast, which was often a year in the planning to celebrate the harvest at the end of September. Formerly known as Michaelmas, then more commonly as Harvest Festival from the seventeenth century onwards, it symbolised a time associated with darker nights and shorter days. In some parts of the country the day was known as Goose Day, (for a number of reasons, including gifts of geese by debt-ridden tenants to keep their landlords happy). This is a tradition that is still maintained in some small towns and villages today and celebrated with a Goose Fair.

In the village of Haddenham, Bucks, there exists an account taken from a local carpenter, Walter Rose, who recalled the feasts in his community during the nineteenth century.

> No institution was more popular, or more deeply rooted in village sentiment, than our annual Feast, which fell on the first Sunday after the nineteenth of September and was always celebrated on the following day ... the village always honoured the Feast with a zest that it brought to no other event ... the ancient celebrations was ... a literal feast of food and drink, with the mirth that goes with these things. It was a whole day of festivity, when, from outlying farms, lads and lasses, hired for the year, were given a day's leave and arrived early, buxom and smiling. Each cottage home was ready for them; the gleaned corn had been ground, the pie of pears had been made from its flour, and a joint of fresh meat had been cooked ... I have heard of ploughmen not able to afford to lose the day's labour, who would rise extra early and be out on the fields when it was barely possible to see the furrows so that they might knock off for the Feast before noon. For the thrill of anticipation was in every heart; it seemed to all to be the violation of deep-rooted sentiment, to work on the day of the feast.[23]

As described above, the annual festival usually commenced in the church followed by a communal harvest supper held for all the farm labourers at the expense of their master. This hospitality was rewarded by labourers with the payment of their rent, or obligatory goose. Harvests reaped, rural labourers would then be given a week-long holiday in order to seek work in the hiring mop fairs.

We read in the *Burnley Express* about how the local mills and workshops in Padiham stopped work on the Wednesday evening of the week beginning 11 August 1890 for their couple of days annual fair holiday. The Padiham fair was a well-known one across the district and also often had a travelling circus. Among the most popular of food stalls were the oyster, candy and fried fish traders.[24]

All Souls, All Hallows, All Saints, Halloween – whatever you call it, October 31 and November 1 even today is a Christian and pagan tradition celebrated very differently according to region, although similar in the overall objective. Humour or light-heartedness is used to remember the dead.

Seed or soul cakes were made at the end of wheat-seeding season (Coinciding with Halloween) in many farming communities around the country, including Staffordshire and Shropshire. On All Souls' Day Peasant girls would go begging door-to-door at farmhouses for soul cakes, and would sing at the door. In Staffordshire their song went:

> Soul, soul, for a soul cake,
> Pray you, good mistress, a soul cake

These cakes were often triangular in shape, which presumably has something to do with the Holy Trinity.

Whereas in Aberdeen cakes called 'dirge-loaf' were baked on All Souls Day and given away as gifts to anyone visiting the house.[25]

The next significant holiday in rural Britain's calendar was Martinmas Day. Celebrated on the 11 November; a month also known as 'blood-month', a period across all of Europe when livestock was slaughtered for the winter months. Martinmas Day was considered the last day when it was possible to eat fresh meat prior to it being salted, dried and preserved for the long cold months ahead. Martin was a Roman soldier who converted to Christianity (and subsequent patron saint of tavern owners). It is believed he was betrayed by a goose that exposed his hiding place from the Romans with a loud honk; hence goose-based dishes were popular to eat on this day. Families worked together to slaughter and butcher the animals. Every part of the beasts were used. In Scotland and the north of England oats were mixed with blood, offal and entrails to make black puddings and sausages. The rest of the meat was salted and hung to dry or buried in oatmeal.[26]

There were numerous Victorian culinary customs practised throughout Britain during the Christmas period, each one relating to different regions with their own traditions. Some of which had their legacy in medieval culture, others that were just particular to the nineteenth century. For example, in Chester, locals would parade and sing through the streets and in parts of Derbyshire, village choirs would meet in the churches, wait until midnight and then visit all the houses in the neighbourhood with a keg of ale, singing 'Christians awake!', they then returned to the same houses a few days later to sing some more and collect money door-to-door. Carol-singing in a similar fashion was carried out across Northamptonshire on Christmas Eve, while in Nottinghamshire many villagers partook in a game in which apples were toasted on a string, until they dropped into a bowl of hot and spiced ale. This beverage – called 'lambs wool' due to its consistency – was then drunk in large quantities. And in Ripon, Yorkshire, all the grocers in the town sent each of their customers a pound or half a pound of currants and raisins as a contribution to a Christmas pudding, while the local coopers sent logs and the chandlers sent candles.[27]

One particular regional favourite of mine was the Christmas custom carried out by fishermen in Folkestone, Kent. Eight of the largest whiting, also known as 'rumball whitings' that were found in any one catch would be put aside and sold separately for a higher price. All the proceeds collected from each boat would then contribute to the Christmas Eve Rumball, an annual festive feast for all the crew, their friends and family.[28]

New Year's Day was often more celebrated than the Eve. For

instance in the Orkney Isles, the houses of the rich were woken by singing from local men in the neighbourhood. These men were then rewarded with ale, bread, a smoked goose or a piece of bread to take back to their own families.[29]

The whole year in Britain was once beholden to the relationship between the land and the seasons, times and tides, both Pagan and Christian in origin. Within this context food played a significant role and featured strongly in annual rituals, festivals and celebrations where traditions and superstitions were upheld, in many cases right up until the early twentieth century. Even today some of these customs remain intact across rural communities and certainly the commercial element of seasonal holidays frequently reminds us to ensure we have our batter mixture ready in February, chocolate eggs in March, our pumpkins at Halloween and our turkeys ready for roasting in December.

It has always been progress and commerce that has ultimately bolstered the food retail trade in Britain and improvements in travel and the opening up of new markets was one of the first. It is disappointing that the standards adopted on board trains in terms of dining have not been retained. One of the few ways to experience the way people originally dined on the rail networks is to travel on the Orient Express, although much of the sophistication of cruise liner feasting is still recognised.

Although the foreign holiday boom in Britain is most strongly associated with the 1960s, the nation's fascination with travel and their relationship with pasta, curry, colourful herbs, spices and exotic fruits and vegetables are long and complex, starting with the early explorers and reaching its climax in the nineteenth century. For most however, the opportunity to eat ice cream, fish and chips by the sea or to even indulge in the best that the countryside could offer was an achievement only to be dreamt of, saved all year for, or experienced only by charitable means.

Recipes

In his best-known book *The Modern Cook* of 1845, Francatelli wrote a recipe for Yorkshire or Christmas pie, which he deems to be an essential for the Christmas table.

Yorkshire or Christmas Pie.
First, bone a turkey, a goose, a brace of young pheasants, four, partridges, four woodcocks, a dozen snipes, four grouse, and four widgeons; then boil and trim a small York ham and two tonges. Season and garnish the inside of the fore-named game and poultry, as directed in the foregoing case, with long fillets of fat bacon and tongue, and French truffles; each must be carefully sewnup with a needle and small twine, so as to prevent the force-meat from escap-ing while they are being baked. When the whole of these are ready, line two round or oval braiz-ing-pans with thin layers of fat bacon, and after the birds have been ar-ranged therein in neat order, and covered in with layers of bacon and buttered paper, put the lids on, and set them in the oven to bake rather slowly, for about four hours: then withdraw them, and allow them to cool. While the foregoing is in progress, prepare some highly-seasoned aspic-jelly with the carcasses of the game and poultry, to which add six calves'-feet, and the usual complement of vegetables, &c, and when done, let it be clarified: one-half should be reduced previously to its being poured into the pie when it is baked. Make about sixteen pounds of hot-water-paste (No. 1251), and use it to raise a pie of sufficient dimensions to admit of its holding the game and poultry prepared for the purpose, for making which follow the directions contained in the foregoing article. The inside of the pie must first be lined with thin layers of fat bacon, over which spread a coating of well-seasoned force-meat of fat livers (No. 247); the birds should then be placed in the following order:—First, put the goose at the bottom with some of the small birds round it, filling up the cavi-ties with some of the force-meat; then, put the turkey and the pheasants with thick slices of the boiled ham between

them, reserving the woodcocks and widgeons, that these may be placed on the top: fill the cavities with force-meat and truffles, and cover the whole with thin layers of fat bacon, run a little plain melted butter over the surface, cover the pie in the usual manner, and ornament it with a bold design. The pie must now be baked, for about six hours, in an oven moderately heated, and when taken out, and after the reduced aspic above alluded to has been poured into it, stop the hole up with a small piece of paste, and set it aside in the larder to become cold.

Note – the quantity of game, &c, recommended to be used in the preparation of the foregoing pie may appear extravagant enough, but it is to be remembered that these very large pies are mostly in request at Christmas time. Their substantial aspect renders them worthy of appearing on the side-table of those wealthy epicures who are wont to keep up the good old English style, at this season of hospitality and good cheer.

Molly Hughes' fondly remembered Banbury cakes for sale at Didcot station are like the Cotswold equivalent of the northern Eccles cake. The recipe is often different from one source to the next and is said to have originated as early as the sixteenth century. They were the favoured railway snack at many Wiltshire and Gloucestershire railway stations.

Banbury Cakes

Take 1 pound of dough made for white bread, roll it out, and put bits of butter upon the same for puff paste, till 1 pound of the same has worked in; roll it out very thin, then cut it bits of an oval size according as the cakes wanted. Mix some good moist sugar with a brandy, sufficient to wet it, then mix some washed currants with the former, put a little each bit of paste, close them up, and put the side that is closed next the tin they are to be upon. Lay them separate, and bake them moderately and afterwards, when taken out, sift sugar over them. Some candied peel may be added, or a few drops of the essence of lemon.[30]

5

CULINARY CULTURE

Public culture and the use of public spaces combining leisure and the arts was a growing and industrious aspect of Victorian society. Where there was cultural enlightenment or distraction, refreshment and facilities now prevailed. Almost every new public building design of the mid-nineteenth century would incorporate the necessary amenities to both attract and satisfy visitors, as well as providing some financial remuneration to line the pockets of the investors.

The proposed aquarium in Brighton with its plans for an open air cafe, where visitors could buy a shilling dinner, St Paul's Cathedral churchyard that combined a confectioners, a luncheon bar, dining room and cafe for reading and smoking and the Blackpool Tower cafe and subsequent proposal for a further bar to be added in 1899 represent just a few from this period.

From the 1860s onwards many galleries, museums and theatres began to serve a wide variety of refreshments.

There were refreshment rooms located at most of the main attractions in London by the early 1850s, including one by the ticket entrance to the Tower of London, the public galleries in the Houses of Parliament, the Museum of Science and Art in

South Kensington (now the Science Museum) and the Royal Academy. However, the people of Edinburgh were clearly not as open-minded as their London counter-parts, as a licence to establish a refreshment room within the Scottish capital's sister Museum of Science and Art (now the National Museum of Scotland) was rejected in 1874 on the grounds that the citizens of Edinburgh were not suitably prepared for the introduction of refreshment rooms in 'places of amusement'[1] Similarly a petition was raised to abolish the refreshment rooms at the Castle Museum in Nottingham in 1878 on the grounds of selling beer and its implications on the wider community.

However it was Salford's Museum and Library that appears to be one of the original advocates of the provision of refreshments for its visitors as early as 1850, when plans to enlarge the venue included the addition of a suitable suite of refreshment rooms in order to better accommodate the public, which were noted as having a 'beautiful approach'.[2]

The South Kensington Museum, largely the site of the current V&A Museum, was founded in 1857 and started life as an omnibus of different museums relating to various arts-based and industrial collections, with the central objective being to deliver educational provision.

There were renovations made to the Museum in 1867 in order to update the building with modern facilities such as hot water and gas pipes. A large refreshment room was installed on the ground floor, with extended offices and kitchens that were well equipped with the latest apparatus and modern kitchen appliances. Three of London's principal kitchen manufacturers were up for tender for the job of refitting these spaces. Jeakes was the company finally selected. It was thought the planned tiles alone for the new refreshment areas would take a significant amount of time to install.[3] The established carpenters, Jeakes were a family firm that opened their offices in Bloomsbury, only to move into larger premises in Great Russell Street opposite the British Museum sometime in the 1830s. The Jeakes' family firm were thought to have been tasked with manufacturing all the lamp posts for the City of London, specialising in kitchen apparatus by the 1830s and were featured in the official catalogue of the Great Exhibition in 1851. As an engineer and inventor, the head of the family William Jeakes patented a number of items for the kitchen. In particular a patent hotplate was more sophisticated than any other rival on the market for at least eighty years after its launch. Many of the large country houses used Jeakes and their list of clients was very impressive including Charles Dickens and Florence Nightingale. The Jeakes family also furbished the kitchens in the House of Lords and installed the central heating for the Palace of Westminster during the 1840s and 1850s. The company continued, first under the brief guidance of William's son John, who sold it to his friend Edward Clements, who respectfully re-branded the firm as Clements Jeakes. They continued to offer a high quality of work up until 1927 when the company finally dissolved.[4]

The attention to detail with the design and furnishing of the refreshment rooms at the new Victoria and Albert Museum, which metomorphosised from the existing South Kensington Museums, were testament both to the importance attached to enhancing total visitor experience and the need to place refreshment and dining at the heart of this experience.

The original central refreshment room was opened in 1867, *The Building News* in 1870 described the room as 'bright and cheerful . . . It looks like one of the richly and gaily-adorned cafés of Paris'. The decoration of the upper part of the room continued into the 1870s. The English artist John Millais contributed to the colour scheme and the original plaster ceiling was replaced to better resemble the trend for metal advertisements on rail stations. Visitors would have eaten at tables designed by the Belgian artist Alfred Stevens.

The Grill Room (also known as the Dutch Kitchen) was decorated in more muted colours and designed by Edward Poynter. Poynter was a painter and designer who also held the position of President of the Royal Academy. He incorporated blue-glazed ceramics, painted by students, and the wall decorations included panels depicting the months and seasons of the year. The room itself took several years to complete, but was praised for both the 'thoroughly artistic' nature of the décor as well as 'the juiciness of the grills'.

The Green Dining Room was also referred to as the Morris Room. William Morris' windows, ceiling and panelled dado complimented figure panels created by the Pre-Raphaelite artist Edward Burne-Jones. The walls and plasterwork of the ceiling was originally green (hence the name) and re-painted in brown some years later.[5]

It is astonishing to think so many iconic artists of the nineteenth century worked on these rooms, for the simple purpose of people to eat in them. It is a testimony both to the prodigiousness of the Victoria and Albert Museum and an example of how dining had become such an important and extravagant pastime.

From this visitor information for the Victoria and Albert Museum, published around 1919, it's clear that the refreshment rooms are still thriving and maintain their original layout.

Admission
The Museum is open free daily, except on Good Friday and Christmas Day from, 10 am to 4 5 or 6 pm according to the time of year. On Saturdays in summer until 8 pm. On Sundays at 2.30 pm.

Entrances
The Entrance to the Main Building is in the Cromwell Road
Entrance to Southern Galleries of Science Museum on west side of Exhibition Road and to Western Galleries in Imperial Institute Road

Nearest Station
South Kensington District Railway and Piccadilly Tube There is a
subway from the station to the Exhibition Road entrance closed
during the War

Omnibus
Any omnibus passing along Cromwell Road to South Kensington
Earl's Court Putney etc will serve

Official Guide
An Official Guide conducts parties daily at 12 noon and 3 pm
starting from the main entrance hall. The tours last about an hour
and are so designed as to cover broadly the whole of the collections
in a fortnight

Refreshment Rooms on north side of the central quadrangle of
the older part of the main building adjoining the Galleries now
numbered 12 to 16. The suite includes Central Room artistically
decorated, Green Dining Room and Grill Room or Dutch Kitchen.
Excellent luncheons teas and dinners are served at moderate prices.
Lavatories etc. adjoin. There is also a buffet in the central hall or
the Southern Galleries.[6]

We are made aware that there were newly opened Refreshment
Rooms in the British Musuem in 1866, for the benefit of readers
and students as well as Public refreshment rooms. And that you
needed to show a 'reader's ticket' before being given access to
the readers' and students' cafe. The former were located in the
basement, the latter in the gallery of antiquities. But in 1841 there
was no provision for refreshments as John Timbs points out in
The Mirror of Literature, Amusement, and Instruction, declaring
rather disdainfully that at the 'Zoological Gardens, and at fifty
other places, where many hours are requisite to see all the sights;

no one can pass seven hours at the British Museum looking at specimens of hares, rabbits, ducks, geese and pheasants, without getting an appetite.'[7]

The Indian Museum; mentioned in many London guide books of the day, exhibiting the story of how Britain took over India, was based in South Kensington. In 1885 the Museum was subjected to a bad fire, which is believed to have started in the kitchens or dining room 'devoted to fish dinners'. In fact we can glean that there were at least two dining rooms in this museum as the *Hartlepool Mail* reports that the other 'Duwal dining-room', was also gutted. This museum no longer exists. Whether this is a result of the highly destructive fire which apparently raged for hours, or the eventual realisation of its shocking inappropriateness is unsure.[8]

There were many rules and regulations during the nineteenth century relating to what constituted legitimate theatre, and one criterion was the differentiation between music halls that allowed eating and the drinking of alcohol in the auditorium itself, and high-end theatre that had designated refreshment areas. Michael Booth notes that extra revenue gained through the sale of refreshments was key to many of the Victorian theatres with bars and refreshment areas hired out from external contractors who provided the staff, food, drink, cutlery and glasses. Some of these deals also involved the same contractor taking a larger fee for selling programmes and running cloakroom facilities.[9] There were also separate refreshment areas allocated for the different classes of audience, to ensure those who enjoyed the stalls, boxes and dress circle privileges would not have to socialise with the labouring class spectators occupying the theatre pit. It became almost essential to offer the provision of food and drink of some sort in all theatres by the mid-nineteenth century. One theatre gained its refreshment rooms as a consequence of one of the biggest tragedies in theatre during the Victorian age. Bristol New Theatre, also known as the

Theatre Royal and finally re-christened The Prince's Theatre in 1884 had become well known for its annual pantomime which played to full audiences year on year. The pantomime of 1869 was Robinson Crusoe. On the opening night of Boxing Day the crowds began to gather at least three hours earlier than the doors opened, keen to get their tickets. The queues had formed a solid wall at the entrance, so that when the doors opened and the crowds surged from behind, people at the front became crushed in the wave. A total of around eighteen people died, with a further forty-odd injured. Following a prolonged closure the theatre itself was completely reconfigured, including new seating and an extravagant refreshment room. According to the *Western Daily Press* of 1902, reflecting on the refurbishments, the facilities for refreshments had previously been very undesirable. Refreshment 'saloons' had been incorporated into each separate area of the auditorium, including one for the orchestra stalls, the dress circle and balcony, the upper circle and the pit. There were also tea and coffee bars, at least two smoking rooms and a bar for alcohol in the gallery. It must have been a very plush establishment indeed. The theatre eventually reopened as the Prince's Theatre and became one of the most successful provincial theatres of the nineteenth and early twentieth centuries. But the success proved short-lived as the theatre was totally destroyed during the Second World War.

The founder of the popular music hall style that we are familiar with today was said to be Charles Morton, a pub landlord who owned and ran the Old Canterbury Arms in Lambeth, London, from 1849. By 1852 he had introduced specialist concert nights, which became so popular that they warranted the building of an accompanying concert hall, next to but separate from the public house itself. Initially fees for these concerts were based on the fact that visitors paid *6d* for refreshments once they had entered the hall. This fee was soon replaced by a concert admission ticket, heralding the first music hall. Although many other establishments were capitalising on the benefits of musical entertainment in public houses all over the country, well before 1849, Morton has attained the credit. This is particularly true of the north of England where venues such as Thomas Sharples's Millstone Inn, Bolton, had established its own concert hall by 1832 and the beer houses of Lancashire and Yorkshire were battling the restrictions of the temperance societies in order to stay in business.[10]

Not all theatres were open to the idea of licensed refreshment areas. The Victoria Opera House in Burnley was still fighting their right to this in 1890, when their application for a licence was refused. According to the *Burnley Express* that year, the patrons of the Opera House argued many of their clientele were rural, often having to leave their homes at five or six in the evening to travel to a performance and not returning until after midnight. As a consequence the theatre would empty out during the intervals while the audience sought refreshment in the local surrounding public houses. The repercussions of this often led to people drinking quickly and in abundance before returning intoxicated from their break. Certainly, of the thirty-two largest theatres in the country in 1890, only five retained a clause which left them unable to obtain a licence to serve alcohol.

Music halls were also places you might visit with your children, making the availability of soft drinks and food imperative. During the 1890s Joseph Stamper regularly visited the People's Palace in St Helen's with his father and ate 'Eccles cakes full of currants'. These cost 'one penny or a halfpenny according to size; pop was one penny a bottle; and oranges were three a penny.'[11]

It was Victoria's successor, Edward VII, who quickly introduced the fashion for dining at the opera during the interval and prior to the performance. Despite the first purpose-built cinema, thought to be in Colne, Lancashire, in 1905, shops, railway arches and halls were being converted into small cinemas, or as they were known then as cinematographs all over the UK as early as the 1890s.

One such event in 1901 is documented in the *Dundee Evening Telegraph* as having taken place at the Victoria Hall. The film being screened was Queen Victoria's funeral procession, after which a service of fruit was brought forth.

A new refreshment house for Bristol Zoological Gardens was proposed in 1895 at a cost of £1,500. Not only were there disagreements between the shareholders about the use of funds for the new premises, there were also moral arguments against the proposed licence to extend sales of beer on site, which was thought to be inappropriate to a respectable family-friendly attraction.[12]

The push and pull of commercialism versus moral responsibility was clearly one that the Victorians frequently anguished over with the numerous meetings between officials that were recorded in the press at the time, from selling alcohol at tourist attractions, to extending refreshment retail sales to include Sunday opening hours from the 1870s onwards.

Frequently dubbed the 'British Tivoli', Vauxhall Gardens was a site for various shows, variety and entertainment between 1661 and 1859. There were pavilions with outdoor orchestras and suppers served outdoors.

But mostly people brought their own picnics. Vauxhall Gardens was also one of the few acceptable places in society frequented by un-chaperoned women and men to go and meet. However this controversial practice gave prostitutes carte blanche to conduct their trade with greater legitimacy. This contributed to the overall decline of the gardens, which started to get a reputation leading to closure in 1859. The gardens were often open every evening except Sundays. The only example of refreshments I could find date to 1822, so a little before the Victorian period, but they offer a detailed list of what was available to visitors on a daily basis. Bearing in mind that a shilling would have been worth around £3–£4 in today's money in 1822, prices were certainly targeted towards the middle and higher classes of society. One assumes the 'plate of sugar' would have been available as an accompaniment to sweeten other dishes or drinks. Salads were popular in Britain from at least the mid-1700s, but it seems there was a trend for eating and mixing salad components separately in 1822, with the individually priced lettuce, cucumber, oil and eggs. What quantity you were provided with remains a mystery, but I imagine this wouldn't be popular today, not just for the inconvenience of it, but due to the fact that it would end up costing a fair amount more to make up a simple salad with all its components, particularly when having to spend around £4 just on the olives! Although it would allow for a more bespoke creation according to taste.

	s	d		s	d
A Chicken	4	0	Jelly	0	9
A pulled Chicken	5	0	Plate of Olives	1	0
Dish of Ham	2	0	Plate of Sugar	0	6
Plate of Ham	1	0	Lemon	0	6
Dish of Beef	2	0	Lettuce	0	6
Plate of Beef	1	0	Cucumber	0	6
Plate of Collard Beef	1	6	Cruet of Oil	0	6
Dish of Potted Meat	1	0	Egg	0	2
Tart	1	6	Slice of Cheese	0	3
Cheesecake	0	6	Pat of Butter	0	2
Custard	0	6	Slice of Bread	0	1
Heart cake	0	4	Pot of Stout	0	8
Shrewsbury Cake	0	2	Pair of Wax Lights	2	0
Biscuit	0	1			

	s	d		s	d
Port	6	0	Frontignac	10	6
Sherry	6	0	Champagne, White	14	0
Bucellas	6	0	Champagne, Red	14	0
Lisbon	6	0	Old Hock	14	0

Vidonia	6	0	Moselle	12	0
Madeira	8	0	Burgundy	15	0
Claret	10	6	Arrack Punch, per quart	12	0
Sauterne	10	6	Ditto, Pint	6	0
Barsac	16	0	Ditto, Half Pint	3	0[13]

Another public venue that gained popularity in the Victorian age was the department store, which became as famous for refreshments as they did for their retail products. Many of the early department store shop workers of the late nineteenth century worked on the controversial truck system of employment, which meant living on the premises, with wages reflecting this contribution to board and lodgings. Despite conditions usually being adequate and respectful, this type of contract was thought to encourage wanton dependence on others. This was an attitude that was very prevalent at the time, for fear that early welfare strategies were leading to a reliance on others, by those who it was thought should ultimately safeguard themselves. Accommodation might have been a bit dingy and close-quartered, but shared bathrooms were often provided as was food. Notwithstanding, the meals were generally reputed to be insufficient and of a poor standard. Staff often did not have the time to sit and eat properly during their hectic work days, as this first-hand account confirms:

> A hot dish for breakfast, a glass of milk at 11 o'clock, a 'relish' for tea, a hot supper, these so-called luxuries are in fact necessities to a growing girl or delicate woman, who is unable to eat the solid but unpalatable mid-day meal ... The anaemia, indigestion, and other forms of debility from which the older women suffer are often attributed to their inadequate diet in those years when they were most in need of good food, but least able to afford it.[14]

Most assistants were allocated just twenty minutes to acquire and eat their meals, although as the stores were so busy many employees were called back into the shop before finishing.

For those working long hours in these new busy stores, but living off-site, there would have been the draw of the public dining halls and tearooms to grab something cheap and cheerful on the way to or from work. Although, as Elsie Webster recalled, her father's job as a shop manager in a large firm of grocers in Liverpool meant that 'he sometimes arrived home after midnight on Saturdays. He left each morning at about 7 a.m., eating his breakfast when he reached the shop. He had to remain on the premises all day when he became a manager, so the shop boy used to come up and get his dinner ... me mother cooked ... perhaps two little chops and ... a little bottle of beer and she used to put that in the bottom of the basket'.[15]

Commerce was big in the nineteenth century and shop owners competed to attract passers-by, while the interiors sought to be as inviting as possible. By the middle of the century department stores provided a system of being able to purchase many different items in one building. Harrods, Harvey Nichols, Liberty's, Fortnum and Mason and many of the old established large luxury stores we are familiar with today were operating during the nineteenth century. Bainbridge & Co in Newcastle upon Tyne, now part of the John Lewis chain, is historically considered the first department store. The restaurant located in Harrod's Stores Ltd in 1895 was situated on the ground floor and sold hot lunches between 12 and 3 p.m. At this time of day you could expect to be served soup, fish, entrees, joints and poultry among other dishes. There was a daily menu or a fish menu to choose from. The most expensive item from the daily tariff was a rump or fillet steak costing one shilling, chops at 10*d*, or ham and eggs, also 10*d*. Or you could delight in hot teacakes, buttered toast, muffins or crumpets for just 2*d*. The fish tariff offered half a lobster for a shilling, or sardines on toast for just 6*d*. If you wanted a drink tea, coffee, cocoa or 'American iced drinks' were available. There is no mention of alcohol, which was probably in line with the strict licensing laws of the period and the all pervading temperance conscious fashion.[16]

William Whiteley's haberdashery store, the Universal Provider located in Westbourne Grove, London, added both a restaurant room and a fish bar to his rapidly expanding empire of a business, which was probably the most diverse haberdashery in the world. So popular was this store that police had to be called out on more than one occasion to mange crowd control issues created by eager customers queuing outside. Specialising in textile fabrics, the Universal Provider also sold jewellery, toys, stationery, books, periodicals, printing, lithography, die stamping, glass, china and upholstery. A general provisions department sold meat, poultry, game, bread, flour, groceries, fruit and vegetables. Whiteley's business interests also ran to auctioneering, house agent, ship broker, coal merchant, insurance agent and banker. The restaurant employed a chef de cuisine, whose menu changed daily and was said to rival any reputable restaurant in London for quality. The staff dining rooms catered for 250 male and 250 female employees separately. It was said 1,200 staff sat down to dinner daily, mostly consisting of the very best quality roasted meat. The store's popularity can be attributed to the fact that they sold the best quality goods for the cheapest prices.[17]

There are several other relevant historical references of interest regarding Whiteley and his store. A great fire raged through the building in 1887 and was forced to move locations. Now labelled the world's biggest store, it seemed there was no stopping the Universal Provider. Alas the same wouldn't apply to William Whiteley. Horace Raynor, a young man claiming to be his illegitimate son, walked into the store one winter's day in 1907 and shot Whiteley dead and then attempted to take his own life, as recorded in the *Lancashire Evening Post* on 11 February 1907. No evidence ever came to light that Raynor was Whiteley's son.

There was a new understanding about the relationship between consumerism and the utilisation of public spaces to accommodate them, emerging from the 1860s onwards. And traders were capitalising on the new movement of respectable, middle-class female clientele, who required refreshment and respite while out shopping, as well as facilities such as lavatories, which had been almost non-existent for women out and about in public during the previous century. Harrods even had the first moving staircase (or escalator) in Britain, unveiled in 1898. Nowhere was this more evident than in the West End where galleries, theatres, hotels and restaurants were thriving. The Grosvenor Gallery in Bond Street applied for a licence to sell alcohol in its newly established gallery restaurant. Its owner claimed that after just three months of opening the restaurant had catered to some three to four hundred diners on a daily basis, providing 'a want which has long been felt to exist in the West End, namely a place conducted on such principles and in such a manner as allows of its being visited for the purposes of refreshment by clergymen, ladies, and others by whom restaurants are considered objectionable'.[18]

Grosvenor Gallery was granted its licence in 1878 and many followed in its wake. The entire west side of Piccadilly in London was occupied by restaurants, taverns, oyster bars and public houses. One such oyster bar, said to be the best in the area, Quin's in the Haymarket which was open until the early hours and often flirted with the press with activities that included a gentleman who scratched his initials on one of the restaurant mirrors, and a complicated dispute involving two ladies, a rowdy diner and a waiter which reached the courts.

The majority of the big stores of the time provided lunch and tea rooms for its predominantly female shoppers. Liberty's offered the ultimate in indulgent shopping with their 'Arab Tea Room', where women could rest their weary limbs and delight in a selection of the finest teas, including Indian, Lotus, Yang-Yin and many others in an environment resembling an exotic far eastern destination. Only a small tea room, it was reasonably priced and served fancy biscuits alongside the beverages. In fact the stores themselves and the task of food shopping became a pastime in itself. Grocers and food and beverage tradesmen were expanding and evolving. By 1894 John James Sainsbury and his wife Mary Ann Staples had opened some six or seven food retail outlets, many of which were affordable for all classes of society. Sainsbury himself described his stores as:

> well lighted, and elegantly fitted with mahogany, the walls being lined with tessellated tiles, while marble slabs and counters give to the whole an inviting air of coolness and cleanliness at the hottest season. The [stock] is of the most comprehensive description, embracing the choicest butters of absolute purity, obtained direct from the farms of Brittany, Dorset and Aylesbury; new-laid eggs; Wiltshire and Irish bacon, York and Irish hams; the finest English, American and Continental cheeses; ox-tongues in tins; fresh and salt dairy-fed pork; and all descriptions of poultry and game when in season.[19]

Tea rooms in the larger stores became popular venues as group and society meeting places for women. The Tea and Shopping Club was founded in 1893 in Regent Street, London. Later renamed the Ladies' Country Club, its primary objective was to provide 'comfort and convenience of ladies visiting the West End for shopping or other purposes.'[20]

Membership stood at 600, before the group even met for the first time and the premises for the club itself took up four floors. Men were allowed access to the first floor only, where luncheons were served.[21] This was the era of grand communal demonstrations of invention and individual talent. Arenas to showcase British skills, aptitude and originality grew.

The French were the first to stage an exposition showcasing industry as early as the 1840s. In response the British Great Exhibition of 1851 provided a platform for international design and innovation, while highlighting above all others the achievements of British manufacturing and industry.

The Great Exhibition of 1851 was an arena not only offering refreshments for those attending, but was a vast showcase for new patented items for the kitchen, cooking and dining, offering a glimpse into the future. According to the official catalogue these included displays by the ceramics manufacturing giant, Minton who showed jelly stands, wine coolers and salt cellars, to many individuals like William Ellis of the Isle of Wight promoting his kitchen range and hot plate over oven, for roasting, boiling, baking and stewing.

The statistics for refreshments consumed throughout the Great Exhibition over some five months were recorded that year and included the following:

Bread (per quarter loaf)	24,536
Coffee (per lb)	9,181
Chocolate (per lb)	3,783
Pound cakes (per lb)	28,828
Savoy cakes (per lb)	20,415
Italiens (per lb)	2,197
Biscuits	33,722
Bath buns	311,731
Plain buns	460,667
Banbury cakes	34,070
Penny cottage loaves	57,528
French rolls	7,617
Threepenny pound cakes	36,950
Pickles (in gallons)	1,946
Milk (in quarts)	17,257
Cream (in quarts)	14,047
Schweppe & Co.'s	

soda-water, lemonade	
and ginger beer	536,617
Ice (in tons)	180
Meat (in tons)	113
Ham (in tons)	19
Potatoes (in tons)	30
Salt (in tons)	16[22]

It was estimated that the caterers present at the 1851 exhibition made profits in the region of 100*l* every day, a staggering £7,000 or £8,000 in today's market.

London's follow-up World Fair of 1862 in South Kensington featured in the region of some 30,000 exhibitors. The six million odd visitors that attended over a six-month period were provided with a wide range of refreshments, which also caused some controversy at the time according to a series of letters that were printed in the press. Complaints were made about the increase in prices over the course of the exhibition. A French stall holder raised some of his prices by 100 per cent from 1*d* to 2*d* for a roll and a 'gelatine' from 1*s* to 1*s* 6*d*. Another letter talked about the lack of available meat products for sale with the exception of pork pies and the unacceptable cost of tips that was expected from waiting staff.[23]

It is understood that the English caterers present at the 1862 exhibition ordered the following utensils for the duration of the event: 20,000 dinner plates, 20,000 dessert plates, 2,000 large dishes, 2000 decanters, 20,000 tumblers, 10,000 sherry glasses, 25,000 champagne glasses, 10,000 coffee cups, 5,000 tea cups, 7,500 knives forks, 11,000 plated forks and spoons, 6,000 yards of damask, 20,000 glass cloths and 3,000 chairs.[24]

What is particularly interesting about these figures is the clear preference by 1862 for the consumption of coffee over tea, exemplified by the quantity of coffee cups over tea by double the amount.

The first specific food exposition was held in London in

1885 at Willis's rooms in London, advertised as 'An Exhibition of High-Class cookery'. After four more similar expositions a number of food trades in London wanted involvement and the Universal Cookery and Food Association was founded in 1889 to organise these events and the cooking fraternity in general. Membership increased from 186 members in 1892 to 1,325 by 1906.[25]

The Universal Food Cookery Exhibitions were held annually in London by the Universal Cookery and Food Association from 1885 until the 1930s. The UCFA originally had their roots founded in the promotion of French cuisine in Britain, but as the country began to change politically, with greater emphasis on the need to roll out a form of national food and cookery awareness, so too did the principals of the UCFA change. The exhibition of 1896, when the association was at the peak of their membership, was patronised by HRH Princess Louise, the sixth child of Queen Victoria and Prince Albert. The stalls were lavishly laid out, with the wedding cake displays receiving a great deal of attention, in part due to the use of real pearls within the decoration, while others rose like 'church spires'. There were also large architectural structures sculptured in sugar and, of all things, mutton fat and wax. And it was observed that a game pie was so ornate that it featured the plumage of a whole pheasant spread across the entire pie. There was also a section dedicated to 'plain' cookery, exhibiting among other choice dishes; beef olives, lamb cutlets, tomato soup, curries, vegetarian rissoles, stuffed eggs, cheesecakes, raspberry buns, soda scones, cherry cake and a variety of blancmanges. The Army and the Marines were represented, with the Army school from Aldershot demonstrating how three good meals could be made at a total cost of just over eight old pence.

The exhibition not only featured food, it also showcased antique kitchen furniture and utensils, old recipe books and menus. There were competitions for children to win scholarships and lectures for adult learners.[26]

Significant event exhibitions were also staged across the country commemorating Queen Victoria's Golden Jubilee in 1887. In particular Manchester's Royal Jubilee Exhibition staged at Old Trafford was one of the grandest. Held over a period of about six months, the site area covered an incredible thirty-two acres, throughout which were located a number of dining rooms catering for different needs. According to the Manchester Guardian the prices were 'distinctly democratic' ranging between three and six old pence for tea and a serving of cold meat or fish.[27]

Liverpool also staged its own large-scale exhibition. Indian-inspired cafes and restaurants dominated many of these exhibitions. An enterprising young Indian waiter called Daniel Santiagoe working in the Ceylon Tea House, at the Liverpool Jubilee event wrote a cookery book titled *The Curry Cook's Assistant or Curries and How to make them in England*. Santiagoe sold 400 of the 500 copies he initially had published, retaining the remaining 100 for friends and family. Due to its success the book ran to a second edition.

Indeed, Britain has a long standing relationship with commemorating Royal Jubilees, with food always playing a significant role in proceedings. The fiftieth anniversary of George III's reign in 1809 was celebrated in Newcastle with street festivals, not dissimilar to our modern-day street parties. Poorer residents of the city were able to dine in groups, al fresco, courtesy of their local parishes. Children attending charity schools were also treated, as were their teachers who were allocated a bottle of wine each. Beef and bread were issued to poor housekeepers, and one lucky congregation based in Hanover Square were presented with beef, bread, porter, tea and lump-sugar to take home with them, by the local church reverend.[28] There were also a number of regular regional organised food fairs, the cheese fairs of Chester, Crewe,

Wrexham, Shrewsbury, Gloucester, Leicester, Derby, Cambridge, Reading and Rugby being among the most popular.

More leisure time in the nineteenth century equated to more ways of entertaining oneself and therefore spending more money, a framework ultimately with food at the heart of it. As well-to-do women with more spending power stepped out of their homes, public dining became an appealing pastime available to them. The last century made no provision for this, but as the great public buildings opened with recreational activities provided, so too were the utilities and facilities with which to cater to their visitors. Socialising outside of the home to eat publically and visit the music halls, theatres and clubs was something increasingly not just for the amusement of men. Small groups of men and women would dine together and for the first time it became increasingly acceptable for women to take tea or a light lunch without a male chaperone. Just as we talk about 'destination' venues today, as somewhere people would expect to go out of their way to visit in anticipation of an experience – whether it is a novelty themed restaurant, or a multi-functional shopping centre with children's activities and fine dining opportunities, the Victorians would have expected a similar adventure. Parks, zoos, public gardens and aquariums were also places to engage with your children as a family. In particular, zoos and aquariums offered a glimpse into Britain's colonial trophies, wild animals and sea creatures captured from the empire for the entertainment of others. Such wonders of the world required appropriate refreshment and respite for visitors. Until the late nineteenth century, increasing attendance to these types of venue led to a multitude of salesmen who would set up their stalls selling drinks and snacks at the building's exit. This trend remains today, often with the obligatory ice cream van parked outside the gates in anticipation.

In particular a barrage of complaints were received from visitors to Regent's Park Zoological Gardens about 'a number of pot boys' hanging around the gates with cans of beer. This led to the zoo's earliest organised refreshments with outdoor seating serving drinks and light edibles to visitors outside both the monkey and elephant houses in the summer of 1835.[29] The provision of public refreshments, however, didn't materialise unchallenged. Women seen to drink alcohol in public were labelled as prostitutes and brothels and salubrious haunts for the depraved often disguised themselves as reputable coffee shops, temperance hotels and dining rooms. It was considered difficult to determine which traders were legitimate and respectable enough for women to frequent and if a respectable store began officially serving refreshments, would this in turn then make them appear to have lost their reputation? Social commentators of the nineteenth century were constantly lamenting upon the evils of urbanisation and commercial growth and how this impacted on the role and image of women in society. In particular, department stores found applications for licences to sell alcohol as part of a lunch menu difficult to acquire without contention.

Leisure itself was even questioned by the Victorians as a potentially immoral practice, considered an unnecessary luxury likely to breed apathy. The younger wealthier generation, blurring of class distinctions and abundance of tempting recreational activities probably contributed to the increase in leisure time pursuits, as did the credible theory that said changes in both environment and activities could yield a better quality of worker.

Recipes

Cheesecake (like that served at Vauxhall gardens)
This is actually an American recipe, but cheesecake recipes were so adulterated, mixed, morphed and influenced by numerous cultures over the centuries, that there was never one model recipe.

The basis of cheesecakes is professedly the curd of milk as turned for cheese, but many are made entirely without it. The following recipe is much approved: Take the curd of eight quarts of new milk; rub the curd in a coarse cloth till quite free from whey, then work into it three quarters of a pound of butter, three biscuits, and an equal quantity of bread crumbs, a little salt, and such spices as you choose, finely powdered. Beat ten eggs (half the whites) with three quarters of a pound of fine loaf sugar, a wineglass full of brandy or ratafia, and a pint of rich cream. Having well mixed all these ingredients, rub them with the hand through a coarse hair sieve; then add a pound of currants rubbed, in a coarse cloth and picked and an ounce of candied citron, cut as small as possible. Line tin patty pans with rich puff paste, put in the mixture, and either entirely cover with paste or put on only bars or leaves. They will take about twenty minutes to bake in rather a quick oven. By substituting half a pound of sweet almonds for currants, and half an ounce of bitter, blanched and beaten to a paste, almond cheesecakes may be made, or lemon orange cheesecakes, by substituting for the currants two or three candied lemons or oranges, pounded in a mortar.[30]

One of the dishes on the 1895 Harrod's Stores menu was a dozen 'Best Whitstable Natives'. Whitstable Natives or oysters were considered some of the best in the world and still are I believe. *Hints for the Table,* an 1866 book of helpful cookery advice and recipes, recommends the best way to cultivate oysters, by placing the live molluscs flat side down in a tub filled with water and salt. The water should be changed daily and the oysters 'fed' with a handful of flour, barley-meal, or oatmeal and wheaten-bran. After five or six days, it was said the oysters would be nice and fat and ready to eat.

The Georgian author and politician Jonathan Swift recorded a recipe for boiling oysters within the long series of letters that he compiled over the years:

Swift's Oysters

Take four oysters, wash them clean, that is, wash their shells clean; then put your oysters into an earthen pot with their hollow sides down, then put this pot covered into a great kettle with water, and so let them boil. Your oysters are thus boiled in their own liquor, and not mixed with water.

As the sale of alcohol was so contentious an issue when combined with shopping and leisure activities in the nineteenth century, I have included here an excellent recipe for 'strong beer'. Whether the reference to the influence of the weather conditions on the final quality of the beer was superstitious or genuine is uncertain, but I would like to know. Perhaps the water was prone to becoming tainted in a storm?

Strong Beer or Ale

Twelve bushels of malt to the hogshead for beer, (or fourteen if you wish it of a very good body) eight for ale; for either pour the whole quantity of water hot, but not boiling, on at once, and let it infuse three hours close covered; mash it in the first half hour, and let it stand the remainder of the time. Run it on the hops previously infused in water; for strong beer three quarters of a pound to a bushel; if for ale, half a pound. Boil them with the wort two hours from the time it begins to boil. Cool a pailful to add three quarts of yeast to, which will prepare it for putting to the rest when ready next day; but if possible put together the same night Tun as usual. Cover the bung hole with paper when the beer has done working; and when it is to be stopped, have ready a pound and a half of hops dried before the fire, put them into the bung hole and fasten it up. Let it stand 12 months in casks and 12 in bottles before it be drank. It will keep fine 8 or 10 years. It should be brewed the beginning of March. Great care must be taken that the bottles are perfectly prepared, and that the corks are of the best sort. The ale will be ready in three or four months; and if the vent peg never be removed, it will have spirit and strength to the very last. Allow two gallons of water at first for waste. After the beer or ale has run from the grains pour a hogshead and half for the twelve bushels, and a hogshead of water if eight were brewed; mash, and let stand, and then boil &c. Use some of the hops for this table beer that were boiled for the strong. When thunder or hot weather causes beer to turn sour, a tea spoonful or more if required of salt of wormwood put into the jug will rectify it. Let it be drawn just before it is drunk or it will taste flat.[31]

6

TRAINING THE MASSES

The concept of a National Training School for Cookery for the benefit of all classes began in 1873 when a committee, consisting of members such as the Countess of Carnarvon and the then Prime Minister's wife, Mrs Gladstone, among others, was established to investigate the best and most appropriate means of communicating the subject for the wider benefit of society. The school was to be an alliance together with the School Board and Training Schools. Eventually established in South Kensington (now the site of the Science Museum), it thrived to become a limited company in 1888 and expanded into a broader school for Domestic Economy from 1902, finally closing its doors in 1962. The school published an official handbook in 1879 that offers a wealth of information pertaining to the content of the daily lessons. These included instructions from how to clean kitchen utensils and stoves, the basic principles of cooking such as roasting, boiling, baking and frying and how to utilise cold cuts and leftovers to specifics on cooking meat, fish, vegetables and poultry, making soups, sauces, pastry's and puddings, cakes and biscuits. There was also instruction on cooking for people who were ill and the importance of diet and its correlation to health. Finally, the guide lists a comprehensive inventory of the necessary equipment needed in a kitchen to be able to train in cooking, including:

3 copper stewpans of various sizes
3 enameld stewpans of various sizes
1 saute pan
iron pot for boiling
stock pot
frying-pan
omelette pan
fish kettle
frying basket
copper preserving pan
roasting jack
steamer
coffee-mill
egg whisk
box of cutters
grater
jelly-moulds
tart pans
pastry brush
rolling pin ...

The list contains some fifty-two items, with variations and different sizes of utensils in addition to this.[1]

In her book *Cookery and Domestic Economy, 1862* Mrs Somerville denotes the necessary qualifications and character needed to become a successful teacher of cookery namely; cleanliness, punctuality, good temper and a thorough knowledge of the 'principles of her art'.

By 1893 there were a number of regional training schools specialising in cookery and it became more of a reputable and professional subject, as well as one deemed essential to assist with the national issue of poor diet and nutrition. In order to be considered good at your craft, it was necessary by the 1890s to study for a Diploma. The Northants and Bedfordshire Training School charged twenty-five guineas for one year's training to obtain such a qualification.[2] Once you'd gained your Diploma you were then free to train others to work towards theirs. A vocation that could earn you around £80 a year or more.[3]

No doubt there must have been a considerable turnover of cookery teaching staff, as the majority were women and once married would have to relinquish their posts. For one such lady a Mrs Edith Sabine, who taught cookery under the London School Board. It would appear her retirement provided the board with an ideal opportunity to capitalise on her absence by taking and using a series of kitchen and scullery props that she invented and made as learning resources for her classes. Edith's props ended up being exhibited nationally, gaining notoriety among the Education fraternity and even making their way to Paris. On discovering what had happened to her models, she approached the board for some compensation. It was estimated that the material value of her work came in at around £100, and that was without all the intellectual and academic worth. Edith requested a modest £20, but was offered a measly five by the board. She took the case to court where the Education Board were found to have acted in 'an extraordinary manner' and forced to pay £75 to Mrs Sabine.[4]

One of the leading cookery schools of the Victorian age was Marshall's, based in Cavendish Square, London and headed up by Mrs Agnes Bertha Marshall. Agnes Marshall was one of those incredible culinary leaders and innovators that have so often been neglected or lack the widespread credit due to them. She wrote prolifically on the subject of iced desserts, delivered lectures all round the country, invented new technology for the kitchen, created a brand with a range of ingredients – including Marshall's Finest Leaf Gelatine, ran an employment agency and of course founded the elite Marshall's School of Cookery in 1883. The school taught a mixture of high-end French and English cuisine. It was thought that if a young would-be domestic graduated from Marshall's they were twice as likely to find employment and secure a higher salary. Admissions to the school were said to have increased 'ten-fold' in just one year. Places were competitive and standards were high at Marshall's.[5]

Restaurant owners were also known to give demonstrations and host cookery courses and lessons, just like they do in today's society. *The Dundee Eve Telegraph* of 1895 advertises two cookery demos by a Mrs Whyte who runs the Commercial Restaurant in Dundee. The first of which promised to teach ladies about an 'entire dinner' while the second focused on an 'entree' dinner for the wives of working men to teach them about the economics of cooking.

The politics of Victorian Britain, as a growing Empire needing to cope with industrialisation and social reform were complex and bureaucratic with boards and committees being established and disestablished, re-structured and re-thought out on a regular basis. It was thought women were best placed to lead on domestic areas of education, despite ironically not even being in receipt of the vote at this time.

The Government's School Management Committee consisted of a number of subcommittees, all of which were predominantly female-led, in particular the Cookery, Laundry and Needlework subcommittee. Later there became a subcommittee of the subcommittee which just focussed on cookery. There appears to have been a great deal of assertion by the women members of these early government boards implemented as part of the wider Education Acts, both in terms of their sex and determination to influence policy, but also among the members themselves who frequently came into conflict about the extent to which girls should be taught more of one subject over another, or whether these subjects should be encouraged towards the poor or the wealthy and what aspects of domestic learning should be grant-aided. This in-fighting resulted in a good many restructures. One Francis Hastings, elected in 1882, lasted only a few years in power as her argument for reducing the curriculum time allocated to sewing was unpopular with the majority of other members.[6]

According to the National Archives, by 1901, the London School Board ran 165 Cookery Centres, 107 Laundry Work Centres and 20 Domestic Economy Schools for schoolgirls. £250 was the allocated budget for each kitchen installed within the new centres prior to 1900, after this time the Education Department increased the budget to £500.[7]

The Work of the London School Board, quoting the then current superintendent of cookery, Emily Briggs's, report notes that there were actually 168 cookery centres in 1900, making the National Archives reference slightly out. The girls being instructed were between the ages of ten and fourteen, with each course consisting of twenty-two lessons, each of which is the same duration as a typical academic lesson. The lessons varied, although the curriculum had to meet the same requirements: to clean and manage stoves, clean utensils, learn every mode of English cooking – roasting, boiling, stewing, grilling and frying. Girls also had to learn how to make soup, bake bread, cakes and pastries, brew tea, coffee and cocoa and manage the art of cookery for the sick and infirm. London schools adopted their own specific approach in that each lesson consisted of a one hour lecture involving cookery demonstrations, followed by the girls replicating what they had observed. Pupils also 'exhibited' their food, almost in the style of Masterchef it seems, to be judged by esteemed London chefs. By 1900 the cooking curriculum was also being extended to the teaching of boys, in order to better equip them in time of war or when joining the services. Briggs' report emphasises the benefits that the teaching of cookery have made to sensory-impaired girls or those with special needs, who gain confidence from being able to achieve the same results as their classmates to take home to their families.[8]

Often cooking in government-funded schools was very much a two birds with one stone approach, as a means of providing girls with the basic skills to cook their own economical meals, while benefiting the wider community. At the Parish Church Girls' National School, Cheltenham – the pupils worked four afternoons and one morning a week cooking in the adjoining cottage kitchen.

On Mondays they cooked a joint of meat with vegetables with a plain pudding which was distributed among the sick and elderly of the local parish. In one year this amounted to 669 meat dinners, 190 portions of pudding and 932 quarts of soup. On Tuesday mornings the girls baked bread which they then sold in the community, while Wednesday, Thursday and Friday afternoons were engaged with washing, ironing and mangling. Similarly at St Peter's Girls' School in Droitwich the girls were expected to cook meat – mutton or beef, potatoes and puddings every Friday to distribute for the benefit of the poor and sick.[9]

The following description is of a cookery school in Arbroath. As was typical of the time, part of the school had been converted for this specific purpose. There was a kitchen and a separate demonstration room, the latter being furnished with a main gas stove and several tiers of benches, enough to accommodate up to fifty pupils and arranged in such a way for everyone to view the main table where the teacher would stand and demonstrate.

The kitchen we are informed was a large, well-lit room containing a range, a gas stove and an assortment of tables and cupboards to store pots, pans and dishes.[10]

It was also quite common for some domestic households to open their doors to girls from poorer labouring families needing domestic and cooking tuition which would be led by the housekeeper and/ or cook. This would often be just one day a week over a course of several months. Whatever the girls made during their lessons could be taken home to their families to eat.

There were numerous cookery schools generally operating across the country during the nineteenth century. These were not new phenomena, with courses available to adults the century before, many of which are discussed at greater length in *Dining with the Georgians*. These were often more intimate and exclusive classes that focussed on specific areas of cooking such as the newly fashionable French cuisine, pastry work or confectionery.

By the latter part of the Victorian era, cookery schools for adult learners were more mainstream and often set up in public buildings to offer part-time provision to large groups of women, keen to experience the new national emphasis on instructional cookery for the masses. The Dundee School of Cookery opened in 1879 at the Gray Street Hall in the city. Apparently the admission charge was 'moderate' and would often cater to some one hundred young women or more. The classes were delivered by the main instructor and one assistant. An example of the type of dishes being taught included sea-pie, or Irish stew, oatmeal biscuits, semolina pudding, soup maigre and methods by which to salt or prepare meats. The emphasis was always on nutritional value and ensuring that women were taught to cook economically and, above all, healthily to contribute to the much wider issues of poverty, malnutrition and ignorance surrounding food and diet.[11]

Catherine Buckton was the first elected woman on the Leeds School Board and she wrote a number of books reflecting on her job and research in the area of instruction for cookery. Her 1879 manual *Food and Home Cookery, a Course of Instruction, as followed in the schools of the Leeds School Board*, provides detailed descriptions on the importance of cleanliness, provides an explanation about some of the basic science behind cooking, what utensils are needed, how people should dress in the kitchen and so on. It is not until around lesson 6 that the real elements of cooking are relayed including instructions for boiling and poaching eggs, grilling a chop or steak, boiling potatoes and making egg sandwiches. Buckton, like many of her peers at the time was thorough in their teachings, going as far as to differentiate between vegetable matter and animal matter for the purposes of discussing where potatoes and eggs come from. There is a wide assumption with all Victorian teaching manuals that the students are completely ignorant. This may well have been necessary when tutoring girls from the poorest of homes with little educational knowledge. But nonetheless they do often interpret as quite patronising. There are at least two pages devoted to the importance of thermometers in cooking, before any egg cooking is demonstrated. Buckton's description for cooking a single chop is worthy of note, for its exacting guidance and resolute conviction of theory; a style synonymous with most cookery training manuals of the time. It is easy when reading old cooking tutorials to feel as if you need a lesson yourself to rethink the basic principles of cooking, as the doctrine is that strong:

We must let the heat of the fire be so great that it will instantly harden the albumen that is on the outside of the meat so that the juices cannot run. The fire must be very hot and the coals all red, not black and smoky; a black fire sends out too little heat to harden the albumen quickly, and the smoke that comes from it would make the chop taste of soot. Our gridiron, which is only a thick iron one, must be put on the fire to get warm before the chop is put on to it, or the raw meat would stick to the cold iron bars. Some cooks have a dirty habit of rubbing grease over the bars, but you must never do this, only make them warm. We will now put the chop on the gridiron with a spoon and knife; take care never to stick a fork into a chop or beefsteak, or the juices will run out of the holes made by the fork. A fine large chop will be well cooked in twelve minutes if it is turned every two minutes; at the famous chop house in Barnsley the chops are turned every minute and take twenty minutes. A chop when properly cooked in this way will be full of gravy and ought to be eaten with a hot potato and a little pepper and salt; never put butter on a chop or gravy in the dish.

Interestingly Whitehead's 1889 guide to party catering, as an American manual pays tribute to England's chop houses and notes the trend for similar models being opened in New York at the time. In particular the Barnsley chop is heralded as the most superior, as Barnsley butchers cut them very thick, from just over the kidney. It is this thickness, according to Whitehead that means the chops should be boiled for at least five minutes prior to cooking, a theory that would no doubt have ruffled Buckton's feathers.[12]

Buckton's manual goes on to instruct on the cooking of boiled potatoes, that they must be washed in cold water, but never allowed to stand in it. Potatoes, we are assured must at all times be cooked with the skins on, due to the fact that 'there is a corky substance in the skin of a potato which prevents any water from entering the potato, and also prevents any of the juices and good things from getting out'. Curiously it was never considered that potatoes could be cut up prior to cooking, as Buckton informs us that potatoes of the exact same size must be selected for the pot, as those of differing sizes will cook at different times.

There was a great deal of literature published on the specialist needs required to cook for sick or invalided individuals. This was also covered under the national teaching curriculum for schools and Buckton's manual along with all other similar guides would outline the necessary training to cook for the sick vulnerable.

Mental Nursing; or, Lectures for Asylum Attendants,1894 provides a more specific approach to cooking for people diagnosed with severe mental health problems or incarcerated in an asylum.

It was thought that there were two divisions of cookery required in the latter situation; those who shared their mealtimes together in the communal dining areas and those 'special cases' where individuals were isolated from the rest of their inmates – I stress the word inmate as nineteenth-century mental health, although improving in its understanding of the human mind, was still a stigmatised illness and people were locked away and experimented on. The guide for 'nursing staff' suggests that any manner of tablecloth put down will be ruined in seconds due to the chaotic nature of the patient, although fresh flowers were thought to evoke a more fresh and colourful environment. It was advocated that all knives and forks should be clean and counted before and after service, for obvious reasons perhaps. Every table needed to be supervised by a member of staff who needed to ensure that each patient sat in the same place every mealtime. This was to allow the nurses to be mindful of individual behaviour and avoid potential chokings, the stealing of food and the overconsumption of food, often leading to sickness. The dining areas were kept orderly and quiet as it was considered that a civilised environment would encourage better behaviour from the patients. No second course would be served to a patient if they neglected to eat their first, regardless of whether they liked it or not. Liquids needed to be kept at a minimum as 'lunatics' were thought to overdrink and this wasn't to be encouraged in the evening for want of too many night time toilet breaks. Epileptics and paralytics were thought to be the most prone to suicide and it was recommended that they be spoon-fed and have their food cut up into small pieces. They were also placed within the direct eyeline of the nurse.

In terms of 'acute maniacs' food was considered paramount to good health as their continued excitement and muscular exertions made them hungrier. Liquid foods only were recommended for this group of patients – milk, eggs or beef tea etc.

There were a number of inventions and improvements in

military cooking during the Victorian age, with the emphasis on cooking economically and in difficult circumstances for large groups of men. Aldershot became the predominant army training school for military cooking, where they pioneered field cooking by cutting a trench, covering this with iron plates and drilling holes in the plates. A fire was constructed at one end of the trench and a chimney at the other.

Rations for both army and navy personnel in the nineteenth century were inadequate and frequently required men to subsidise their diets from their own additional resources. The cost of feeding the navy in 1811 amounted to 1s and 3¾d per head per day and consisted of the following provisions:

Bread	16 ounces	Butter	7/8 ounce
Beef	4 ½ ounces	Sugar	7/8 ounce
Pork	2 ¼ ounces	Cheese	1 ¾ ounce
Flour	3 ounces	Beer	1 quart
Suet	¼ ounce		

This was supplemented with some small quantities of peas, oatmeal, raisins and vinegar. In comparison the Army were issued 1 lb of bread and 1 lb of meat a day.[13]

As a consequence of these deficiencies new methods were frequently being considered in terms of the levels of determining the levels of nutrition needed to sustain the military, as well as the means to achieve it.

By 1870 the Queen advocated that one sergeant cook was to be appointed to every regiment in the military and that each one had to undergo a course in cookery at Aldershot before taking up their position. Horace Wyndham, enlisted in 1890, was a prolific author of military novels; he served in many locations within the Empire, including Aldershot. Wydham wrote an article about the Army School of Cookery in 1903 which revealed much about the activities that took place there and the value of the work being undertaken. The school was established in 1872. The officers in charge at the time of writing were very high-ranking and experienced, including a Major Goldfrap (officer in charge), Sergeant Major Macmillan and four instructors. Wydham informs us:

The numerical strength of the class under instruction at the school is generally forty at a time. Of these, the larger proportion are Regulars, the remainder coming from the militia. Their training is of a very practical nature, and extends (except in the case of the militia) over a period of four months. This is carried out in three different kitchens, in each of which a separate routine is in force. Thus, in the first, instruction is given in roasting and baking; in the second, in stewing, steaming, boiling, and frying; while the third is reserved as a class room for lectures.

Before a soldier is eligible to be received at the Army School of Cookery he must be a non-commissioned officer (of at least the rank of Corporal) and be in possession of a second-class certificate of education. On his application to undergo a course of instruction being approved, he reports himself with the other candidates for similar honours at Aldershot. Each class, therefore, is composed of representatives of every branch of the Army, the men forming it coming to it from all parts of the Kingdom. Breakfast in the Army, which is served at 7.45AM, consists of a pint of tea or coffee, with half a pound of bread and an "extra "in the way of porridge, fish, bacon, butter, or jam. At 8.30AM the class assembles again, and is employed until 12.45PM in preparing dinner. As this meal is the chief one of the day, it is accordingly of a substantial nature. The government ration is three quarters of a pound of meat per man (a much more liberal amount, by the way, than that to which the majority of recruits are accustomed prior to their enlistment), and to these are added regimentally vegetables and pudding. Soup also frequently figures in the menu, as this is readily made from the bones and odds and ends of meat that cannot otherwise be disposed of. From 2.30PM to 3.30PM a proportion of the cooks attend a lecture or examination on the work up to date, while the remainder make the afternoon's supply of tea. The blend that is approved of by the military authorities is, it may be mentioned, Black Congou, from China. It is served at four o'clock, and is consumed with half a pound of bread and a small allowance of butter or jam. The meal is quite an informal one, and the men are not compelled to be present at it, as is the case at breakfast and dinner. When the orderlies have taken the 'cup that cheers' to the barrack rooms, the cooks have (with the exception of cleaning the kitchens and utensils) finished their labours for the day. They are then, accordingly, free to attend to their own devices until the following morning.

At the end of the course of instruction in the different kitchens the members of the class spend a short time at the Army Service Corps supply depot, where they are given practical lessons in the art of killing and cutting up meat. Having shown the necessary amount of proficiency in this and the other branches, they are granted parchment certificates, and return to the battalions. They then, as soon as a vacancy in the position occurs, are appointed sergeant cooks, and draw on this account an extra six pence per diem.[14]

Not only does this indicate that, in less than a century, army daily rations were far more satisfying, but they were also committed to ensuring the very best in understanding the dietary needs of the military and the importance attached to the knowledge of educated cooking practices.

Another area of national instruction, albeit less formal, was with the work of the Universal Cookery and Food Association. This was a voluntary organisation originally established around the 1870s to promote fine dining and French cuisine. Its key members were French migrant chefs now established in London. Its growth was rapid. In 1892 it boasted 186 members, which increased to 917 in 1897 and by the end of Victoria's reign in 1901 it stood at some 1,200 members. By the 1920s membership had levelled. The French element of the association factioned off and by 1887 the group was more concerned with charitable enterprise, with their main objective

'To promote and encourage the advancement of cookery in every grade among all classes of the community'.

The Association ran annual large scale exhibitions in London for over forty years, the proceeds of which went to pay for trained cookery teachers to help instruct the less fortunate, provide food to needy children and establish scholarships.[15]

Contrary to the extent with which culinary improvement sought to permeate every aspect of British life from the middle of the nineteenth century, many cooks in domestic service did not rely on recipe books, rather they worked to their own measures and times and had their own methods of communicating to the rest of the kitchen staff. Instead of requesting a tablespoon of fat, they might instead ask for a 'nut' of butter, which the other kitchen maids would automatically translate as a nut-sized portion. Kitchen and parlour maids learnt to be cooks from observing their superiors as well as learning from their own mistakes. Recipes, especially successful ones, were not to be shared and were more often than not just memorised and locked away for safe-keeping. That being said, the market for recipe writing and theoretical cooking was at its height during both the eighteenth and nineteenth centuries. These were not written by the 'plain cooks' who laboured in the kitchens of the middle classes, or by the vast majority of sophisticated well-trained European cooks. They were mostly compiled by the ladies who were the head of a large household, or by Housekeepers, ladies of leisure, men of influence and the very high-end, well-known gastronomes in society.

Some of these important culinary characters cross-over from the Georgian era, which yielded a wealth of early 'celebrity chefs'. By the nineteenth century, recipe writers assumed the readers of their books would have some knowledge of cooking, so in one sense they omitted some of the details that eighteenth century cookery writers provided, but in other ways recipe writing became more specific and included information on timings, quantities and approximate temperatures.

Names such as Maria Rundell, Eliza Acton, Charles Elmé Francatelli, Margaret Dod, Alexis Soyer, Colin MacKenzie, John Massey, Jules Gouffé, Urbain Dubois, Auguste Escoffier and many more besides, are all synonymous with Victorian culinary writing. Many were also highly respected cooks and restaurateurs.

Although recipes were frequently copied and pirated in the eighteenth and nineteenth centuries, from generation to generation, many of the well-known ideas and philosophies of Isabella Beeton actually belonged to Eliza Acton. A clever plagiariser, Beeton even stole Eliza's novel method for measuring every individual item of ingredients. Ironically, and rather sadly for Eliza, this was one of the unique developments in culinary literature that made Mrs Beeton famous. Her *Book of Household Management* was published two years after Eliza's death, leaving her with no opportunity to challenge her usurper. Eliza Acton's book *Modern Cookery for Private Families* was in many ways a truly original style of cookery writing that spoke about the economies of food, the amounts required for individual dishes and the exact cooking timings. Acton was also an active campaigner for better quality produce and an advocate for reducing the country's expenditure on food. Essentially Mrs Beeton wrote good household manuals, while Eliza Acton wrote cookery books, so the two were incomparable.[16]

Charles Elmé Francatelli, a British born second-generation

Italian, was trained under the notorious Marie-Antoine Carême. Francatelli was best known as chief cook for Queen Victoria and was alleged to have invented that very British colonial dish coronation chicken, in honour of Queen Victoria's accession to the throne. He also started the trend for eating just two courses – a main and a dessert. He was frequently in trouble during his employment in the royal kitchens, known for his bullying, rude insults and bad language. He was eventually suspended for his behaviour and went to work at the Reform Club. Like many of his contempories during this period Francatelli was a prolific author on the subject of cooking and published *The Modern Cook* in 1845, of which there were some twelve editions due to its popularity, *A Plain Cookery Book for the Working Classes* in 1852, *The Cook's Guide and Housekeeper's & Butler's Assistant* in 1861 and finally *The Royal English and Foreign Confectionery Book* in 1862. Incidentally Francatelli's cousin Laura was one of the few survivors of the *Titanic*. Another cook made famous for his work at the acclaimed Reform Club, Alexis Soyer was probably the best known of all the celebrity chefs of the Georgian and Victorian ages. An advocate for the poor and social change, Soyer became an advisor to government and established a number of large-scale soup kitchens, particularly in Ireland during famine, and invented innovative cooking equipment that could be used out in the fields during combat. He was sent to the Crimean War to mobilise special kitchens and design military hospital kitchens. Soyer wrote extensively on the art of economical cooking for the masses and his role in social reform during this period was considerable.

Jules Gouffé worked under the tutelage of Marie-Antoine Carême, one of the few great French gastronomes not to have worked in Britain. Gouffé's renowned books, most notably *Le Livre de Cuisine* and *Le Livre de Pâtisserie* were translated by his brother Alphonse, who also happened to be pastry cook to Queen Victoria, for the English market, making him a respected household name in the Victorian annals of culinary influence, with one British newspaper citing him as 'undeniably the great culinary authority of our day'. Gouffé's instructions to his readers were thorough and detailed. Like Eliza Acton, in his preface to *Le Livre de Cuisine*, he is critical of the trend for cookery writers to simply rework old and existing recipes that repeat the same errors and lack any precision where measurements, quantities and cooking times were concerned, noting 'I have not written down a single one of my elementary directions without having continually my eyes on the clock and my hand on the scales.' Gouffé also raised the issue of recipe writers frequently and incorrectly mixing high-end cuisine with domestic cookery. Rather Gouffé divided his works into two separate and specific categories.[17]

Christian Isobel Johnstone made a decision to use a pseudonym when writing – Margaret Dods, who was actually a fictional character in a novel by Sir Walter Scott called *Saint Ronan's Well*. Dods is the owner of a guest house, Cleikum Inn, in Scotland. Christian was primarily an early prolific feminist fiction writer, so the *Cook and Housewife's Manual* was somewhat of a departure from her usual style. An unusual book, the *Cook and Housewife's Manual* provides an insight into the culinary heritage of Scottish border fare through the eyes of the Cleikum Nabob, or Walter Scott's original character, Peregrine Touchwood. It starts with the crude nature of hunting, moving to soups and recipes with barley, ending with Scotland's eventual grasp of good French cuisine.

A less well-known recipe writer, Charles Silby published under the pseudonym of Tabitha Tickletooth. Writing in 1960 and sporting a rather comical picture of what appears to be a cross-dressing man on the inside cover, Silby provides a comprehensive guide to cooking from table etiquette to kitchen cleanliness. Silby (aka Tickletooth) suggests providing each guest with a menu and a small vase of flowers nearby. This, he assures, will aid any momentary flags in conversation as the guest can refer to his or her menu, or distract themselves with the flowers in order to make the lull less painful and then revive the general discourse.[18]

From the military, to schools and for the benefit of commercialisation and commerce – cooking and how best to accomplish it played a significant role in nineteenth century Britain. So many experts wanted to impart their knowledge to the wider public and share dialogue on the subject of culinary discourse. The relationship between health and nutritional cooking instruction is one which still dominates aspects of political debate in the commons. Recent National Curriculum directives to place cooking and knowledge relating to the origins of food back on the education agenda for young children is evidence for this. Similarly, Britain still craves the expertise offered within the vast culture of the celebrity chef media.

Recipes

The following recipe is taken from the Dundee School of Cookery and was taught in the evenings to fee-paying young women with a desire to improve their cookery skills, like so many did during this time.

Semolina Pudding

Semolina is a preparation from pure wheat, and is very nutritious. Two tablespoons semolina soaked overnight in water, two breakfast cups of milk, one egg, and dessert spoon pounded sugar. Put the semolina and milk into a saucepan and stir until it boils and thickens – about seven or eight minutes. Then add the sugar and a little ground nutmeg or other seasoning. Lift the saucepan to a side before adding the egg; when quite off the boil add the egg well whisked, pour into a buttered dish and bake ten minutes in oven or before the fire. Immediately on removing from the oven sprinkle the top with a little pounded sugar and cinnamon or nutmeg. Sup with milk or stoned fruit.[19]

Despite the fact that we no longer eat small domestic garden birds like the lark anymore in this country, the following recipe taken from Jules Gouffé's *Le Livre de Cuisine*, or *The Royal Cookery Book*, as its translated English title was given, demonstrates the exactness with which Gouffé offered instructions to his readers. The recipe, unlike many of its time provides weights, timings, precise directions – everything that we would expect to see in a recipe today. It is this, as much as his talent as a chef, that make Jules Gouffé one of the most important and influential cookery writers of the nineteenth century.

Lark Patties

Line 18 small pie moulds with paste, as directed for Patties a la Monglas (vide recipe above);

Put 7 oz of grated bacon in a sauté pan, with 10 oz of chicken livers; Season with salt pepper and spice; fry for four minutes; and, when cold pound in a mortar; and press the forcemeat through a hair sieve; Bone 18 larks; open them, and season them slightly; spread a little of the forcemeat on each lark, place a piece of truffle, about the size of a nut, on the forcemeat, and roll the lark up into a ball, to enclose it;

Put a thin layer of forcemeat at the bottom of the lined moulds; place in each, one of the prepared larks, and spread another thin layer of forcemeat on the top; cover the patties with paste, as described for Patties a la Monglas; egg the tops, and lay on each a round of puff paste, cut with a l ¼-inch fluted cutter; egg the top, and bake the patties in a hot oven for twenty minutes. Cut out the covers pour in a spoonful of Espagnole Sauce with Essence of Larks; replace the covers; and serve.[20]

1. Queen Victoria, after George Baxter, *c.*1860. (Yale Centre for British Art)

2. Copper kettle, c.1870.
(©Museum of Kitchenalia)

3. Pair of butter patters,
c.1890, Late Victorian/
Edwardian butter paddle,
nineteenth century butter
wheel. (©Museum of
Kitchenalia)

4. The Soup Kitchen
William Strang.
(Yale Centre for
British Art)

5. Victorian cut glass bowl. (©Museum of Kitchenalia)

6. Lambeth Ragged School: women teaching girl students, 1846. (Courtesy of the Library of Congress)

Poor little Rose

7. Poor little Rose. (Yale Centre for British Art)

8. Christmas tree at Windsor Castle, 1848. (Courtesy of the Library of Congress)

9. Home sweet home, W. Dendy Sadler, 1900. (Courtesy of the Library of Congress)

10. J. Schweppes glass bottle, 1831–1895. (©Museum of Kitchenalia)

11326—In Kensington Gardens, London, England.

11. In Kensington
Gardens, 1901.
(Courtesy of
the Library of
Congress)

12. A Life on the Ocean Wave, George Sala. (Yale Centre for British Art)

A life on the Ocean Wave!

13. The Jetty, Margate, 1890. (Courtesy of the Library of Congress)

14. Dining car, (Delaware, Lackawanna and Western Railroad), 1900. (Courtesy of the Library of Congress)

15. May Day, William Collins, 1811–12. (Yale Centre for British Art)

16. 'Chapman' china tea plate, c.1889–1906, Cartwright and Edwards tea cup and saucer, c.1912–1936, Willow pattern teapot, late Victorian 'Teaette' silver plated infuser spoon, silver plated mustard pot with blue glass liner, solid silver condiment spoon, c.1815. (©Museum of Kitchenalia)

17. The Pavillion Theatre, 1834. (Yale Centre for British Art)

18. Dandies Having a Treat, Robert Cruickshank, 1818. (Yale Centre for British Art)

19. Scene at Vauxhall Gardens, George Cruickshank. (Yale Centre for British Art)

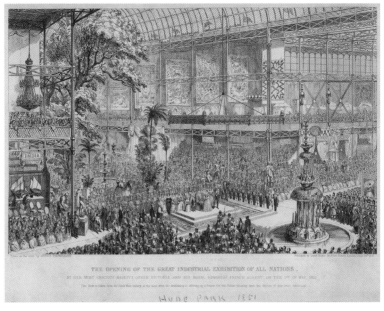

20. Opening of the Great Industrial Exhibition, George Cruikshank, 1851. (Courtesy of the Library of Congress)

21. Nailsea nineteenth-century painted glass rolling pin, nineteenth-century bone and wood pastry cutter, nineteenth-century carved patterned biscuit mould. (©Museum of Kitchenalia)

22. Cooking house, 8th Hussars, 1858. (Courtesy of the Library of Congress)

23. Two round brioche tins, early 1900s. (©Museum of Kitchenalia)

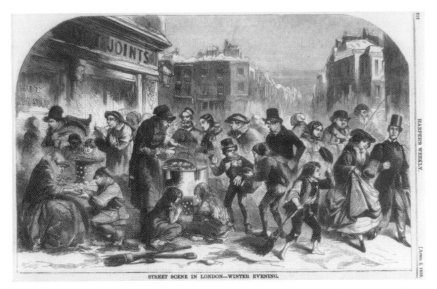

24. Street scene in London – winter evening, 1859. (Courtesy of the Library of Congress)

25. Silver plated muffin dish, early twentieth century, James Deakin & Sons food/plate warmer, 1890s, small late Victorian drinking glass. (©Museum of Kitchenalia)

26. London, English bar
and barmaids, 1893.
(Courtesy of the Library
of Congress)

27. Cartwright and
Edwards tea cup and
saucer, c.1912–1936,
c.1900 wooden handled
copper coffee/chocolate
pot, J. E. Bushell
silver plated chocolate
pot early twentieth
century, copper kettle,
c.1870. (©Museum of
Kitchenalia)

28. London central fruit and vegetable market, Mr Horace Jones, 1880. (Courtesy of the Library of Congress)

29. Hotels Cecil and Savoy, 1901. (Courtesy of the Library of Congress)

30. Early Victorian spice tin with grater, tinware Gill measure early 1900s, bronze pestle and mortar nineteenth century. (©Museum of Kitchenalia)

FEMALE ATTENDANTS.

31. Female Attendants, Sir Charles D'Ogly, 1781–1845. (Yale Centre for British Art)

7

PUBLIC DINING (AND EVERYTHING IN BETWEEN)

In the most basic of terms the towns and cities of Victorian Britain were provided with 'eating-houses' and 'dining-rooms', with the lower classes opting for the former and the middling and higher echelons of society preferring the latter. Dining rooms mostly evolved from the need of traders and clerks, working late and living long distances from home, to dine at a later hour after work. There were also a myriad of independent public houses and a scattering of coffee rooms, a throwback from the century before but still providing simple fare in addition to hot drinks and some alcohol. While the Georgian coffee emporiums and taverns served the aspiring business men, merchants, artists, wits, wenches and wantons, by the middle of the nineteenth century business and enterprise moved into the gentlemen's clubs and the middle classes all but deserted the public houses, which, as the nineteenth and early twentieth century progressed, slowly morphed into the epitome of working-class social culture.

Writing in 1900 Robert Hichens confirms that the restaurant dinner in London was as popular as it was in Paris and notes the frequency with which homes were abandoned for the alternative of entertaining friends and family in public. He also reflects on the older population who typically found this trend somewhat vulgar, determined to write off public dining as a fad, destined for dissolution. Undoubtedly this same group of citizens would have been very dissatisfied by the fact that in London women were able to eat in hotels and independent restaurants by the late 1880s. In 1888 in Mortimer Street, London, the Dorothy, an exclusively female restaurant was opened by three enterprising ladies to serve women workers, students and 'weary' shoppers.[1] Said to be reasonably priced, a lunch consisting of a choice of two joints of meat, two types of vegetables and bread could be purchased for 8*d*. Or a rasher of ham could be bought for just 2*d*, a small cup of tea or coffee for 1*d*, mutton hash for 4*d* or beef pudding or pie for 4*d*, among other popular dishes of the day.[2]

Murray's handbook of London for 1851 lists the best restaurants in the city at the time, namely Verrey's – also a renowned confectioner – of Regent Street, the celebrity chef Alexis Soyer's, Universal Symposium at Gore House Kensington, and the Sabloniere Hotel where dinners were also served to guests hiring out private apartments. Bertolini's and Girauld's, both in Leicester Square, and Mouflet in Knightsbridge it is said all served excellent French cuisine at reasonable prices.[3]

Murray's follow-up book *London in 1857* reveals the specialities of many of the restaurants favoured in the capital. For example the turtle served at the Ship & Turtle in Leadenhall Street, Joe's in Finch Lane famed for its steaks and chops served on metal plates, or the Three Tuns Tavern in Billingsgate celebrated for its fish. And at the Salutation in Newgate Street, if you arrive for 5 p.m. you are guaranteed three courses including bread, beer and cheese for just 1*s* 6*d*, but only on the understanding that you purchase wine or beer after the meal.[4]

The dining rooms of Covent Garden and the Haymarket were largely dominated by actors, artists and migrants and a number of French restaurants providing opportunities for women to dine un-chaperoned. *The Penny Magazine of 1843* informs us that at the time there were two main ways to order; either by restaurants who employed waiters to recount every dish available to their diners, or from a printed 'bill of fare', with a price list. The cheaper soup houses for the poor and labouring classes were mostly situated around St Giles, Broad Street and Holborn Hill and displayed large steaming bowls in the windows to entice customers in.

The 'chop houses' of the last century, by the late Victorian period known better as 'grill rooms' simply sold either steaks or chops, for six pennies or nine pennies. Similarly the 'ordinaries' or fixed time, fixed price menu establishments were also still operating after their emergence in the seventeenth and eighteenth centuries, although the writer indicates there are a lot fewer of these by the Victorian period.

In contrast the Victorian French critic and historian Hippolyte Taine was very disparaging of all restaurants across England noting:

Excepting in the very best clubs and among continentalised English people, who have a French or Italian chef, [the cooking] is devoid of savour. I have dined, deliberately, in twenty different inns, from the highest to the lowest, in London and elsewhere: huge helpings of greasy meat and vegetable without sauce; one is amply and wholesomely fed, but one can take no pleasure in eating. The best restaurant in Liverpool cannot dress a chicken. If your palate demands enjoyment, here is a dish of pimentos, peppers, condiments, Indian vinegars: on one occasion I carelessly put two drops into my mouth. I might just as well have been swallowing a red-hot coal. At Greenwich, having had a helping of ordinary 'whitebait', I helped myself to more but from another dish: it was a dish of curried whitebait – excellent for taking the skin off one's tongue.[5]

Karl Baedeker's 1878 guide to London confirms that most first-class restaurants in the capital were French, and charged high prices for the privilege, with most of these opening for dinner between 4 and 8 p.m. with customers choosing to drink beer on draught or from the bottle to accompany their food. Wine was considered too expensive and the quality was not consistent, although sherry and port remained popular. There were also a number of lunch bars generally open from 11 a.m. till 3 p.m., selling chops or small platters of hot meat, bread and vegetables, very reminiscent of the century before.

The Food Journal of 1872 provides a detailed description of the City Restaurant situated at 34 Milk Street, Cheapside, whose somewhat cheesy advertising strap line read,

Among other questions asked when parties are visiting the great Metropolis is "where shall we dine?" the reply which is becoming as "familiar as household words" is "Why, at the City Restaurant where the best and cheapest Dinner is served in the most unique style in the City of London."[6]

The first room on entering the City Restaurant was a *salle à manger* or dining room, 'elegantly ornamented' with 'capital lighting and ventilation', then a bar and saloon led to lavatories, a gentlemen's ante-room and a smoking and billiards room – spaces that sounded as if they would not be out of place in a refined gentleman's club, with its Moroccan-inspired furnishings and contemporary periodicals.

A further staircase took the customer to the ladies lavatory and the first sounds of sizzling food and a chop room were audible, where guests could dine à la carte or from an all-inclusive menu. Traditional dishes such as mock turtle soup, turbot, saddle of mutton, bread, cheese and vegetables, whitebait, chicken fricassee, duckling, and so on were all available to eat in this space. The ground floor acted as a 'luncheon bar' with a variety of dishes ' to satisfy the most inveterate a snapper-up of unconsidered trifles in the way of snacks, beside certain hot and substantial refreshments … a very handsome compromise for dinner.'

Soups, cold meats, savouries, pastries, ices, wines, ales and liqueurs as well as hot beverages were all served at two counter bars, or at little tables.[7] This was apparently very typical of a busy multi-functional 'city restaurant' of the time.

City Restaurant was said to have staged major regional chess championships like the one between London and Bedford in 1874, where twelve players from each town battled it out over ten games, with the London team winning eight of them.[8] Another advertisement for the City Restaurant in the *London Daily News* of 1872 notes that this provision extended to draughts and domino matches.

Other large cities such as Manchester may have taken a very different approach to dining. One account in the 1857 *Visitors Guide to Manchester* observes that, in contrast, ladies were very rarely seen out in public. Dining rooms did not serve what the guide describes as 'unintelligible gibberish', such as 'curryrabbysoups and vegibles' but rather offered simple choices of a selection of different joints of meat that arrived swiftly together with the bill. Waiters went out of their way not to speak to you and the dining areas were often devoid of any conversation. The most polite and noiseless of the city being the Merchants of Market Street, Brown's Chop House, The Albion Dining Rooms, the Refectory and the Exchange Dining Rooms which was somewhere ladies could dine in a separate segregated area.[9]

Dublin rather boastfully modelled its public fine dining establishments on London in many ways. The Red Bank restaurant opened in 1845 in D'Olier Street, taking its name from the oysters of the same name which grew on the beds located in County Clare, owned by the proprietor. 'Red Bank' oysters were sold in season at the D'Olier Street restaurant. There was a 'suite of luncheon, dining and supper rooms for ladies'. Just a year later the restaurant took new ownership and was remodelled 'in the London fashion' with a spacious bar and counter serving luncheons. Coffee and dining rooms were provided for gentlemen on the ground floor, while the 'luxurious ladies' dining rooms were located upstairs. The whole establishment was lit by electricity.[10]

There are numerous advertisements for large holistic dining rooms combined with shops in the nineteenth century like Shilson's of Lewes, who not only professed to be a pastry cook and confectioner selling ices, creams, jellies and so on, but were also large-scale caterers for functions and maintained an 'old-established' restaurant and dining rooms serving soups, hot joints, steaks and ales. Similarly St Giles' Restaurant in Oxford, another cook and confectioner, offered hot joints at lunch time, desserts and soups, wines and ales and an external catering service for wedding breakfasts. And then there's Edwards' 'High-Class' restaurant and confectioners, who not only sold chops and steaks from the grill, but offered a broad hot and cold lunch menu and a variety of hot drinks and specialist teas as well as providing a separate Ladies' Dining Room and acting as an external catering company for banquets, balls, suppers and weddings. This type of multi-functional catering must have been hard work, labour intensive and complicated to manage, yet there were enough of these establishments to suggest that the rewards were forthcoming. There is a trend today for small retailers to introduce a coffee bar area, or for delicatessens to open in the evening as bistros. This has largely emerged out of a need for small businesses to diversify and generate more income. Perhaps the commercialisation and increasing competition in the Victorian food business market had a similar effect.

Plain fare at cheaper prices could be found at dining rooms across cities and larger towns to cater for employees who were unable to get home to eat at a sociable time. Selling roast, boiled or baked meats, broths, bread cheese and vegetables. The city offering the best variety of this type of eatery in the nineteenth century was Glasgow. Cheap, comfortable and clean, one such establishment located in Jamaica Street employed fast and efficient waiting staff, where 'the wants of each customer were attended to in an almost incredibly quick way'. On entering customers paid for a ticket at a machine from a choice of one penny, two pence or more in exchange for a brass token displaying the sum paid. This was then handed to one of the waiting staff, who would serve the food according to price paid. The room was large, scrupulously clean and neat with rows of neat tables around six feet long, each with a glass carafe of sparkling water, four to six tumblers, salt and pepper and mustard. A meal of broth, hot boiled beef, potatoes and plum pudding could be ordered for five pence. The equivalent in London for this type of meal was estimated at a much higher price of one shilling, three pence. This Glasgow model of economical, but quality dining was introduced across Manchester with great success in the disused cotton mills at the height of the Cotton Panic in the early 1860s when manufacture exceeded demand.[11]

The cafes of the nineteenth century were not akin to the cafes we associate here in the twenty-first. They were a type of restaurant. Among the most notable of these in London included Verrey's, the Café Parisian at the Savoy and 'if you want to see English people at their most English', according to the great theatrical actor-manager, Sir Herbert Beerbohm Tree, you had to 'go to the Café Royal, where they are trying their hardest to be French'. Originally named Cafe Restaurant Nicols after its founder the wine merchant Daniel Nicholas Thévenon in 1863, this establishment of princesses and peers moved to Regent Street and much bigger premises offering a grill room, billiard room and private banqueting hall. Once reputed to have the world's greatest wine cellar, the newly named Café Royal was more of a dining club than cafe; a social meeting place for the country's finest writers, artists, including Oscar Wilde and Lord Alfred Douglas which served to give the Café Royal a less salient reputation among London's less open-minded fashionistas.[12] Today the Café Royal is now one of the premier hotels in London and continues to retain celebrity attention worldwide.

Tea room society began to dominate towns and cities across the north and south by the end of the nineteenth century. The very first chain of supermarkets established in the north west of England, *Booths*; founded in the mid-1800s and still owned by the same family today, began opening small cafes, as we would recognise them today, in their stores from 1901.

For a more detailed narrative of the history of tea and coffee drinking in Britain, the reader should refer to *Dining with the Georgians: A Delicious British History*. Undoubtedly the role of the Victorian tea shop was founded in the emergence of the temperance societies. Pioneers such as Kate Cranston had the foresight to commission one of the era's most talented and innovative artists, Charles Rennie Mackintosh, to design the fixtures, fittings and even the waitresses outfits for what has now internationally become one of the most famous tea rooms in the world, the Willow Tearooms, in Sauchiehall Street, Glasgow. Her chain of public house-alternative businesses started as early as 1878, with the Crown Tea Rooms, Argyle Street, under the trading name of Miss Cranston's Tearooms.[13]

The English avant-garde equivalent to Cranston's empire, which included some five or six successful shops for the Scottish entrepreneur, was Lyons. Lyons opened their first teashop in London's Piccadilly in 1894. Up until the Second World War this chain of high street cafes would increase to some 250 branches across the country. Lyons also founded the legendary restaurants Lyons Corner House and the Trocadero. Lyons products infiltrated the retail market with their red and green label teas, its 'Kup Kakes' and ice cream products. In short this family-run tea and cake-inspired business became a vast empire, which also included large-scale catering services for high-level events such as Wimbledon and Buckingham Palace garden parties. The starched-aproned waitresses affectionately christened 'Nippies' for their speedy service to deal with the long string of daily queues, served superior tea at just two pence a cup.[14]

Mass production of baked goods was rapidly on the increase during the Victorian era and none is more demonstrable of this than the Aerated Bread Company (ABC). Founded in 1862 by Dr John Dauglish. Dauglish had perfected a method of developing a healthier product, with fewer additives, no yeast and a perfectly risen bake. Essentially carbonic acid was forced into an air-tight machine, along with water, flour and salt. From these containers some 2,000 pounds in weight of bread could be manufactured annually. This equated to ten times the amount an average commercial baker could produce.[15] A bit like pawnbrokers and betting shops have crept onto our high streets today, by the late 1880s the ABC shops had bought up numerous corner plots in popular commercial areas across London and the north of England. By 1889 there were some seventy shops selling breads, cakes and pastries adopting techniques to ensure that customers did not linger too long. There were no newspapers and only a few of their stores allowed smoking. The baked goods were not manufactured on site either. All the baking was carried out at the company's headquarters in Camden Town on the Regents Canal and then distributed out to individual stores to sell.[16]

The ABC tea shops were known for being cheap and cheerful establishments open from early in the morning, and they frequently came under scrutiny in the media for the long hours and low pay they provided their female staff with. Other businesses with their foundations rooted in Victorian temperance and mass consumerism in the public dining arena, include John Pearce's British Tea Table Company, whose motto was 'we best serve ourselves by serving others best' were running some twenty-nine cafes in London by

1898 and Lockhart's Cocoa Rooms, who maintained a chain of stores in both England and Scotland.[17] *The Sunderland Daily Echo and Shipping Gazette*, 1878 wrote about the opening of the second Lockhart's store in Sunderland. On entering the shop there was a big room with a long bar at one end and tables and chairs the other. Tea, coffee and cocoa were served from the bar to the waiting tables, or could be purchased directly from the bar itself. Behind this façade were a passage and a further room, bigger than the first, which would open in the evenings only, again to serve tea, coffee and cocoa to the working man. The store also provided smoking rooms and lavatories. By 1878 a total of nine of Mr Lockhart's temperance-themed bars were operating in the north, located in Newcastle, Sunderland and Shields.

Nineteenth-century public dining wasn't all sober and civilised. Much like the Eating Houses of the Georgian age, the Victorian media was full of stories of brawls, rows and disputes. In 1891 in an Eating House in Dundee, James Reid and Cornelius Short were charged with assault and 'malicious mischief', resulting in a one-month prison term for the former and a small fine or fourteen-day jail sentence for the latter. The court heard that the two men walked into the Eating House and helped themselves to food on display, and when reprimanded Reid struck the owner and Short attacked the owner's wife who had gone to defend him. They then smashed the glass frontage.[18] Again in Scotland, this time Aberdeen in 1901, Mary Wood was attacked and strangled by a labourer, William Robertson, who pleaded not guilty, but was fined ten shillings or offered three days imprisonment.[19] Often frequented by customers already drunk from a night on the town, or by the labouring and poorer classes, just about able to afford a humble meal, Eating Houses had a reputation spanning right back to the century before for drink-related crimes and the crimes of the hungry and desperate. Perhaps one of the more amusing of these is recalled in a Bristol newspaper of 1889, where it was said many a well-meaning passer-by would get caught out by a regular downtrodden figure of a man who would stand outside a local Eating House dressed in rags, with holes in his shoes, staring longingly at the food on display in the window. His demeanour and desperate expression would have onlookers digging in their own pockets to give him enough money to purchase a meal. The man would take the money and make his way to the door of the eatery. Once out of site however, he would pocket the money and return to his position outside the window waiting for his next gullible victim.[20]

Another significant change in the Victorian period for owners of eating and coffee houses was the establishment of the Coffee and Eating House Keepers' Association, in London, a charity which provided pensions and financial relief to elderly or sick workers in the trade, or those who needed support for their families. As Britain was growing commercially and expanding its trade in all areas, many of the old industries also had to diversify with the new culture and this would have impacted greatly on a number of businesses.

Street sellers were at their height in the preceding era and much can be read about the different types of early food retailers in *Dining with the Georgians: A Delicious History*.

Charles Booth describes an area around Brand Street, North London, off Hornsey Road, well known for its severe overcrowding and low moral character where traders sold whelks, vegetable refuse, cats meat and cooked horse flesh, from which Booth assures us, they earned a 'good living' from the desperate neighbouring poor residents.

The best records for determining Victorian food street-sellers can be found in Henry Mayhew's reports of 1851.

In particular his investigations of capital and income generated from street food sales provides a thorough breakdown of the types of food and their popularity in London in the mid-nineteenth century, including among others: Around 300 pea soup and hot eel sellers, 150 whelk sellers, 300 selling fried fish and sheep's trotters, 60 selling ham sandwiches, 200 selling baked potatoes, 150 misc meat sellers, 4 hot green pea sellers, 25 bread sellers, 1,000 selling dog and cat meat, 800 selling coffee and tea, 1,700 engaged with the sale of soft drinks such as ginger beer, lemonade and sherbet, 6 specialising in plum puddings, 150 cake and tart sellers, 5,000 hot-cross bun sellers (seasonal), 500 muffin and crumpet sellers and around 20 ice cream merchants. Cat and dog meat as listed here was not sold in its literal sense, rather it was meat fit for cats and dogs, but doubtless the very poor may have purchased it cheaply for their own consumption, as suggested by an article published in the *Sunderland Daily Echo and Shipping Gazette,* 1901, expressing concerns about a prevailing trade in cat's meat (mostly horse flesh) being used to manufacture sausages and other meat based products. A London-based medical officer of the time is quoted as saying 'I have absolutely no doubt that there is an enormous amount of filthy poisonous food (of course deeply masked with condiments) dealt in, and that regular well-established markets and agents exist for this purpose'. By 1901 this lucrative band of traders had re-named themselves as 'Domestic Animal Providers'. The pet-meat traders would hawk their wares on long skewers over their shoulders to attract the neighbourhood pets and strays and therefore catch the eye of potential buyers. It was also one of the highest income generators in the city where street food selling was concerned together with tea and coffee, baked potatoes, ginger beer, miscellaneous meat and assorted bread products. Sweets and pies also attracted high numbers of sales. Overall Mayhew estimates that the total sales of all street food in London in the mid-1800s to be around £203,115, possibly equivalent to £15 million in today's money.

Just as Georgian Britain provided the street customer boundless choices in food, the Victorian market continued the trend. In

London fish was available in abundance at Billingsgate, vegetables or 'greens' could be picked out at Covent Garden and Sunday dinner purchased at the all night Saturday street markets.

The following extract from an 1838 edition of *The Magazine of Domestic Economy* provides an overview of market prices and produce that year in London.

Notwithstanding the backwardness of the season, the crops have a promising appearance. The young wheat's seem well planted and the spring corn has been got into the ground in good order. There is a tendency to a slight reduction in the price of grain, owing doubtless to the want of employment in the manufacturing districts, which lessens the demand for consumption by abridging the means of buying. Although the agricultural interest may be said to be thriving, and the farmers are getting high prices those infallible indexes the customs and excise returns prove that the public generally is not so prosperous and it has become a general subject of remark, that although corn is more than twenty per quarter dearer than in 1835, the revenue which was then on the increase is now on the decline, a plain proof that cheap prices are quite necessary for national prosperity. The present Mark Lane prices may be quoted as follows: – Wheat from fifty one shillings to sixty five shillings, Barley thirty shillings to thirty five shillings. Oats twenty shillings to twenty seven shillings per quarter, Flour from forty three shillings to fifty five shillings per sack. The Market has been well supplied with town and country killed meat throughout the month of May; on certain days greatly overstocked and prices lower: – Beef two shillings four pence to three shillings four pence, Mutton two shillings one penny to three shillings six pennies, Veal three shillings six pennies to four shillings six pennies, Pork three shillings to four shillings, sixpence per stone of eight pounds., Lamb five shillings to seven shillings. Poultry still continues dear the prices being nearly the same as last month. Plovers' eggs are two shillings per dozen.

The price of fish has varied greatly throughout the month of May; at times Turbots of equal size and quality could be bought for six shillings to seven shillings which a few days before or after would fetch thirty shillings or forty shillings. Persons to whom the particular day on which they choose to indulge in a good dish of fish is immaterial, should watch these gluts of the Market and make their purchases at favourable seasons, for the price altogether depends on the supply of the Market, not on the quality, and the cheapest fish is often the best. Salmon is now from one shilling to one shilling fourpence per lb. Some mullet are also at Market Vegetables are still dear. In colonial articles no alteration.[21]

The food markets of Victorian Britain were loud, brash and undoubtedly frightening as this account of London's Leather Lane Sunday market suggests with the 'never-ending cries of Buy! buy! buy!' coming from the cheesemonger, while the 'somewhat threatening' shout of the butcher as he sharpens his large knife repeating the words 'Meat, meat, meat' in quick succession leaves the passer-by feeling quite unnerved. All this among a myriad of other retailers all vying for attention with the constant background sounds of the rattling barrows over the cobbles, dodging police from illegal touting.[22] One of the most intimidating food markets of the nineteenth century would unquestionably have been Smithfield meat market, perhaps best summarised by Charles Dickens in his 1830s serial *Oliver Twist or The Parish Boys Progress*:

The ground was covered, nearly ankle-deep, with filth and mire; and a thick steam, perpetually rising from the reeking bodies of the cattle, and mingling with the fog ... All the pens in the centre of the large area, and as many temporary ones as could be crowded into the vacant space, were filled with sheep; tied up to posts by the gutter-side were long lines of beasts and oxen, three or four deep.

Countrymen, butchers, drovers, hawkers, boys, thieves, idlers, and vagabonds of every low grade, were mingled together in a dense mass ... the bellowing and plunging of oxen, the bleating of sheep, the grunting and squeaking of pigs ... the hideous and discordant din that resounded from every corner of the market; and the unwashed, unshaven, squalid, and dirty figures constantly running to and fro, and bursting in and out of the throng, rendered it a stunning and bewildering scene.[23]

It cost a significant amount to acquire a licence to sell game – in the region of £130,000 and £160,000 annually. It was shot and transported to market with great speed by rail to avoid being spoilt. The two predominant game and poultry markets in London were situated at Leadenhall and Newgate and they would certainly have provided good returns for those trading; with Leadenhall reaping the benefits from some 1,310,000 sales of game and fowl and Newgate in the region of 542,000.[24]

The most popular licence of the period was that which enabled the retail of alcohol. The total number of independent persons licensed to brew their own beer for sale in England and Wales between 1848 and 1849 that could be sold and drunk on the premises was 12,201. The number of brewers licensed to sell beer on the premises in the same year was 34,800. The latter was 154 in Scotland and just ninety-six in Ireland. Although the number of licences issued to Publicans, decreased across the UK between 1840 and 1849 by about 1,000. This may correlate to the steady increase in duty that also had to be paid throughout this period.[25]

Prior to 1800 little was needed to establish yourself in business with a tavern, dining room or coffee house with specially adapted rooms in domestic dwellings often serving as public spaces. Visitors would be able to identify these establishments by simple signage and window displays.

Initially public houses were tap rooms that served beer directly from the cask, with a couple of long benches and tables. The more discerning establishments might have a separate parlour and some soft furnishings, but in the main they attracted the country's poor and labouring classes from street and market stall holders to seasonal migrant workers, domestic servants, factory workers, the homeless and transient lodgers. As this market grew, so too did the buildings themselves with tap rooms evolving into saloon bars with larger more functional spaces now offering counter service. The invention of hydraulics meant that the beer casks could be stored out of site and beer pumped directly to the customer waiting at the bar. Working men began fitting the pub around their daily routine, combing a drink with a simple lunchtime meal consisting of a sandwich, fried fish or bread and cheese and the opportunity in some venues to take along your own food to be cooked on the premises for a small additional fee.[26]

The Victorian age was the age of the grand hotel, with its equally grander dining rooms. Colonel Newnham describes the Savoy Hotel dining rooms in 1900, with their great marble mantelpiece and oriental ornamentations. There are two dining areas, a more formal *table d'hôte* or the hotel's Cafe and Grill where they also served curries cooked by the infamous Victorian Indian chef 'Smiler'. The fine dining restaurant was run by a French restaurant manager, who would come and speak to customers directly if they needed to establish the cost of their haute cuisine in advance.

It was discouraged in such establishments to order hors d'oeuvres although they were frequently cited on menus. One marvels at the strange contradictory etiquette of dining at this time. The fish dishes on the Savoy *table d'hôte* menu in 1900 included: Sole de Breteuil, Sole a la Riechemberg, Filets de Soles Aimee Martial, Sole D'Yvonne, Pommes de Terre de Georgette, Sole Dragomiroff, Pilaff aux Moules, Homard a la Cardinal, Homard Lord Randolph Churchill, Queue de Homard Archiduchesse, Homard d'Yvette, Darne de Saumon Marcel Prevost, Filets de

Macquereau Marianne. Clearly you would know when you had made it as a celebrity in the Victorian period, when your name appeared as a dish on an exclusive restaurant menu.[27] 'Smiler' was a renowned Indian chef who worked at the famous 'Sherry's' of New York, before being head-hunted across the Atlantic by the grand Cecil Hotel, once located between the Strand and Thames Embankment, now demolished. 'Smiler' was then employed by the Savoy Hotel.

Colonel Newnham also made observations of Claridge's with its silent waiters, high-backed chairs, heavy purple and red curtains and oak panelled and olive wood walls. He describes the menu precisely:

Hors d'oeuvre
Consommé Sevigne Bisque d'Ecrevisses
Filets de Sole Florentine
Poularde a la d'Albufera
Troncon de Filet de Boeuf Richelieu
Becassines bardees a la Broche
Salade de Saison
Asperges vertes. Sauce Mousseline
Ponchardin d'Ananas
Comtesse Marie. Petits Fours
Soufflé au Parmesan
Dessert

One of Claridge's specialities at that time were their ices, which came in a hard shell and when cracked revealed a fusion of many different flavours.[28]

Built in the 1870s, Piccadilly's Criterion, although not a hotel, provided all the opulence of Victorian Hotel dining. It was one of the first restaurants designed with women in mind, from its beautiful feminine furnishings to its delicate fanciful dishes. Once a segregated restaurant with à la carte dining one end and a table d'hôte the other, by 1914 the two had merged, with the only difference being the type of menu and prices. The cheaper seven-and-six menu offered the following:

Hors d'oeuvre
Consommé Rossolnick
Creme aux huitres
Truite de riviere Dona Louise
Selle d'Agneau Mascotte
Pommes nouvelles
Poularde du Surrey a la broche
Salade
Parfait au moka
Friandises
Dessert

While a half-guinea would provide all of these treats, with the added bonus of *cailles à la Grecque* (Greek style quail)and *chou de mer, sauce vierge.* (Sea cabbage)[29]

As the catering industry became more commercialised in Victorian Britain, the restaurants of the time reflected the Continental ownership of the big plush designs particularly reminiscent of French style. Potted palms, orchestras, gilt mirrors, red and purple plush velvet upholstering, carpets and flowers were all indicative of this.

The Langham Hotel which opened in 1865 provided a ladies' coffee room, several saloons for formal balls and dinners and a staff dining area catering for 260. The ovens were bespoke to fit up to 2,000 plates and a small tramway system was also integrated into the kitchen to transport goods.

It wasn't just the capital that was bathing in the culinary marketability of the large hotel. As the Victorians accrued more leisure time and the growth in tourism and holidays increased, many seaside resorts such as those in the far north and south of England enjoyed a boom in hotel dining. The Grand Hotel, Scarborough, employed a French head chef and served breakfast at 9 a.m. prompt for the sum of three shillings. For this the customer received tea, coffee and a carte du jour. Luncheon again was prompt at quarter past one and cost just two shillings while guests could expect a 'semi-dress' dinner of five shillings at 6 p.m. consisting of soups, fish, entrees, roasts, entremets and dessert. Served of course in the new fashionable à la Russe style of one course at a time.[30]

The abundance and choice of public dining venues in Britain during the nineteenth century from the grill-room and cafe, to the inns and taverns, temperance dining halls, tea rooms, club and hotel restaurants and other recreational establishments harbouring eating areas offered something for everyone. Even the very poor were in receipt of charitable food dispensaries and soup kitchens designed for destitute adults and children alike.

There were some unremarkable changes compared to the century before, like those to be found in the taverns and on the streets, together with some extraordinary revolutions in public dining. The tea room phenomenon and high-class restaurant to some extent emancipated women and radically altered the way that people socialised, taking eating out of the domestic dining room and out into society. The preferred cooking style remained French, as it had in the Georgian era, although English food was integral to the marrying of the two cuisines on any respectable menu.

Recipes

Crayfish soup was a very popular dinner dish during the Victorian period and as this chapter notes, was on the menu at Claridges in 1900.

Bisque d'Ecrevisses (Cray FishSoup)

Wash half a hundred of crayfish, and boil them on a brisk fire, with salt,whole pepper, a little nutmeg, and a piece of butter ; toss them and stir them without intermission, a quarter of an hour will suffice. When they are all red, take out the meat from the shells; and from the belly take the gut which goes to the end of the tail. Fry some bread till brittle and brown and pound it with the meat, reserving a few fine pieces dilute with light veal consommé, to the thickness of cream: add the butter in which your crayfish were done, coloured with red lobster spawn; pound it well and add it to your puree; then pass the whole through the tammy, and keep it hot au bain marie. Serve with fried bread cut in dice.[31]

In the magazine supplements that would eventually be published as her *Book of Household Management*, Isabella Beeton first mentioned John Dauglish about a year before his tea rooms exploded onto British society and detailed his method of aerated bread products that would make him a commercial success.

Aerated Bread

It is not unknown to some of our readers that Dr. Dauglish, of Malvern, has recently patented a process for making bread 'light' without the use of leaven. The ordinary process of bread-making by fermentation is tedious, and much labour of human hands is requisite in the kneading, in order that the dough may be thoroughly interpenetrated with the leaven. The new process impregnates the bread with carbonic acid gas, or fixed air by the application of machinery. Different opinions are expressed about the bread; but it is curious to note, that, as corn is now reaped by machinery, and dough is baked by machinery, the whole process of bread-making is probably in course of undergoing changes which will emancipate both the housewife and the professional baker from a large amount of labour.

In the production of aerated bread, wheaten flour, water, salt, and carbonic acid gas (generated by proper machinery), are the only materials employed. We need not inform our readers that carbonic acid gas is the source of the effervescence, whether in common water coming from a depth, or in lemonade, or any aerated drink. Its action, in the new bread, takes the place of fermentation in the old.

In the patent process, the dough is mixed in a great iron ball, inside which is a system of paddles, perpetually turning, and doing the kneading part of the business. Into this globe the flour is dropped till it is full, and then the common atmospheric air is pumped out, and the pure gas turned on. The gas is followed by the water, which has been aerated for the purpose, and then begins the churning or kneading part of the business.

Of course, it is not long before we have the dough, and very 'light' and nice it looks. This is caught in tins, and passed on to the floor of the oven, which is an endless floor, moving slowly through the fire. Done to a turn, the loaves emerge at the other end of the apartment, and the aerated bread is made.

It may be added, that it is a good plan to change one's baker from time to time, and so secure a change in the quality of the bread that is eaten.[32]

8

POPULATION AND EMPIRE

Two new committees were appointed in 1888 with the specific remit to look at Emigration and Immigration in relation to its impact on Britain as a whole.

Figures for emigration certainly outweighed those of immigration to the UK from 1890 to 1893. In total in 1893 702,995 passengers left the UK to travel to both Europe and the Continent, while only 93,299 entered UK shores that year. Taking into consideration the fact that some of these travellers were leaving for leisure or business purposes only, a total of 15,791 immigrants have been calculated to have arrived in the UK in 1893 with the intention of finding work/to live, with 109,090 UK residents leaving the same year to live outside of Europe. However these figures can only act as an approximate guide. Other figures such as the number of migrants travelling to the UK that weren't seamen in 1893 travelling without tickets for onward journeys past the UK are worth investigating further and by their country or origin. In 1893 these included 7,721 Russian and Polish travellers, 4,597 Norwegians, Swedes and Danes, 6,562 Germans, 880 Dutch, 977 French, 644 Italians and 2,221 from other unspecified countries. According to the *Alien immigration Reports on the volume and effects of recent immigration from Eastern Europe into the United Kingdom, 1894*, the most likely of these migrant travellers to stay in the country were the Russian and Polish contingent. 70 per cent of these arrived in London, with Hull and Grimsby being the next major disembarkation locations. A large proportion of these migrants were also Jewish. Many of the country's fine dining restaurants and hotels that flourished during the Victorian period were masterminded by wealthy Europeans from the continent, particularly the French and Swiss and companies including Lyon's had their roots in German-Jewish ownership. Restaurants like Schmidts founded in 1901 exploited Britain's love-affair with migrant entrepreneurialism, becoming as equally well-known for its German cuisine as for its rude German waiters. The Board of Trade, perhaps somewhat optimistically, estimated some 4,000 German bakers operating in London in 1887, while census returns suggest around 2,000 practising German bakers nationally between 1881 and 1911.[1] Germans were also influential in Britain's sugar refining industry and established themselves as reputable pork butchers across the country. One of the earliest was George Friedrich Hohenrein, who was trading in Hull in 1850 selling 'home-cured ham and bacon, warranted pure lard, celebrated Brunswick sausages and Cassel polonies as well as all kinds of German sausages'.[2]

Britain and Ireland exported a lot of food and drink items abroad during the late Victorian period, such as meat, fish, pickles, vinegar, sauces, condiments, confectionery, beers and ales and spirits. This was at its peak in 1897 with some £12,130,000 worth of food and drink items leaving the country for foreign shores.[3]

So what were the British eating from abroad in the nineteenth century? Raisins were chiefly imported from Malaga and Smyrm and consumption steadily increased from 12,642 tons in 1847 to 13,816 in 1851 and of course grapes in abundance from France.[4]

The nation became increasingly dependent on coconut oil from Manila and Ceylon, importing 750 tons in 1847 to 3,815 tons in 1851 as well as dried tongues from Russia and Germany.[5] Walnuts from France and Holland declined tremendously in popularity between 1847 and 1849 from 1,222 tons to just 740. As well as growing them natively Britain imported some 324 tons of hops from the USA, Belgium and France between 1849 and 1850. Similarly Britain, despite producing tens of thousands of tons of apples each year, also imported different varieties from the USA, France and Holland – as much as 8,277 tons in 1848 into London alone. The UK imported 17,640 tons of foreign bacon and ham in 1851, worth £529,200, mostly from Ireland and the USA. Britain imported 980 tons of turmeric in 1850, a huge increase on the 191 tons the previous year, and up from just 18 tons in 1848. This may be attributed to the increased popularity for curried dishes, particularly as rice imports into London reached almost 13,000 tons in 1850 and staggeringly in excess of over 37,000 tons into Liverpool in the same year. Cardamoms were also a regular import into Britain. The UK was partial to continental cheeses, with imports into London alone exceeding over 9,500 tons. Primarily these came from Holland, the USA, Italy (Parmesan), France, Denmark and a small number of cheeses from the Hanseatic towns.

One of the most imported goods was, of course, sugar, with over 180,000 tons entering London in 1850; coffee consumption had also superseded tea, a trend continued from the Georgian era. Some other imports of note that the Victorians liked to indulge in included capers, of which around 40 tons came into the country annually from France, caviar and champagne also came from France. Cranberries from Russia and North America, currants at over 20,000 tons a year from the Ionian Islands, cloves from Malaysia, ginger from the East and West Indies and some 30,000 lb worth of grapes came into the country from France, Spain, Portugal, Italy and Germany each year. Despite being extensively cultivated in England, by the mid-nineteenth century Britain had also begun to import onions from Portugal.

With the new burgeoning rail, road and existing canal networks internal trade included items such as cockles from Lancashire to the south coast and bacon and hams from Ireland to London, Liverpool and Bristol. Butter-making in Ireland was synonymous with the manufacture of the 'firkin', a measure of butter packed and exported out in earthenware dishes or 'pan mugs'. Ireland also produced the largest amount of eggs, supplying the whole of the UK market with around 500 million. The remaining 100 million or so eggs consumed in the UK each year were exported from Europe. It was typical for upwards of 1 million eggs to be transported daily from Ireland to Liverpool and then distributed countrywide. Celery principally grown in London, Birmingham and Manchester was transported in bulk out to the manufacturing districts who consumed the largest quantity of this vegetable. Cherries were cultivated throughout the counties of Kent and Hertfordshire, and then transported to the London markets for wider distribution. Truffles were in high demand, especially in restaurant cooking, and were cultivated on the Salisbury Plains. While most of the lard used in the UK was once supplied by Ireland, in 1849 it was importing some 16,000 tons from America at a value of almost £453,000. At about twelve shillings per hundredweight cheaper than Irish lard, this probably accounts for the switch. Many more general everyday provisions were being imported from the United States in Victorian Britain including beef, pork, bacon, hams, eggs, cheese, butter, fish and poultry among others. Although Britain was exporting widely during the century before, the nineteenth century marks the start of a radical departure away from domestic British production and arguably the onset of the demise of the British food industry.[6]

The food influences from Britain's imperial past started to permeate society during the Georgian age. By the time of the Victorians and sophisticated transport networks, the potential to experiment with the cooking and eating of new ingredients was open to a much wider audience. Queen Victoria's love of curry was no secret and was enhanced greatly by her relationship with Abdul Karim, her controversial twenty-four-year-old servant and confidant, that began in 1887. It was at Osborne House where Karim first cooked for the Queen using a spice box that he carried with him from India. It was a chicken curry daal, with a fragrant pilau and from that meal onwards the Queen requested Karim's curries with great regularity; in fact during the last decade of her life, curry was ordered to be cooked on a daily basis, and always served to visiting Indian royalty.[7]

In time the Queen reconfigured large parts of Osbourne House to replicate the architectural and cultural styles of India and had recruited a small team of Indian chefs to work alongside her European kitchen staff. One member of the Royal kitchens noted, while observing the Indian coterie:

> For religious reasons, they could not use the meat which came to the kitchens in the ordinary way, and so killed their own sheep and poultry for the curries. Nor would they use the curry powder in stock in the kitchens, though it was of the best imported kind, so part of the household had to be given to them for their special use and there they worked Indian style, grinding their own curry powder between two large stones and preparing all their own flavouring and spices. Two Indian in their showy gold and blue uniforms worn at luncheon always served the curry to Queen Victoria and her guests.[8]

Curry was never served at dinner, only for lunch, as was also customary for the British living out in India. Dinner was for French and English cuisine only. This rule of thumb is often reflected in the restaurant menus of the time, like the newly opened Pizzini and Co. in Cheltenham in 1893, serving traditional British roast beef and strawberries and cream, alongside fillet of sole, bordelaise and curried mutton and rice. Yet the name would seem to conjure up the notion of an Italian-run establishment. Perhaps the braised beef, Italian style, served as their token dish.[9]

Curry was in and out of favour throughout the Victorian era. Perhaps writing at its height of popularity, Thackeray inflicts one on the aspiring Becky Sharp in *Vanity Fair* in his novel of 1847:

'Oh I must try some, if it is an Indian dish', said Rebecca. 'I am sure everything must be good that comes from there.'

'Give Miss Sharp some curry, my dear, ' said Mr Smedley, laughing.

Rebecca had never tasted the dish before.

'Do you find it as good as everything else from India?' Said Mr Smedley.

'Oh, excellent!' said Rebecca, who was suffering tortures with the cayenne pepper.

'Try a chilli with it, Miss Sharp', said Joseph, really interested.

'A chilli, ' said Rebecca, gasping. 'Oh yes!' She thought a chilli was something cool, as its name imported, and was served with some.

'How fresh and green they look!' she said, and put one into her mouth. It was hotter than the curry; flesh and blood could bear it no longer. She laid down her fork. 'Water for heaven's sake, water!' she cried.[10]

In terms of Indian cuisine. Spices were introduced at a very early age into Britain and began permeating cultural culinary society long before the Victorian period. *The Yorkshire Evening Post* advertises that an Indian restaurant has opened in London in 1898, although the first Indian-inspired coffee house, the Hindostanee opened in 1811 serving 'Indian dishes in the highest perfection'.[11] Bengali seamen or Lascars worked on British ships and undoubtedly this would have influenced the culinary offerings across port cities around the UK.

Local newspapers were full of advertisements for curry paste. There were numerous weekly 'curry clubs' that took place round Britain run by elder Indian expatriates from the 1880s and beyond. Curry was also seen as a solution to the poor crisis by an article that appeared in the 1871 *Orkney Herald, and Weekly Advertiser and Gazette* for the Orkney & Zetland Islands, proclaiming it '*less expenditure, better health and more satisfaction, than any other element*'. Similarly in 1845 the Duke of Norfolk recommended that the poor add a pinch of curry powder to warm water to drink before going to bed as a substitute for supper.

British men took their families to settle and work throughout Britain's vast colonies in a variety of roles from government administrators and trade operations managers, to soldiers and labourers. The influences of all these countries culinary attributes would have become absorbed into British culture. Ingredients, recipes and the utensils needed to prepare them were brought back and integrated into British society.

The Nabob's (Nawab's) Cookery Book – A manual of East and West Indian Recipes, 1870, was written intriguingly by someone who just signs themselves POP. Clearly a native of India, the writer of the book provides a brief preface to clarify that all of the ingredients required to make the dishes outlined in the book can be obtained in England.

The classic imported dish and one that Britain still consumes today, mulligatawny soup, appears in this book. By 1875 there are regular advertisements in the press for Crosse and Blackwell's canned version and it first appears with any regularity from as early as 1815, on sale in coffee houses as a spicy warming meal:

Mulligatawny Soup
Skin, and cut up a rabbit or fowl into small joints, and brown them in a frying pan, then put them into a stewpan with five fried onions a small piece of garlic, and three pints of stock, into which you

have previously mixed two tablespoonfuls of currie powder. Simmer gently for two hours, then add one ounce of pounded almonds, which mix well, and a little lemon or mango juice, with a good lump of butter and salt to taste. Serve very hot and send up a large dish of boiled rice with it or the rice may be put into the soup if preferred.

Life must have been difficult for the wives and families of men working in these countries, and for the majority of women accompanying their husbands, the only contact they would have had with local people would have been their domestic servants. Coming to terms with the climate, environment, the customs, culture and of course the food must have been challenging, particularly in countries that were then a great deal more impoverished with far less amenities than both today, and compared to Victorian British society.

As their servants were such a significant part of their lives they would have dominated their journals and letters home and shaped their whole opinion of that culture.

Of the many who initially migrated to India, they were not of the higher echelons of society, rather they would have belonged to the aspiring middle and lower-middle-class sectors of British society and unlike the three or so domestic staff they may have been able to employ at home, in India they could afford a whole team of staff. There would have been huge communication barriers to overcome, issues of prejudice and sex discrimination. While the majority of domestic servants in Britain were, by the Victorian period, women, in India they were predominantly male, which may have concerned the mistresses of the house, in terms of personal safety and trust. The only female member of staff employed in the kitchen would be the Tanniketch, or scullery maid, whose duties included washing the cooking utensils, boiling rice, grinding spices and general sweeping up. There would have been a cook's boy, a waiter and more often than not a *bheesti* or water carrier, as well as messenger boys and *punkahs* or coolies who would work between house and kitchen.

It had also become illegal to physically punish domestic staff in Britain by the mid-nineteenth century, but in India it was apparently common for servants to be beaten as punishment. Writing in 1864, an anonymous 'Lady Resident' in India advises against the use of physical force:

> I am often told it is a proof of weakness to show consideration for servants, – that the better a native is treated the more ungrateful he is; but I cannot divest myself of the idea that he is – if a very bad specimen of the "man and brother" – at all events, a fellow creature, and I really cannot persuade myself or others that it does well to treat him like a brute; to deny him every opportunity of relaxation, or to prevent his having his meals or sleep in peace.[12]

The same author describes the best attributes to look for when recruiting a cook in India:

> In small households goes to market in others confines his attention to the kitchen. A first rate native cook is indeed a *rara avis*: he should be able to send up a thoroughly well dressed dinner for any number of guests, including jellies, made dishes and confectionery. An ordinary good cook has a large *repertoire* of made dishes, but they generally bear the most peculiar names, strangely transmogrified from their original ones. Considering the very primitive kitchens and cooking pots, the total absence of stoves, hot closets, and every convenience for dressing a dinner, it ought to be a matter of astonishment that anything is ever sent up fit to eat. As it is, a native cook will frequently put to shame the performances of an English one; soups cutlets and made dishes in particular. Their abilities vary greatly and so does their pay from seven to fifteen rupees or more.

The basic equipment provided for a cook included a table, a chopping board, several different sized choppers for meat and wood, some knives and spoons, a couple of ladles, a bamboo rice strainer, bamboo shovels, a pestle and mortar for pounding rice and a stone roller for grinding seeds, bellows for the fire and brooms for sweeping. Cooks were also given a set of copper pans (tinned once a month), chatties (to hold water), enamelled saucepans and stewpans, a kettle, grid iron and frying-pan. Interestingly the real primitive nature of Indian kitchens is revealed by the fact that small dogs were often still used to turn the spits for roasting meat, a tradition that died out in Britain during the early eighteenth century.[13]

Some women made the mistake of buying pots and pans with handles, as the Indian cooks disliked them and would hammer them off. Anne Wilson writing about her time in the Punjab provides us with a good description of what a typical kitchen would have resembled, recalling it as "a little darkroom, with a board on the mud floor to hold the meat, two tumble-down brick 'ranges' in one corner, a stone receptacle in another into which the water is thrown, to run out through its hole in the wall into a sunk tub." There was no running water and the oven was often little more than a tin box surrounded with bricks. The nineteenth-century snobbery around chefs translated from England to India, with the most sought after being the Mughs who resided on the Burmese border and elevated in status as 'the French cooks of India'. Many Indian cooks however were renowned heavy drinkers, if they weren't Muslim and frequently untrustworthy. *The Complete Indian Housekeeper and Cook* encouraged British migrants to 'do anything' in order to secure a reliable cook. Good households would expect the cook to present himself each morning in a clean uniform and submit all the accounts from the previous day before menu planning with the *memsahib,* who would then allocate the day's supplies to the cook from the storeroom.

Waiters were equally important to the process of dining, known as *khitmutgar* in northern India, *masaul* in Bombay and *matey* in the south. They operated from a small pantry just off from the kitchen. For some reason; possibly the need to sleep in the heat between jobs, these roles were characterised by their slovenliness, beyond anything conceivable in Britain.[14]

The social and cultural differences that India presented had a wide impact on domestic servitude for British employers, in terms of persuading various kitchen staff to handle different types of meat and serve or cook with alcohol. Having to be tolerant and understanding of the complexities that emerged when working with servants from various religions was unfamiliar and confusing to the British living out in India.[15]

George Franklin Atkinson's *Curry and Rice* is a nineteenth-century satirical and fictional portrait of British officials living in India, published in 1859. Semi-biographical, the characters are probably similar to those Atkinson encountered during his time as a Captain stationed with the Bengal Engineers. The book is full of accurate and humorous observations that mock both British officials and local Indian citizens. His very disparaging accounts of 'Our Cook Room' provide a similar description to those documented by the mothers, wives and daughters living in the British Empire in India. It is a book of its time that uses language we now consider derogatory and offensive to describe native Indians, but it must be remembered it is of its time and therefore not a reflection of my own opinions.

His description of an 'oriental' kitchen is as follows:

> If your eyes are not instantly blinded with the smoke, and if your sight can penetrate into the darkness, enter that hovel, and witness the preparation of your dinner. The table and the dresser, you observe are Mother Earth; for ... Orientals ... – have that peculiar faculty which characterises the ape and the kangaroo: they can only

stand erect on an occasion. The preparation for your dinner must therefore be performed in the earth's broad lap, like everything else in this Eastern land. As a matter of course, you will have curry, the standing dish of the East. There are the slaves busy at its preparation. The chase for the fowls has terminated in a speedy capture. Already the feathers are being stripped, and the mixture of the spicy condiments is in course of preparation. There on his hams, is the attractive-looking assistant, grinding away the savoury stuff which is soon to adorn that scraggy chicken … .Observe the kitchen-range, I beseech you: a mud construction, with apertures for the reception of charcoal, upon which repose pans of native mould, in which the delicacies are cooked.

Atkinson goes on to describe how meat is roasted, not with a smoking jack to turn a spit, but by the cook himself, usually a wise old sage whose job it was to hand turn the meat. He adds that even with all the new technology afforded to the kitchens of the burgeoning affluent UK households, undoubtedly the Indian cooks are capable of creating far superior dishes than those of their British counterparts.[16]

The abolition of the slave trade in 1807 left behind a bitter legacy of black populations influenced by Britain's role in Africa, Americas and West Indies. Images of black people dominated English culture in many forms, in books, on stage and in a wide range of consumerable products and Britain's streets, homes and work places had visible numbers of black African and West Indian men and women, although this was still primarily true of the larger trading port locations and there were certainly greater numbers of men than women. How the two cultures related to one another was complex in terms of status, prejudice and community, as the transition from slavery to freedom unfolded. There is a lack of accurate statistical data about the black population in Britain. Even the censuses of 1841 and 1851 do not offer any further evidence, as the question of ethnic origin and colour only emerged in a voluntary capacity on the forms as late as 1991. Some of the best sources of information can be found in the press and media of the time and from court, probate and coroners' reports.

From the documented total black male convicts recorded in the UK between 1812 and 1852, eighteen were cooks, two were sea cooks and one was a pastry cook. This suggests there were a potentially significant number of skilled black cooks working throughout the UK during this period, particularly if these figures are just reflective of the ones who committed a crime. One such criminal was Jacob Morris, a fifty-seven-year-old cook and seaman, who having drunk the good town of Uxbridge dry one night, decided to seek comfort in a woman. With no means to pay for this pleasure, he assaulted and mugged a man for the sum of £60 down an alleyway. Following his conviction, Morris was sentenced to transportation for life.[17]

Stories like that of Mr Vincent, the son of Caribbean parents who finally settled in Cardiff having worked as a cook at sea and became a stalwart member of the community, even becoming grandmaster of the local Oddfellows benevolent society, were quite common in some societies and there are many accounts of mixed-race marriages in both rural and urban communities. As was the case of the Vincents who ended up opening a boarding house together, selling tea and soup that catered specifically to West Indian sailors. Racism was rife in Britain in the nineteenth century, certainly black migrants were considered of lower intelligence and there were many displaced former black seamen, soldiers and former slaves creating pockets of communities throughout the major port towns and cities.

Another group and by far the largest of immigrants in England during the nineteenth century were the Irish, with over 600,000 recorded by the 1850s.[18] The main reason for this mass influx was the great potato blight. But the Irish also contributed significantly to England's great food store. Irish butter was a staple for many Victorians, particularly in the north of England, although towards the end of the nineteenth century this allegiance had been usurped by the more palatable butters from the continent. Potato cake recipes are frequently cited in the English Victorian press. Recipes such as champ and colcannon were popularised as a means of disguising the taste of the early inferior potato crops with onion, cabbage or kale. It became a favoured dish of the higher classes in England. Undoubtedly one of Ireland's biggest exports during the Victorian era was Guinness. By 1855 it had become the largest brewery in the world, with its very own railway.[19] Shares in the brewery went on sale in 1886, applications for which were reported as filling up in minutes, with the amount of shares required being fulfilled twenty times over.[20]

The nineteenth century witnessed the largest expansion of the empire as the British took greater possession of the West Indies. They also settled in Australia and New Zealand and competed for further territorial control of Africa. Asia too yielded Singapore, Burma and Hong Kong to the British army.

Chinese food began to permeate British culture from the middle of the nineteenth century, with one newspaper quoting 'in cookery the Chinese hold a middle position, below the French and above the English'.[21]

During the 1880s and 1890s the Limehouse borough of East London became synonymous with Chinese migrants and Manchester's Chinatown was emerging from the overspill of communities settling in Liverpool. London's six-month International Health Exhibition of 1884 chose to place Chinese cooking within the heart of the collection focusing on China, with a full-scale Chinese restaurant featuring as one of the exhibits. An article published in the *Exeter Flying Post* that year described it thus:

The hungry sightseer may with confidence order bird's nest soup. As served in a tiny slop-basin, it is excellent. It will have a great success in London, and will probably be naturalized in England from and after 1884.

Chinese food could be found being sold on the streets of England in the nineteenth century, but many go undocumented and were probably run by ex-seamen or were exclusively patronised by their own communities, rather than the wider public. New York was well ahead of London in terms of embracing this exotic culinary delight, with the township of Manchester assuming the label of 'Chinatown' and housing some 250-odd Chinese restaurants by 1901, although Chinese restaurateurs in the US Capital existed at least as early as the 1870s.[22]

According to J. A. G. Roberts the first officially recognised Chinese restaurant did not open in London until at least 1908 and was believed to have been located in Piccadilly and called the Tanhua Lou.[23] There is also mention of 'a high-class Chinese restaurant' called the Cathay in Piccadilly Circus in 1910, where chopsticks were laid out on the tables and customers had to request a knife and fork.[24]

Certainly by the beginning of the First World War, London was abuzz with establishments not only selling Chinese, but also Japanese cuisine.

The Georgian era witnessed Britain's love affair with Italy. Pasta, particularly macaroni with cheese, was already becoming something of a national dish, with numerous recipe books of the time citing macaroni and vermicelli dishes. Most towns and cities enjoyed the presence of Italian confectioners and ice cream makers and some Italian cooks like Francatelli rivalled the French experts employed in the big houses, clubs and hotels. Naturally these Italian migrants married into British society and the Italian culture embedded itself with some significance into communities across the UK, which has impacted on the country's generational relationship with Italian culture and cuisine.

An interesting criminal case involving a number of Italian ice cream vendors and confectioners occurred in Glasgow in 1890 during a wedding between a local Italian-born ice cream vendor and confectioner and a British-born woman. It appears that once word got round about the union in the Italian community a group of Italian nationals attempted to interrupt proceedings. Initially turned away, they returned in greater numbers that evening. The group were admitted to the celebrations, but then thrown out. Even more Italian men engaged in the ice cream trade appeared and what followed was a large-scale street brawl. The fight ended with one man being fatally stabbed and one seriously wounded. Several of the men ran away and it was the screams of the female onlookers that alerted police. This sounds like some sort of creamy dessert-based West Side Story drama, but it also hints to more important underlying issues within the Glasgow community at the time. Was there violent rivalry among Italian food traders, or was the argument related to animosity surrounding mixed marriages? Were there organised gangs being run by the Italian community in Glasgow at this time. And if so, was this particular to the ice cream and confectionery traders?[25]

There are numerous crimes reported in the media involving Italian cooks and, in particular, ice cream vendors. Stephen Pacitto used an 'ice pricker' to stab a young British national while walking with a group of other Italian ice cream traders in Wolverhampton in 1889,[26] another ice cream vendor Rocco Valente was charged with seriously assaulting a British national in Aberdeen in 1901,[27] two Italian ice cream sellers brawling in Gloucester in 1900 involving a knife and a stick ended fatally for one.[28] Incidentally many of the group fights between Italian and British men that ended in serious injuries or deaths were often explained away in terms of a quarrel or dispute, and there are many cases of Italians being accused by British nationals of poisoning their ice products. One sentence stands out quite tellingly in a newspaper article of 1900, when a case against one Italian ice cream trader is dismissed, with the court declaring 'these people had been unnecessarily persecuted lately'.[29]

This suggests that there was tension surrounding the presence of these workers during the nineteenth century. They were accused in the press of everything from shameful Sunday trading, to adulterated ice cream, violence, fraud and general dishonesty. Despite Britain's love of Italian food and cooking, they were a community undoubtedly persecuted and frequently provoked.

One Italian who was highly revered in Britain during the nineteenth century was the Italian General Garibaldi. In 1864 Queen Victoria staged a large-scale banquet in his honour which was held at the Fishmongers Hall in London. Garibaldi was considered the founding father of the united Italy we are familiar with today and he was hugely respected and supported by both the United Kingdom and the United States in all of his military campaigns. The London biscuit factory Peak Freans developed and manufactured the Garibaldi biscuit which retains his legacy in this country.

Many cultures influenced the way people ate during the nineteenth century, from the established French ideals to the contribution that migrants living in the country brought with them and from the increasing foreign imports market. Many of the staple foods we are familiar with today can be attributed to sources other than that of British origin. The fried fish accompanying our nationally identifiable fish and chips was thought to have originated from the Jewish communities of London, considered the lowliest class of street-food sellers. Jewish communities frequently preserved their fish by coating it in a thick batter, as relayed to us by Hannah Glasse in her 1781 edition of *The Art of Cookery Made Plain and Easy*.

'Take either salmon, cod or any large fish, cut off the head, wash it clean and cut it in slices as crimped cod is, dry it very well in a cloth; then flour it, and dip it in yolks of eggs, and fry it in a great deal of oil, till it is of a fine brown, and well done; take it out, and lay it to drain, till it is very dry and cold.'

The concept of fried fish and chips is, however, frequently credited to the north of England. Potatoes became integral to the British diet from the middle of the nineteenth century, largely as a consequence of the Irish, but in England potatoes were traditionally grown in greater abundance in Lancashire. *The New Guide for the Hotel, Bar, Restaurant, Part One* of 1885 refers to fish and chip shops as fish and batter shops, but by the 1890s they were also called fried fish and chipped potato shops. In the town of Batley, West Yorkshire there were thirty six of these establishments, this is apparent from a court case in which claims were made against the shops themselves as a nuisance to society, due to the number of customers they attracted and the over-powering smell.[30]

Most of the foods that have shaped Britain's national identity can be traced back to the influence of other culture's, largely as a consequence of the nation's legacy of empire and broad diversity of migrant communities. Immigration remains one of Britain's most contentious political issues in the twenty-first century, but undeniably the country's rich mix of cultures has contributed significantly to the broad availability of delicious multi-ethnic fare which binds us all.

Recipes

German Puddings or Puffs

Melt three ounces of butter in a pint of cream; let it stand till nearly cold; then mix two ounces of fine flour, and two ounces of sugar, four yolks and two whites of eggs, and a little rose or orange flower water. Bake in little cups, buttered, half an hour. They should be served the moment they are done, and only when going to be eaten or they will not be light. Turn out of the cups and serve with white wine and sugar.[31]

Italian Cream

Having sweetened a pint of cream, boil it with the rind of a lemon, cut very thin, and a small stick of cinnamon; strain and mix with it a little dissolved isinglass, while hot add to it the yolks of eight eggs well beaten, and stir it till quite cold.

Another way: this is made by thickening in a saucepan a pint of good milk, the beaten yolks of three eggs, a table-spoonful of potato or wheaten flour, about two ounces of sugar, and some grated lemon peel stirring constantly. It is served in the following way: – cover the bottom of the dish with some sponge cake, dipped in white wine or liqueur, (the latter is preferable) and pour the cream upon it; whisk the whites of two new laid eggs and half an ounce of pounded and sifted sugar into a good froth, and cover the cream with it, or lay the froth in detached portions of almost the size of a large apple in the cream. If the cream be covered with the froth it may be browned with a hot shovel.[32]

China Chilo has disappeared from recipe books in the twenty first century. It resembles and tastes a lot like Chinese stir fry. It may have been inherited by Britain from the days when the East India Company engaged in trade with China; it is a recipe that has been linked to those British ports that were actively trading with China. As Elisabeth Ayrton notes in her book English Provincial Cooking, the dish was 'Traditional in the families of certain nineteenth-century sailors who, returning from a voyage to the China seas, described a Chinese dish. This was the nearest their wives could get to what they wanted.'[33] Lettuce would be the substitute for bok choy and peas for bean sprouts.

China Chilo

Mince a pound of an undressed loin or leg of mutton, with or without a portion of its fat, mix with it two or three young lettuces shred small, a pint of young peas, a teaspoonful of salt, half as much pepper, four tablespoonsfuls of water, from two to three ounces of good butter, and, if the flavour be liked a few green onions minced. Keep the whole well stirred with a fork, over a clear and gentle fire until it is quite hot, then place it closely covered by the side of the stove or on a high trevet that it may stew as softly as possible for a couple of hours. One or even two half grown cucumbers cut small by scoring the ends deeply as they are sliced, or a quarter pint of minced mushrooms may be added with good effect or a dessertspoonful of currie powder and a large chopped onion. A dish of boiled rice should be sent to table with it.

Mutton 1 pint green peas 1 pint young lettuces 2 salt 1 teaspoonful pepper 4 teaspoonful water 4 tablespoonsful butter 2 to 3 ozs 2 hours Varieties cucumbers 2 or mushrooms minced pint or currie powder 1 dessertspoonful and 1 large onion.[34]

9

EMPIRE TO EMANCIPATION

The exceptional commercial and industrial expansion Britain encountered during the nineteenth century had not alleviated the long term issues of the poor and their insubstantial diets, despite philanthropic and well-meaning attempts by some groups to tackle the problems. One of the key indicators for this was the British sociologist, reformer and son of the chocolate manufacturer, Joseph Rowntree, Benjamin Seebohm Rowntree's 1900 publication *Poverty, A Study of Town Life*.

It is a damning portrayal of the poor in the city of York, the revelations of which failed to capture much attention from the public. Nonetheless Rowntree's overall findings did contribute to Liberal party reforms in the early part of the twentieth century and his further comparative studies in the 1930s and 1950s helped shape the modern welfare state.

Food is a theme which runs significantly through Rowntree's publication. He presented a serious correlation between diet, cooking and physical and mental health. He calculated that the necessary minimum weekly expenditure for food should have amounted to three shillings for adults and two shillings, three old pence for children. This was based on a complicated system of breaking down the required nutrients, proteins and carbohydrates needed to give men, women and children adequate fuel to function to their best ability, and to ensure that the items selected would be cost effective. Rowntree's selected standard diet included the following:

Flour 1s.4d. per stone
New milk 1 ½ *d* per pint
Skim milk ¾ *d* per pint
Oatmeal 2d per lb less 5 percent
Dried peas 2 ¼ *d* per lb less 5 percent
Bacon 6d per lb
Cheese 6 ½ *d* per lb
Sugar 1¾ *d* per lb
Potatoes ½ *d* per lb
Margarine 8 *d* per lb, less 5 percentage
Butter 1 s per lb
Biscuits 4 *d* per lb
Cocoa 1*s* per lb, less 5 percent
Tea 1s 5 *d* per lb
Coffee 1 s per lb, less 5 percent
Treacle 1 ¾ per lb, less 5 percent
Onions ½ *d* per lb
Yeast 8d per lb
Currants 3 ½ *d* per lb
Suet 8d per lb

It was still customary for people to make their own bread in York in 1900, which is why flour and yeast are cited rather than bread itself.

Rowntree also noted that this proposal did not take into consideration the need for proper cooking facilities and utensils and the necessity to educate people in more practical and nutritional cooking and preparation methods. He noted that time was also a factor for the poor and labouring classes to consider, in that preparing a breakfast of porridge required more preparation than that of the typically consumed tea, bread and butter.[1]

Just as the previous century had witnessed the growth of soup kitchens and public 'cooking depots' to provide the poorer classes with healthy economical 'fast food', National Kitchens were established by 1918 to counteract the scarcity of fuel and continued rationing following the end of the First World War. At first these were located in towns and cities but were eventually expanded to rural areas, where village halls and school kitchens were utilised for the purposes of preparing and distributing 'soup, good puddings, fish dishes, and other things which organized marketing and economical cookery would make available at low prices'.[2]

Certainly, somewhere between 1900 and 1935, Rowntree's subsequent studies revealed that poverty reduced by 50 per cent on the streets of York, so clearly the enduring work of governments, philanthropic individuals and charities was succeeding in breaking the cycle of depravation in Britain.

It wasn't only York that was researching its communities and attempting to find a solution for the poor situation. Bradford City Council began investigating the diets of its children in 1907. The Bradford Feeding Experiment, which was initially funded by the mayor, set out to 'ascertain what effect the giving of food had upon the children ... it was thought that the experiment might prove useful as a practical guide to the character and meals to be provided, and the best methods to adopt in the serving of them.'[3]

The report noted that the forty children included in the experiment were closely observed during the times when they were fed the breakfast and dinner menus provided. Breakfast consisted of oatmeal porridge with milk and treacle. It was noted that there was some reluctance by the children to eat the porridge, but by the end of the experiment they all enjoyed it so much that they as good as rioted if it was substituted with anything else. The dinners were varied from lentil soup and ginger pudding, to savoury batter, gravy and beans and rice pudding with currants. The children were also given baked lentils, stewed fruit and something called 'Yorkshire Cheese Pudding', cheese and potato pie, meat hash and cottage pie, among other well-thought-out dishes. The experiment relied on the children being weighed before and after each week, which were inconclusive as turnout of participants for the weighing was poor and the school premises had to be closed during the final week of the experiment. However the evidence the committee did provide resulted in the introduction of a free school meals service being rolled out across the city. Similar experiments were carried out in Edinburgh and London in the same years.[4]

In terms of children, and the impact food and cooking continued to have on their lives, in 1906, the Provision of Meals Education Act made it possible for local authorities to provide elementary schools with meals. These meals could be free or available for a small charge, depending on the authority. For this reason the meal system, together with the fact that many children did not want to be labelled poor, was not popular. Less than half of all the education authorities across England and Wales signed up to the scheme by 1912.

Bradford commissioned the first central cooking depot, distributing meals across the city from 1907. Within six months of opening they had served over 2,000 daily meals.[5]

Clearly some regions were more willing to adopt the scheme than others, Bradford being an area then known for its high levels of poverty.

The cookery teaching frenzy of the century before, with the intention of making economical and nutritious cooking mandatory, was in full swing by the Edwardian era, but the quality and structure of the classes had come up for criticism.

In 1906, following an investigation titled *Suggestions for The Consideration of Teachers and Others Concerned in the Works of Public Elementary Schools*, the summarised findings confirmed the system of teaching cookery as lacking. Less than satisfactory demonstrations were not followed up with practical instruction. Funding and resources generally meant that teachers were not able to deliver as competently as they should have been. As food was sold on after the lessons, much of the instruction focussed on cakes and buns, rather than roasting meat. As a consequence of the report, new regulations were adopted, including a proposed change to the structure of the classes, less time between theoretical and practical instruction and a reduced emphasis on elaborate cooking skills. Eventually the subject was broadened to include laundry work and housewifery.[6]

By 1910 some half a million school girls were benefiting from this new holistic domestic tuition.

As the century progressed the expense of food and greater emphasis placed on nutrition made kitchens and cooking more sanitised and intelligent. America was also making great strides; in fact overtaking Britain in the race to manufacture new kitchen gadgets that would make cooking, cleaning and washing easier and less demanding of women's time. The early twentieth century witnessed the first use of the word 'gadget' as a term associated with new kitchen apparatus. As the North Devon Journal commented, 'Gadget is a fairly common term, used for almost any mechanical apparatus which performs its work successfully'. The word itself derived from a seafaring term for miscellaneous items found on board ship.[7]

In 1905 Lucy H. Yates wrote *The Model Kitchen* as a guide to setting up a domestic kitchen in a modern urban flat. She lists all the necessary equipment, together with prices. This includes a refrigerator, the most expensive item, costing £6 6s. Other items deemed essential requirements consist of an asparagus boiler, a game pie dish, an omelette pan, a coffee mill and a cafetiere, a frying pan with a shield, a tea infuser, egg poacher, pastry cutters, glass lemon squeezer, gravy strainer, bread mixer, egg beater, can opener, apple corer, oyster knife, a refuse holder, sink tidy, fruit stoner, meat saw, a 'Spong' chopper, grey granite enamel ware saucepans and jugs and so on. Yates estimates that the cost of equipping a kitchen flat with all modern items should equate to around £16 6s 1d. In today's currency this would amount to approximately £1,000 or slightly more. Compared to 150 years before and the records acquired from a weaver's cottage kitchen that lists its contents of earthen pans and earthen jugs, wooden bowls, tea caddies, wooden whisks, skewers and an open fireplace to cook on, the types of equipment that Yates lists are far more sophisticated and labour-saving.[8] She also talks at length about the merits of gas and electric cooking but notes that in smaller flats and self-contained domestic settings, which she terms 'lower-rented ones' neither electricity or gas are usually fitted making oil stoves the best solution for cooking.[9]

In keeping with the kitchenalia revolution that emerged as early as the eighteenth-century culinary and household kitchen and dining inventions became much more sophisticated by the Edwardian age. In 1922 George Sprake invented a combination sideboard and dresser with fitted cupboards and drawers. While the Staines Kitchen Equipment Co. patent an early dishwasher in 1922 and the Kitchen and MFG Co. invented a food mixing machine in 1928, although the Americans had pioneered this about ten years before.

Ethel DM Robson was a Domestic Science teacher during the first two decades of the twentieth century, having trained prior to the First World War. There remains a useful body of her work detailing miscellaneous items and 'housewifery notes' associated with the management of kitchens during this period. These vary from line drawings illustrating how to peg out handkerchiefs and sheets on the line after washing to cut and pasted pictures of saucepans, a plate rack, a gas stove with a kettle and pot on the hob and an open oven revealing pies and meat cooking inside to other images of items including a hostess trolley, a knife cleaner with a tuning handle, miscellaneous crockery and various household brushes.[10] All of these records provide excellent documentation of the types of items likely to be used on a daily basis in the average household kitchen *circa* 1912.

The crowded dining tables of the Victorian era with their grand floral displays, coloured glass, ornate runners, elaborate candelabras, baskets of sweets and other grand adornments became streamlined in the Edwardian period with a simple arrangement of flowers, perhaps a bowl of fruit and small lamps with tiny lampshades casting a low glow across the diners.

There were many inventions worthy of noting in this chapter, during the nineteenth and early twentieth centuries. Too many to address here, but there were a number that were ground-breaking in their ability to change the way we both eat and prepare food. Evaporated, condensed and powdered milk all emerged during the mid-1800s. Past experiments by a number of scientists led to evaporated milk being patented in 1847 by T. S. Grimwade. A by-product was condensed milk, which is essentially evaporated milk with added sugar. The vacuuming and sealing of Grimwade's condensed milk led to other forms of preservation and his products were utilised on long-haul expeditions to the Arctic. Less than ten years later, he patented powdered milk, using a technique to dry it after evaporation had taken place.

Canning and refrigeration all have their origins in the Georgian period, but it was during the nineteenth century that these inventions developed and flourished and became more of an everyday reality by the beginning of the twentieth century.

Fast-acting yeast, self-raising flour, baking powder, custard powder, egg powder, mass-produced factory cheese, margarine, dried vegetables, dried soups, preserved and bottled pickles, sauces and so on were all rapidly on their way to filling up the kitchen cupboards of Britain.

The cast-iron open range transformed the middle and upper class domestic kitchen, with the closed range right behind it. Combination cooking, boiling, frying, and baking was now a possibility, together with a vast range of new cooking utensils and tin ware for baking, cutting and moulding.

Kitchens and cooking was becoming terribly avant-garde in some societies by the Edwardian period.

The American custom of providing engaged couples with a kitchen shower became popular in Britain during the turn of the twentieth century, particularly in Scotland.[11] This was a gift giving party as a means of supplying the bride-to-be with all the necessary items she would need for her kitchen once she was married. Again this is indicative of both the emphasis being placed on this room in the house, and the notion that more householders were taking control of their own kitchens and cooking.

Greater technology, labour-saving devices and the emancipation of women in the work place made the need for domestic servants and household cooks less of an essential by the turn of the twentieth century. But for the very wealthy, cooks remained integral to their social and domestic needs and they could demand a high salary if they were competent and versatile, as the contents of this letter from Joan Kennard to her mother Florence Oglander in London demonstrates:

Your card has only just arrived and am so afraid you may not have this before interviewing the cook on Tues. It sounds delightful. It is such a good thing to have a really nice woman, whom one can trust, to be in charge downstairs, but after the experience of Wheeler, I must have someone who cooks really nicely, for Auberons sake. Wheeler was absolutely alright for us alone, but hopeless for anything outside her small list of homely dishes. Having always to get in things, we found came to a great deal. I do want someone who has other ways of doing fish, except plain fry! and can do just one or two really nice entrees. Our kitchen maid helps Edith to do their bedroom, does the cooks room, all rooms in basement (including man's bedroom) ... .I think up to £40 would be right for wages. One who requires more would be too grand. We should want her any day between March 18th and 25th, probably the 20th. I do hope she will do, for it is such a good thing to have someone one knows of.[12]

By 1918 The National War Labour Board cited domestic servants as some of the lowest paid workers in the country, which was justification for a higher minimum wage and equal pay for men and women. It lists the average salary for a kitchen maid as £1 14s 6d. In today's currency that would total around £36 per month.[13]

The late nineteenth and early twentieth centuries also witnessed the growth of worker's Unions and worker's rights. In eighteen seventy two domestic kitchen staff had formed their own separate Trade Union, that requested one Sunday off work each fortnight, and a half-day during the week. Cooks also proposed that they wanted to become their own mistress after 7 p.m., make the protective cap they wore over their heads redundant and be allowed to wear whatever jewellery they chose. These unions started to rise in Dundee and rapidly spread as far down as Leamington that same year.[14] Additionally, domestic staff were demanding higher wages, greater prospects and more free time generally. The cost of living rose considerably after the First World War, which meant that the growing affluent middle classes of the century before were choosing to relinquish their servants. This is reflected in the number and variety of publications at the time, written to instruct and advise people on how to manage their own homes without staff.[15]

Together with their salary, domestic staff were provided with meat, sugar and daily beer rations. By the turn of the twentieth century this allowance totalled as much as one and a half pounds of meat daily, four pounds of sugar monthly and at least one pound of tea a month. Supper consisted of the leftovers from the day's meals. *Cassell's Household Guide* reminded employers of the importance of maintaining these supplements:

> For some reason or other, which it is difficult to account for, many housekeepers do not undertake to find grocery and beer, but allow money for those articles of consumption Either such things are necessary to the diet of servants, or they are not. If they are necessary, it is better by far to provide tea, sugar, and beer, than to give money, which may not be applied to its proper use. In point of economy, the money payment is a losing one, because a housekeeper having to feed a certain number of persons daily, the better all the meals are supplied, the more regular is the consumption likely to be. A girl that goes without a good tea is more likely to prove an inordinate supper-eater than one who has previously enjoyed a good meal.
>
> With regard to beer money. If beer be a necessary, the money ought to be spent in buying the required nourishment; if not, there is no sense in giving wages in lieu of it.[16]

The late Victorian through to the Edwardian period was the age of the kitchen garden. Throughout the latter half of the nineteenth century, the popular *Penny Illustrated Paper* ran a regular column on kitchen gardening, and other newspapers of the time frequently promoted advertisements for seeds to plant in your kitchen garden, the most popular including peas, broccoli, turnips, cress, onions, parsnips, lettuces, cabbages, cucumber, celery, radishes, tomatoes and marrows. At two shillings and six pence for a packet, the equivalent of about £6.50, these seeds were certainly not cheap to buy. The general housekeeping manuals made so popular in the previous century remained so by 1900. Some examples include *The Housewife's Manual of Domestic Cooking,* with particular reference to how to cook with gas, alongside *Daily meals for small households* and *Cookery for two and more.* These manuals, as their titles denote, were becoming more practical and humble as society began to embrace a new approach to cooking that involved taking responsibility as an individual, as opposed to relying on domestic staff.

Similarly Randall Phillips' 1920 book *The Servantless House* dedicates an entire chapter to instructions of how to manage a kitchen and scullery. He suggests merging the two and designing a more practical space where daily items are more accessible. And the layout moves fluidly from sink to dresser. He also notes the importance dressers with enclosed shelving can make to create a cupboard effect to mitigate dust and promote hygiene. Randall makes reference to the phrase 'kitchen cabinet', including drawers and separate compartments for utensils, which he confirms is already in popular use in America. He also recommends that old stone-flagged floors should be replaced or covered with something like cocoa-nut matting or with modern linoleum. He advocates good draining boards with metal plate racks and fitting sanitary sinks with taps, such as those to be found in hospitals.[17]

Layout and hygiene were now becoming fundamental to kitchen design after the First World War, alongside the new concept that housework should no longer be viewed as a chore, to be made quicker and less labour intensive with the introduction of electricity and increase in modern electrical appliances. Essentially this shift in attitude and technological advancement would begin to reduce the gap between the working and middle classes.

The Savoy and Claridge's dominated the high-class hotel

restaurant industry in the nineteenth century and it was the management team of Auguste Escoffier and his partner Cesar Ritz who also established the legendary Ritz hotel where, allegedly, the best food in London was cooked in the early twentieth century. Having initially been thrown together into the hotel business on the French Riviera and then Germany, Escoffier and Ritz took London by storm, with the latter as manager and the former as chef at the Savoy Hotel. The success of this pairing cemented their partnership and led to Escoffier designing the kitchens and recruiting teams of the best staff to work in Cesar Ritz's Europe-wide hotel syndicate.

Their departure from the Savoy was clouded, with Ritz being accused of fraudulent activity. Staff loyalty to Ritz was so strong that many key workers also chose to leave and follow in his next success. Later, as word circulated, customers of the Savoy also removed their loyalties and chose to dine at London's latest salubrious and fashionable hotel the Carlton. In a complicated story involving several large-scale hotel corporations, the Carlton Hotel Company tendered for Cesar Ritz's management team which included Escoffier. The Carlton menus, designed by Escoffier, included a prix-fixe menu at a cost of twelve shillings and six pence a head, for four diners and included:

Melon Cocktail
Veloute Saint-Germain
Truite de rivere meuniere
Blanc de poulet Toulousain
Ritz Pilaw
Noisette d'agneau à la moelle
Haricots verts à l'Anglaise
Pommes Byron
Caille en gelée à la Richelieu
Salade romaine

Asperges d'Argenteuil au beurre fondu
Mousse glacé aux fraises
Friandises[18]

A much more elaborate menu was also available at a cost of one guinea each for twenty people, including buckwheat crêpes and caviar among other dishes. The Carlton Hotel was sadly demolished after the Second World War had left it little more than a ruin, but observations of this grand new and shiny establishment at the height of its popularity are recorded in the media at the time:

> The most striking feature is undoubtedly the hall, or Palm Court, which is entered from Pall-Mall. This is a large glass covered quadrangle decorated in the Louis XVI style. The walls are a rich cream colour, broken up with coloured marble pilasters with gilded capitals supporting a cornice ornamented with gold. The furniture consists of appropriate fauteuils, bergéres, settees, &c., with a profusion of Oriental rugs, while tall and graceful palm trees, as its name indicates, play an important part in the decoration. On the same level is the restaurant, access to which is reached by ascending a flight of steps. This is a charming room in the Adams style, with pink marble columns, upholstered in cream white and old rose, the latter colour in graduated tones being used in the carpet, the chairs and the shades of the table lights. Meals will also be served in the dining rooms, which are in the Charles II style and are intended for the table d'hôte ... Another feature of the hotel will be the grill-room in the basement, which is in the Jacobean style, and is treated in white.[19]

One lesser known fact about the Carlton is that it was reputedly where the Communist revolutionary leader and one-time president of Vietnam, Ho Chi Minh, trained as a pastry chef between 1913 and 1917. Although there is no conclusive evidence to support this claim, a plaque commemorating Ho Chi Minh's position under Escoffier remains on the site of where the old hotel once stood. It seems a strange diversion for someone of his reputation to have taken up such a position. Nonetheless there are many other accounts of Ho Chi Minh working as a cook and cook's assistant as he travelled and worked his way around Europe during the first decades of the new century.

Just six years after the Carlton opened, the Ritz Hotel in Piccadilly, heralded as 'the most artistic Hotel in Europe', revealed its Edwardian elegance to the world. Just as the Carlton had a Palm Court, so too did the Ritz. This room had steps leading up to it in order to provide ladies with a dramatic entrance to take tea. The fountain with its central nymph lay at the back of the room bordered by panelled mirrors. The frosted glass ceiling and chandeliers illuminated the entire room in a soft light pink.[20]

Interestingly, the Ritz chain of hotels across Europe was the first to provide private bathrooms in each room or suite.[21]

Although coffee houses and tea rooms were established as early as the Georgian era and began to appear more regularly during the nineteenth century, the Edwardian era epitomises their success. New tea rooms were being advertised everywhere throughout the country by the turn of the twentieth century, on the high streets, in the larger hotels and across the new department stores, in parks, galleries and museums. They were also places frequently renowned for their gossip; as places to be seen and to see, to romance, to plot and to fall in love. One such story published in the Lincolnshire Echo in 1903 recalls the tragic suicide of a young man who, having fallen in love with one of the tea room cashiers, a love that clearly was not reciprocated, chose to shoot himself in the heart during a busy afternoon sitting at the teashop where she worked. It is said many of the ladies taking tea at the time fainted, while others fled the premises.

In addition to all the big culinary names of the Victorian and Edwardian era, many of which have been acknowledged throughout this book, there is one who embodies the spirit of the early twentieth century, as a woman and as a pioneering chef and hotelier. Rosa Lewis bought and ran the Cavendish Hotel in Jermyn Street from 1902 until 1952. Her humble beginnings in domestic service, elevating to that of cook, saw Lewis privileged enough to work in private households such as the Churchill's and also learn the craft from chefs like Escoffier along the way. By the age of thirty, anyone who was anyone in British society wanted Rosa to cook for them.

Fictionalised in literature and on screen as the *Duchess of Duke Street* in the 1970s, Rosa Lewis was quite a character in an age when women were more liberated and independent. It was rumoured she had an ongoing affair with Edward VII, who openly complimented her skills as a cook and had his own private suite of rooms at the Cavendish.[22]

The Cavendish became one of the most fashionable and entertaining establishments in London in the early years of the twentieth century. In Anthony Masters' book *Rosa Lewis: An Exceptional Edwardian*, he describes the Cavendish Hotel as a 'naughty nursery' where the rich 'sowed their spurious wild oats and tippled champagne', with Lewis at the heart of it as the 'amoral nanny'.

After the opulence, romance and heady liberating days of the early years of the twentieth century, the First World War plunged Britain into austerity as rationing and food shortages left millions wanting. Women baked and delivered bread both at home and for the troops along the British Western Front as one of the key roles within the Women's Army Auxiliary Corps. Those baking in their own homes were provided with an extra flour ration allowance by the Ministry of Food, which continued for several years after the war.[23]

By 1917 there were considerable limitations on the availability of food and prices and supplies were heavily controlled due to the war and shortages in production. The war efforts involved public demonstrations on the cultivation of vegetables, together with advice on preserving, drying and bottling.[24]

By 1918 significantly large quantities of food were being imported from abroad by the Ministry of Food. In particular America became our largest supplier. But not it seems where flour was concerned. In 1917 the Flour Mills Control Committee placed restrictions on how much foreign flour entered the country owing to the fact that too many complaints were being communicated about the colour of people's loaves due to the difference with the colour of imported flour.[25]

New food regulations were implemented between 1914 and 1918 including the Public Meals Order. Typically rationed foods included sugar, butter, margarine, all meats and lard. Customers taking tea or coffee in hotels, restaurants, clubs, cafes and refreshment rooms had to provide their own sugar. In addition it became illegal to serve anyone a glass of milk at any time during the day and people staying in hotels, clubs or boarding houses were forbidden meat, poultry or game at breakfast. A meatless day was applied to all public eating areas later in 1918.[26]

The making of light pastries, muffins, crumpets, tea-cakes and other similar baked delicacies was strictly prohibited. Cakes, scones, buns and biscuits however were permitted although they were only allowed to contain a certain amount of sugar and flour. Cakes and biscuits had to contain no more than 30 per cent flour and 15 per cent sugar, while buns and scones could only include 10 per cent sugar and 50 per cent flour.[27]

If you consider the average traditional Victoria sponge cake contains around a third equal portions each of sugar and flour, this doesn't sound too limiting in terms of flavour. One also wonders how something so exacting and widespread could be enforced and monitored. It conjures up visions of bureaucrats running around tea rooms armed with test tubes and weighing scales.

Soldiers however received on average one pound of meat and bread and a handful of vegetables daily in the trenches.

Military kitchens were developing and evolving into well-designed and efficient spaces during this period. The new 'Arrow Camp' kitchen was constructed to cook for 250 men in the formation of a quadruple arrow shape, including four feeding trenches.[28] And portable cooking apparatus were developing consistently throughout this period for use in the field. In particular Captain Warren's Cooking Pot, a three-tiered series of chambers that enabled meat and vegetables to be cooked in their own vapour when left on a fire. This item quickly also became popular in domestic kitchens among less experienced or competent cooks.[29]

After the war opportunities in travel and tourism exploded with Billy Butlin opening his first permanent fairground stall on Barry Island in 1925, which would soon escalate into one of the biggest holiday camp businesses in British history and the newly formed Hotel and Restaurant Association of Great Britain established itself in 1926, with a view to leaping on the bandwagon of impending prosperity for the industry.

Within this context of hospitality and leisure would emerge a new wave of culinary evolution and diversity that would eventually change the way Britain ate yet again, both for better and worse.

Recipes

These delicate, intricate millefeuille pastries would undoubtedly been served at the Ritz Palm Court tearooms in Edwardian Britain. Certainly they were served at the Ritz Paris at this time and anything the French ate, the British higher echelons of society wanted to eat, and particularly as a French man ran the kitchen. The recipe below is one that was taken from a popular early nineteenth-century cook book and is representative of the ongoing desire to embrace French cuisine and the art of pâtisserie baking from an early age in Britain.

Mille Feuilles Recipe

Make two pounds and a quarter of puff paste, twelve times rolled; roll it out in sheets; cut four rounds, eight inches in diameter – four seven and a half – four seven – and five six and a half, with a two inch cutter; cut out the middles of all these except one of the last egg them prick them with the point of the knife here and there; bake them at a moderate heat; take them out when the paste is quite dry. When cold place one of the large sheets on a sheet of pate d'office (No 744) nine inches in diameter; mask it with half a pot of apricot marmalade; put on another sheet of the next size, which mask with currant jell,y the next with apple jelly. There must be no fruit on the edges of the paste, either in the middle or on the outsides. Whip six whites of eggs, and mix them with half a pound of sifted sugar, mask the cake with this all round as quickly as possible, mask this again with sugar, merely crushed and glaze it .The top sheet, the one not cut in the middle, must be meringue; round the edge place a circle of small meringues. Put an ornament on the middle, which fix with white of egg; sugar the whole and put the sheet of puff paste in the oven to take the same colour as the socles of the cake: when cold decorate the top with various sweets. To serve, fill the inside with whipped cream and put on the top.[30]

The Win-The-War Cookery Book published in association with The Ministry of Food in 1917, was compiled following a lengthy campaign by members of the public requesting simple recipes to work from during rationing. It was sold for 2*d* and written simply to appeal to everyone.

Fish sausages became very popular, not only during, but after the war. The recipe itself may have originated in Germany, as a newspaper in 1916 published an article about the extensive market in Germany, Norway and Copenhagen for fish sausages using minced fish and spices which were often smoked to enhance the flavour. The recipe published in The Win-The-War Cookery Book, which is rolled in breadcrumbs, resembles something more akin to the fish finger of today. The recipe notes reassuringly that it is a nourishing way of serving fish for children or grown ups.

Fish Sausages *(for four people)*

Two teacups of cooked fish.

Two tablespoons of cooked rice (or more if liked).

Half a teaspoon of dried herbs.

Salt and pepper to taste.

One small egg or a tablespoon of the water the rice was boiled in.

Pound the fish smoothly, having taken out out all bone and skin, add the rice, herbs, seasoning and egg or stock. Add stock as required to moisten. This depends on the consistency of the cooked rice. Mix thoroughly, form into small sausages, roll in dried breadcrumbs, maize flour, or oatmeal and fry in boiling fat.[31]

NOTES

Introduction

1. R. Roberts, *The Classic Slum: Salford Life in the First Quarter of the Century* (Penguin, 1990).
2. Punch, Vol XX (London,1851), p. 65.
3. J. Scott-Keltie, (ed.), *The Statesman's Year Book* (Macmillan and Co. Ltd. London, 1899), p. 24.
4. F. Hayward Severance, *Studies of the Niagara Frontier*, (Heritage Books, USA, 2009), p. 155.
5. The British Newspaper Library, *Northampton Mercury*, (Saturday 14 September 1889), p. 10.
6. P. Horn, *The Victorian Town Child* (Sutton Publishing, Gloucestershire, 1997), p. 173.
7. *Charity and Food: Report of the Special Committee of the Charity Organisation Society Upon Soup Kitchens, Children's Breakfasts and Dinners, and Cheap Food Supply*, (Spotiswoode & Company, London, 1887), p. 36.
8. F. Engels, *The Condition of the Working Class in England in 1844*, (George Allen & Unwin Ltd, 1892), p. 40.
9. R. Kerr, *The Gentleman's House: Or, How to Plan English Residences, from the Parsonage to the Palace; with Tables of Accommodation and Cost, and a Series of Selected Plans* (J. Murray, London, 1865), pp. 96–97.
10. S. and S. Adams, *The Complete Servant* (1826), p. 380-381.
11. Board of Trade, *Alien immigration Reports on the volume and*

effects of recent immigration from Eastern Europe into the United Kingdom, (HM Stationery Office, 1837) p. 15.

12. J. Duckworth, *Fagin's Children: Criminal Children in Victorian England*, (A&C Black, 2002), p. 121.

13. The Carlyle Letters online, Thomas Carlyle to Alexander Carlyle, 8 December, 1848.

14. The English note-books of Nathaniel Hawthorne volume I, (Leipzig, 1871).

15. P. Barr, *I Remember: A Tapestry for Many Voices* (Macmillan, 1970).

16. M. Llewlyn Davies, (ed), *Life as we have known it* (Virago Press Ltd, 1977), p. 16.

17. J. C. Drummond, A. Wilbraham, *The Englishman's Food* (Pimlico, 1939), pp. 363-365.

18. T. Hughes, *Tom Brown's Schooldays* (Leipzig, 1863), p. 81.

19. M. Carpenter, *Ragged Schools: their principles and modes of operation* (Partridge&Oakey, 1850), p. 82.

20. The Church of England Magazine, Vol LXXI (S. D. Ewins and Sons, 1871), p. 128.

21. C. Dyhouse, *Girls Growing Up in Late Victorian and Edwardian England*, (Routledge, Oxon, 2012), p. 90.

22. E. A. Youmans, (ed), *Lessons in Cookery, Hand-Book of the National Training School for Cookery*, American edition, (D. Apleton and Company, New York, 1879).

23. The Magazine of Domestic Economy, Volume 2 (W. S. Orr & Co, London, 1837), p. 185.

24. J. Jennings, *Two Thousand Five Hundred Practical Recipes in Family Cookery*, (Sherwood, Gilbert and Piper, London, 1837), p. 259.

1 Regency to Regina

1. V. Woolf, *Orlando* (Oxford, Oxford University Press, 1992), p. 218.

2. C. Harvie, *Nineteenth-Century Britain: A Very Short Introduction*, (Oxford University Press, Oxford, 2000).

3. N. Verdo, *Rural Women Workers in Nineteenth-Century England: Gender, Work and Wages* (Boydell Press, Suffolk, 2002), p. 89.

4. M. Llewelyn Davies,(ed), *The voices of working-class women* (Virago, 1977), pp. 2–3.

5. F. M. Eden, *The State of the Poor*, I (London, 1797), p. 531.

6. K. Foy, *Life in the Victorian Kitchen: Culinary Secrets and Servants' Stories* (Pen and Sword, 2014), p. 22.

7. G. Nostradamus, *Consult the Oracle: A Victorian Guide to Folklore and Fortune Telling* (Osprey Publishing, Oxford 2013).

8. N. Fiddes, *Meat: A Natural Symbol*, (Routlege, London, 2004,), p. 153.

9. A. Frost, *Death And Disaster In Victorian Telford*, (Amberley Publishing, Gloucestershire, 2013).

10. The British Newspaper Library, *Taunton Courier, and Western Advertiser* (Saturday 26 November 1938), p. 4.

11. The British Newspaper Library, *Whitby Gazette* (Friday 06 April 1917), p. 6.

12. The British Newspaper Library, *Liverpool Daily Post* (Tuesday 19 November 1867), p. 7.

13. K. Kvideland, *Sin-Eating* (International Society for Folk Narrative Research, Volume 35, 1984), p. 28.

14. The British Newspaper Library, *Aberdeen Evening Express* (Friday 11 October 1889) p. 959.

15. I. M. Beeton, *The Book of Household Management*, (1862), p. 959.

16. A. Broomfield, *Food and Cooking in Victorian England: A History* (Westport, USA), pp. 25–26.

17. B. Poole, *Statistics of British Commerce: Being a Compendium of the Productions, Manufactures, Imports, and Exports, of the United Kingdom* (W. H. Smith & Son, London, 1852), p. 160.

18. B. Poole, *Statistics of British Commerce: Being a Compendium of the Productions, Manufactures, Imports, and Exports, of the United Kingdom* (W. H. Smith & Son, London, 1852), p. 66.

19. The British Newspaper Library, *Hartlepool Mail* (Monday 16 March 1896).

20. M. French, J. Phillips, *Cheated Not Poisoned?: Food Regulation in the United Kingdom, 1875–1938*, (Manchester University Press, Manchester, 2000), pp. 32–53.

21. R. Miller, *Memoirs of George III., Chiefly Illustrative of his Private, Domestic and Christian Virtues*. Second edition, (London, 1820), pp. 41–45.

22. The London Quarterly Review, Volume LVI, (Theodore Foster, New York, 1838), p. 255.

23. J. Lane, *A Right Royal Feast: Menus from Royal Weddings and History's Greatest Banquets* David & Charles Ltd, Cincinnati, 2011), p. 37.

24. S. and S. Adams, *The Complete Servant* (1826), pp. 233–234.

25. J. Davies, *The Victorian Kitchen*, (BBC Books, 1989), p. 28.

26. Freeman's Journal, (Monday 13 November, 1837), pp. 2–4.

27. J. Gouffe, A. Gouffe, *The Royal Cookery Book. (Le Livre de Cuisine)* (Spottiswoode and Co., London, 1869), p. 189.

28. S. Woodworth, (ed), *The Ladies' Literary Cabinet*, Volume One, (Woodworth and Heustis, 1819), p. 197.

29. I. M. Beeton, *The Book of Household Management*, (S. O. Beeton, London, 1861), p. 751.

2 The Poor, Philanthropy and Plenitude

1. The British Newspaper Library, *Grantham Journal* (Saturday 2 March 1895), p. 7.

2. The British Newspaper Library, *The Gloucester Citizen* (Thursday 18 September, 1884).

3. *Charity and Food: Report of the Special Committee of the Charity Organisation Society Upon Soup Kitchens, Children's Breakfasts and Dinners, and Cheap Food Supply* (Spotiswoode & Company, 1887), p. 33.

4. *Charity and Food: Report of the Special Committee of the Charity Organisation Society Upon Soup Kitchens, Children's Breakfasts and Dinners, and Cheap Food Supply* (Spotiswoode & Company,1887), pp. 27–28.

5. *Great Britain. Poor Law Commissioners, Report of the Poor Law Commissioners, upon the Relief of the Poor in the Parishes of St Marylebone and St Pancras*, (W. Cowes and Sons, London, 1847), p. 18.

6. C. Shaw, *When I was a Child* (Churnet Valley Books, 1998), pp. 66–70.

7. The British Newspaper Library, *Leeds Mercury* (Saturday 7 December, 1872).

8. R. O'Day, D. Englander, *Mr Charles Booth's Inquiry: Life and Labour of the People in London Reconsidered* (Hambledon Press, London, 1992), p. 123.

9. D. D. Gray, *London's Shadows: The Dark Side of the Victorian City*, (Continuum, London, 2010), p. 205.

10. J. C. Drummond, A. Wilbraham, *The Englishman's Food* (Pimlico, 1939), p. 368.

11. E. Kay, *Dining With The Georgians* (Amberley Publishing, Gloucestershire, 2014), p. 51.

12. J. C. Drummond, A. Wilbraham, *The Englishman's Food* (Pimlico, 1939), p. 401.

13. F. Macdonald, *Victorian Servants, A Very Peculiar History* (Andrews UK Limited, 2012).

14. S. Hardy, *The Real Mrs Beeton: The Story of Eliza Acton* (The History Press, Gloucestershire, 2011), p. 203.

15. L. Lethbridge, *Servants: A Downstairs History of Britain from the Nineteenth Century to Modern times* (W. W. Norton and Company, USA 2013), p. 74.

16. A. Cobbett, *The English Housekeeper: Or, Manual of Domestic Management, Etc.* (London, 1835), p. 81.

17. The British Newspaper Library, *Dundee Evening Telegraph* (Monday 17 May 1886), p. 4.

18. The Family Oracle of Health, Volume II (1824).

19. K. Foy, *Life in the Victorian Kitchen: Culinary Secrets and Servants' Stories* (Pen and Sword, 2014), p. 135.

20. F. K. Prochaska, *Women and Philanthropy in Nineteenth-Century England* (Oxford University Press, Oxford, 1980), p. 21.

21. *Charity and Food: Report of the Special Committee of the Charity Organisation Society Upon Soup Kitchens, Children's Breakfasts and Dinners, and Cheap Food Supply* (Spotiswoode & Company,1887), pp. 76-79.

22. The British Newspaper Library, *Edinburgh Evening News* (Tuesday 26 December, 1893).

23. R. Goodbody, *Quakers and the Famine, 18th -19th Century History, Features* (The Famine, Volume 6, 1998, Issue 1).

24. M. D. Button, J. A. Sheetz-Nguyen, *Victorians and the Case for Charity* (McFarland, USA, 2013), p. 193.

25. The London City Mission Magazine Vol. XXXIII (Seeley, Jackson and Halliday, London, 1868, p. 157-158.

26. A Shilling Cookery for the People: Embracing an Entirely New System of Plain ... By Alexis Soyer, 1855, Routledge, London, p. 18.

27. H. E. Hatton, *Largest Amount of Good: Quaker Relief in Ireland, 1654-1921,* (McGill-Queen's University Press, Canada, 1993) p. 140.

28. E. Clarke, *High-class cookery recipes* (H. Allen and Co., London, 1885)

3 Childhood and the Victorian Family

1. E. Gordon, *Public Lives: Women, Family, and Society in Victorian Britain* (Yale University Press, 2003)

2. The British Newspaper Library, *Western Daily Press* (Tuesday 25 March, 1873), p. 3.

3. C. Redding, W. C. Taylor, *An illustrated itinerary of the county of Lancaster,* (How and Parsons, 1842), p. 248.

4. J. T. Ward, *The Factory Movement, 1830-1855,* (Macmillan, London 1962), p. 182.

5. Reminiscences of James Holt, (Lancashire Record Office, DDX/978/1/8/9).

6. P. Horn, *The Victorian Town Child* (Sutton Publishing, Gloucestershire, 1997), p. 45.

7. G. Haw, *Workhouse to Westminster. The Life Story of Will Crooks, MP* (1911), p. 3–5.

8. J. Duckworth, *Fagin's Children: Criminal Children in Victorian England* 2002 (A&C Black), p. 139.

9. Local Reports on the Sanitary Condition of the Labouring Population in England: In Consequence of an Inquiry Directed to be Made by the Poor Law Commissioners (W. Clowes and Sons, 1842), p. 44.

10. A. B. Soyer, *A Shilling Cookery for the People,* (Routledge and Company, 1854).

11. P. Horn, *The Victorian Town Child* (Sutton Publishing, Gloucestershire, 1997), p. 62.

12. B. Bosanquet, *The Standard Life* (Macmillan and Co, London, 1898), p. 25.

13. Knightsbridge Barracks: The First Barracks, 1792-1877 Survey

of London: Volume 45, Knightsbridge. (London County Council, London, 2000), pp. 64-68.

14. K. Theodore Hoppen, *The Mid-Victorian Generation, 1846-1886* (Oxford University Press, Oxford, 2000), p. 345.

15. Journal of the Gypsy Lore Society, (Gypsy Lore Society), p. 223.

16. The Old Bailey, Ref: t18370130-607, James Mason, Theft, simple larceny, 30 January 1837.

17. R. Dennis, *English Industrial Cities of the Nineteenth Century: A Social Geography* (Cambridge University Press, 1986), p. 41.

18. H. Mayhew, *London Labour and the London Poor*, Volume 1 (G. Woodfall, London 1851), pp. 112–114.

19. The Old Bailey, Ref: t18370403-920 John Rixon, Bridget Rixon, Mary Ann Rixon, miscellaneous, other, 3 April 1837.

20. J. C. Drummond, A. Wilbraham, *The Englishman's Food* (Pimlico, 1939), p. 445.

21. J. C. Drummond, A. Wilbraham, *The Englishman's Food* (Pimlico, 1939), pp. 449–450

22. J. C. Drummond, A. Wilbraham, *The Englishman's Food* (Pimlico, 1939), p. 408.

23. J. Perkin, *Women and Marriage in Nineteenth-Century England*, (Routledge, 1988), p. 144.

24. I. M. Beeton, *The Book of Household Management*, (S. O. Beeton, London, 1861).

25. The British Newspaper Library, *Western Gazette* (Friday 20 January 1899), p. 2.

26. P. Jalland, *Death in the Victorian Family*, (Oxford University Press, Oxford, 1996), p. 5.

27. I. M. Beeton, *The Book of Household Management*, (S. O. Beeton, London, 1861).

28. *The handbook of dining, based chiefly upon the Physiologie du goût of Brillat-Savarin* (Brown, Green, Longmans & Roberts, Longman, London, 1859), p. 124.

29. *Charles Dickens and the Sciences of Childhood: Popular Medicine, Child Health and Victorian Culture* By Katharina Boehm (2013, Palgrave Macmillan), p. 173–175.

30. P. Horn, *The Victorian Town Child* (Sutton Publishing, Gloucestershire, 1997), p. 131.

31. H. Mayhew, *London Labour and the London Poor*, (Cosimo Inc, 2007), p. 7.
32. M. Bills, V. Knight, *William Powell Frith: Painting the Victorian Age* (Yale University Press, 2006), p. 15.
33. The British Newspaper Library, *Sheffield Daily Telegraph* (Saturday 7 August 1880), p. 10.

4 High Days and Holidays

1. K. Baedeker, *Italy: Handbook for Travellers: third part, Southern Italy, Sicily, the Lipari Islands* (Williams and Northgate, London) p. XX.
2. K. Baedeker, *Belgium and Holland: Handbook for Travellers*, (Williams and Northgate, London, 1869). p. 109.
3. J. C. Drummond, A. Wilbraham, *The Englishman's Food* (Pimlico, 1939), p. 288.
4. P. Horn, *Pleasures and Pastimes in Victorian Britain*, Amberley Publishing, Gloucestershire, 2012).
5. The British Newspaper Library, *Cheltenham Chronicle* (Tuesday 30 March 1858), p. 3.
6. M. Hughes, *A London Child of the 1870s* (Persephone Books Ltd, London, 2005).
7. The Official Guide to the London and North Western Railway: The Royal Mail West Coast Route between England, Scotland, Wales, and Ireland: also between the continents of Europe and America. London (Cassell, 1894), p. 31.
8. The British Newspaper Library, *Aberdeen Evening Express* (Friday 19 October 1888).
9. The British Newspaper Library, *Nottingham Evening Post* (Wednesday 23 September 1891), p. 2.
10. J. Hamilton, *Thomas Cook: The Holiday Maker* (The History Press, 2005), p. 239.
11. C. Dickens, *Household Words*, Volume 1, 1850), p. 535.
12. S. Poole, A. Sassoli Walker, *P&O Cruises: Celebrating 175 Years of Heritage* (Amberley Publishing Limited, 2013).
13. D. A. Butler, *The Age of Cunard: A Transatlantic History 1839–2003* (Lighthouse Press, Annapolis, 2004), p. 153.

14. J. Wagner, *A History of Migration from Germany to Canada, 1850–1939* (UBC Press, Canada, 2011), p. 63.

15. E. Dakin Voolich, *A Ring and a Bundle of Letters, an immigrant's story and the family's stories back home: with genealogical information on Eric Helsten's family* (Lulu.com, Somerville, MA, 2013), p. 67.

16. F. Coussée, G. Verschelden, H. Williamson, (ed), *The History of Youth Work in Europe: Relevance for Youth Policy Today*, Volume 3 (Council of Europe, Strasbourg, 2012), p. 58.

17. The British Newspaper Library, *Dundee Evening Telegraph* (Wednesday 10 April 1901), p. 3.

18. W. Plover, (ed), *Kilvert's Diary, 1870–1879, Reverend Francis Kilvert* (Jonathan Cape, London, 1944) pp. 44–45.

19. W. Levy, *The Picnic: A History* (Rowan and Littlefield, Plymouth, 2013), pp. 38–39.

20. T. F. Thiselton Dyer, *British popular customs, present and past; illustrating the social and domestic manners of the people: arranged according to the calendar of the year* (William Clowes and Sons Ltd., London, 1875), p. 81.

21. The British Newspaper Library, *Yorkshire Post and Leeds Intelligencer* (Friday 12 March 1937).

22. W. Hone, *The Every Day Book, Or, A Guide to the Year*, (William Tegg, London 1866), p. 285.

23. M. Higgs, *A Visitor's Guide to Victorian England* (Pen and Sword, 2014).

24. The British Newspaper Library, *Burnley Express* (Saturday 16 August 1890), p. 6.

25. T. F. Thiselton Dyer, *British popular customs, present and past; illustrating the social and domestic manners of the people: arranged according to the calendar of the year* (William Clowes and Sons Ltd., London, 1875), p. 410.

26. A. Broomfield, *Food and Cooking in Victorian England: A History* (Greenwood Publishing Group, USA, 2007), p. 81.

27. T. F. Thiselton Dyer, *British popular customs, present and past; illustrating the social and domestic manners of the people: arranged according to the calendar of the year* (William Clowes and Sons Ltd., London, 1875), p. 447–452.

28. A. Guilmant, *Victorian and Edwardian Kent* (Amberley Publishing Limited, 2013).

29. T. F. Thiselton Dyer, *British popular customs, present and past; illustrating the social and domestic manners of the people: arranged according to the calendar of the year* (William Clowes and Sons Ltd., London, 1875), p. 19.
30. C. Mackenzie, *Mackenzie's Ten Thousand Receipts: In All the Useful and Domestic Arts: Constituting a Complete and Practical Library*, (Pennsylvania, 1866), p. 201.

5 Culinary Culture

1. The British Newspaper Library, *Edinburgh Evening News* (Friday 01 May 1874), p. 3.
2. Corporation of Salford. The annual report of the receipts and expenditure of the several committees of the council on account of the township fund ... ' (William Francis Jackson, Salford, 1850), p. 59–60.
3. Reports from Commissioners, House of Commons (1867), p. 232.
4. P. Sambrook, *A Country House at Work: Three Centuries of Dunham Massey* (National Trust Books, 2006), p. 46.
5. Victoria and Albert Museum Survey of London: Volume 38, South Kensington Museums Area. Originally published by (London County Council, London, 1975), p. 97–123.
6. *A Pictorial and Descriptive Guide to London and Its Environs* (Ward, Lock & Co., Ltd, London), p. 167.
7. J. Timbs, *The Mirror of Literature, Amusement, and Instruction*, Volumes 37–38 (Hugh Cunningham, London 1841), p. 359.
8. The British Newspaper Library, *Hartlepool Mail* (Friday 12 June 1885), p. 3–4.
9. M. R. Booth, *Theatre in the Victorian Age* (Cambridge University Press, Cambridge, 1991), p. 38.
10. D. Russell, *Popular Music in England 1840-1914: A Social History*, (Manchester University Press, 1997), p. 84-85.
11. J. Stamper, *So Long Ago*, (Chivers, 1960).
12. The British Newspaper Library, *Western Daily Press* Thursday 19 September 1895, p. 7.
13. C. F. Partington, *A Brief historical and descriptive Account of the Royal Gardens, Vauxhall.*, (Gye and Balne, London, 1822), p. 40–42.

14. L. Sanders, *Consuming Fantasies: Labor, Leisure, and the London Shopgirl, 1880-1920* (Ohio State University Press, 2006), p. 35.
15. P. Horn, *Behind the Counter: Shop Lives from Market Stall to Supermarket*, (Amberley Publishing Limited, 2015).
16. Harrod's Stores, Ltd. *Victorian shopping: Harrod's catalogue 1895*, p. 186.
17. The British Newspaper Library, *Luton Times and Advertiser* (Saturday 11 November 1876), p. 6.
18. E. D. Rappaport, *Shopping for Pleasure: Women in the Making of London's West End*, (Princeton University Press, USA) pp. 34, 201.
19. M. Higgs, *A Visitor's Guide to Victorian England* (Pen and Sword, 2014).
20. The British Newspaper Library, *Aberdeen Evening Express* (Monday 22 January 1894), p. 2.
21. The British Newspaper Library, *Dundee Evening Telegraph* (Tuesday 05 December 1893), p. 2.
22. The British Newspaper Library, *Inverness Courier* (Thursday 23 October 1851), p. 2.
23. The British Newspaper Library, *Belfast Morning News* (Wednesday 14 May 1862), p. 4.
24. The British Newspaper Library, *Liverpool Daily Post* (Tuesday 18 February 1862), p. 8.
25. A. B. Trubek, *Haute Cuisine: How the French Invented the Culinary Profession* (University of Pennsylvania Press, 2000), p. 122–23.
26. The British Newspaper Library, *London Daily News* (Tuesday 28 April 1896), p. 6.
27. The British Newspaper Library, *Manchester Guardian* (16th May 1887).
28. *Historical Account of Newcastle-Upon-Tyne Including the Borough of Gateshead* (Mackenzie and Dent, Newcastle-upon-Tyne, 1827), pp. 66–88.
29. T. Ito, *London Zoo and the Victorians, 1828–1859* (Boydell & Brewer ltd, Suffolk, 2014), p. 44.
30. *Cook and Confectioner* (Leary and Getz, Philadelphia, 1849), p. 157.
31. M. Rundell, *A New System of Domestic Cookery, Formed Upon Principles of Economy, and Adapted to the Use of Private Families* (Thomas Allman, London, 1840), p. 248.

6 Training the Masses

1. R. O. Cole, E. A. Youmans, T. King, *Lessons in Cookery: Hand-book of the National Training School for Cookery* (Applewood Books, Massachusetts, 1879), p. 373.
2. The British Newspaper Library, *Bedfordshire Times and Independent* (Saturday 08 April 1893), p. 4.
3. The British Newspaper Library, *Manchester Courier and Lancashire General Advertiser* (Saturday 29 October 1898), p. 2.
4. The British Newspaper Library, *Manchester Courier and Lancashire General Advertiser* (Saturday 01 February 1902), p. 9.
5. The British Newspaper Library, *Bath Chronicle and Weekly Gazette* (Thursday 12 February 1885), p. 5.
6. G. McCulloch (ed), *The Routledge Falmer Reader in the History of Education* (Routledge, London, 2005), p. 128.
7. T. J. Bailey, *The Planning and Construction of Board Schools*, (School Board for London 1900), p. 12.
8. T. A. Spalding, T. Stanley, A. Canney, D. Reay, *The Work of the London School Board* (P. S. King & Son, 1900), pp. 226–227.
9. Report of the Committee of Council on Education (England and Wales), with Appendix, (HM Stationery Office, 1861), p. 32–33.
10. The British Newspaper Library, *Arbroath Herald and Advertiser for the Montrose Burghs* (Thursday 21 May, 1896), p. 6.
11. The British Newspaper Library, *Dundee Evening Telegraph* (Thursday 20 March 1879).
12. *The Steward's Handbook and Guide to Party Catering* (Jessup Whitehead, Chicago, 1889).
13. J. C. Drummond, A. Wilbraham, *The Englishman's Food* (Pimlico, 1939), p. 344.
14. H. Wydham, *The Army School of Cookery*, (1903).
15. Mennell, S, *All Manners of Food: Eating and Taste in England and France from the Middle Ages to the Present* (Basil Blackwell, Oxford, 1985), p. 185.
16. S. Hardy, *The Real Mrs Beeton: The Story of Eliza Acton*, (The History Press, Gloucestershire, 2011), pp. 203–205.
17. The British Newspaper Library, *Morning Post* (Monday 10 August 1868), p. 3.

18. C. Silby, *The Dinner Question or How to Dine Well and Economically* (Warne and Routledge, London, 1860), p. 10.

19. The British Newspaper Library, *Dundee Evening Telegraph*, (Thursday 20 March, 1879).

20. J. Gouffé, *The Royal Cookery Book (Le Livre de Cuisine)* (Spottiswode and Co., London, 1869), p. 309.

7 Public Dining (and Everything In Between)

1. E. D. Rappaport, *Shopping for Pleasure: Women in the Making of London's West End*, (Princeton Uni Press, USA) p. 102.

2. The British Newspaper Library, *Dundee Evening Telegraph* (Saturday 17 November 1888), p. 2.

3. J. Murray, *Murray's handbook for modern London: Modern London or, London as it is* (Peter Cuningham 1851).

4. J. Murray, *London in 1857*, (Peter Cuningham, 1857), p. xxxviii.

5. M. Higgs, *A Visitor's Guide to Victorian England* (Pen and Sword, Yorkshire, 2014).

6. K. Baedeker, *London and Its Environs*, (London, 1885).

7. J. M. Johnson, *Food Journal*, Volume 3, (London, 1873), p. 266.

8. The British Newspaper Library, *Sheffield Daily Telegraph* (Tuesday 16 June 1874), p. 3.

9. *The Visitor's Guide to Manchester; and Handbook to the Attractions of the City and Suburbs Pub* (W. Kent and Co. London, 1857), p. 7.

10. M. MacConIomaire, *Public Dining in Dublin: the History and Evolution of Gastronomy and Commercial Dining 1700–1900*, Martin, (Dublin Institute of Technology, 2013), p. 18.

11. *Once a Week*, Volume 4 (1860), pp. 517–518.

12. N. Fitch, A. Midgeley, *The Grand Literary Cafés of Europe* (New Holland Publishers, 2006, London), p. 107.

13. P. Kinchin, *Taking Tea with Mackintosh: The Story of Miss Cranston's Tea Rooms*, Pomegranate, 1998).

14. G. Ferry, *A Computer Called LEO: Lyons Tea Shops and the World's First Office Computer* (Harper Collins, 2003), pp. 3-11.

15. J. Benson, L. Ugolini, (ed), *Cultures of Selling: Perspectives on*

Consumption and Society Since 1700 (Ashgate Pub Ltd, Hants, 2006), p. 86.

16. The British Newspaper Library, *Pall Mall Gazette* (Thursday 21 November 1889), p. 3.

17. A. D. King, (ed), *Buildings and Society: Essays on the Social Development of the Built Environment* (Routledge, London, 2003), p. 134.

18. The British Newspaper Library, *Dundee Evening Telegraph* (Saturday 4 April 1891).

19. The British Newspaper Library, *Aberdeen Journal* (Thursday 4 July 1901).

20. The British Newspaper Library, *Western Daily Press* (Saturday 5 January 1889).

21. The Magazine of Domestic Economy, Volume 3, (W. S. Orr and Company, 1838), p. 376.

22. The London City Mission Magazine Vol. XXXIII (Seeley Jackson and halliday, London, 1868), p. 69.

23. The Shorter Novels of Charles Dickens (Wordsworth Editions, Hertfordshire, 2004), pp. 149–150.

24. B. Poole, *Statistics of British Commerce: Being a Compendium of the Productions, Manufactures, Imports, and Exports, of the United Kingdom* (W. H. Smith & Son, London, 1852), p. 169.

25. B. Poole, *Statistics of British Commerce: Being a Compendium of the Productions, Manufactures, Imports, and Exports, of the United Kingdom* (W. H. Smith & Son, London,1852), pp. 4-5.

26. R. Tames, *The Victorian Public House* (Osprey Publishing, 2003), pp. 6–7.

27. Col. N. Davies, *A Gourmet's Paradise in Homes of the Passing Show*, (The Savoy Press, London, 1900), p. 42.

28. Col. N. Davies, *Two Restaurants for Kings in Homes of the Passing Show* (The Savoy Press, London, 1900), p. 45.

29. Col. N. Davies, *The Gourmet's Guide to London* (Brentano's, New York, 1914).

30. Grand Hotel Scarborough. Hotel Information and Charges, etc. (A Guide to Scarborough) (A. Heywood and Son, 1867), p. 2.

31. J. Simpson, H. W. Brand, *Simpson's Cookery, Improved and Modernised* (Baldwin and Craddock, London, 1834), p. 74.

32. I. M. Beeton, *The Book of Household Management* (S. O. Beeton, London, 1863), p. 834.

8 Population and Empire

1. *Alien immigration Reports on the volume and effects of recent immigration from Eastern Europe into the United Kingdom, 1894,* (Board of Trade, HM Stationery Office, 1894), pp. 6-10.
2. S. Manz, M. Beerbühl, J. R. Davis, W. de Gruyter, (ed), *Migration and Transfer from Germany to Britain, 1660–1914* (Verlag, Germany.2007), p. 157.
3. Board of Trade, Statistical Abstracts for the Principal and Other Foreign Countries (HM Stationery Office, 1899), pp. 71–72.
4. B. Poole, *Statistics of British Commerce: Being a Compendium of the Productions, Manufactures, Imports, and Exports, of the United Kingdom* (W. H. Smith & Son, London, 1852), p. 236.
5. B. Poole, *Statistics of British Commerce: Being a Compendium of the Productions, Manufactures, Imports, and Exports, of the United Kingdom* (W. H. Smith & Son, London, 1852), p. 76.
6. B. Poole, *Statistics of British Commerce: Being a Compendium of the Productions, Manufactures, Imports, and Exports, of the United Kingdom* (W. H. Smith & Son, London, 1852).
7. S. Basu, *Victoria & Abdul: The True story of the Queen's Closest Confidant* (2011), p. 56.
8. S. Basu, *Victoria & Abdul: The True story of the Queen's Closest Confidant* (2011), pp. 128–130.
9. The British Newspaper Library, *Gloucestershire Echo* (Tuesday 15 August 1893), p. 4.
10. WM. Thackeray, *Vanity Fair*, (Wordsworth, London, 1992) p. 22.
11. L. Collingham, *Curry a tale of Cooks and Conquerors* (Oxford University Press, New York, 2006), p. 129.
12. *The Englishwoman in India: information for ladies on their outfit, furniture etc.*, 1864, by a lady resident, (Smith, Elder and Co., London, 1864), p. 57.
13. *The Englishwoman in India: information for ladies on their outfit,*

furniture etc., 1864, by a lady resident, (Smith, Elder and Co., London, 1864), pp. 45–72.

14. M. Macmillan, *Women of the Raj*, (Random House, New York, 2007), pp. 170–172.

15. N. Chadhuri, *Memsahibs and their Servants in 19c India* (Kansas State University, 2006), p. 552.

16. G. F. Atkinson, *Curry & Rice, on forty plates, or, The ingredients of social life at "Our Station" in India*, Volume 1 (Day and Son, London, 1860), pp. 34–35.

17. D. Killingray, *Africans in Britain* (Routledge, 2012), pp. 61–65.

18. R. Swift, *Irish identities in Victorian Britain*, (Routledge, 2013), p. 25.

19. A. Garvette, D. Cook, *Traditional Irish Cooking: The Fare of Old Ireland and Its History* (Garnet Publishing Ltd, 2008).

20. The British Newspaper Library, *Manchester Courier and Lancashire General Advertiser* (Tuesday 26 October 1886), p. 4.

21. The British Newspaper Library, *Southern Reporter and Cork Commercial Courier* (Friday 05 February 1858), p. 4.

22. The British Newspaper Library, *The Manchester Courier and Lancashire General Advertiser* (1902).

23. J. A. G. Roberts, *China to Chinatown: Chinese Food in the West* (Reaktion Books, 2004), p. 156.

24. The British Newspaper Library, *Hull Daily Mail* (Tuesday 14 June 1910), p. 4.

25. The British Newspaper Library, *Dover Express* (Friday 7 November 1890), p. 6.

26. The British Newspaper Library, *Hull Daily Mail* (Friday 10 May 1889).

27. The British Newspaper Library, *Aberdeen Journal* (Friday 26 July 1901).

28. The British Newspaper Library, *Gloucester Citizen* (Thursday 13 September 1900).

29. The British Newspaper Library, *Sunderland Daily Echo and Shipping Gazette* (Tuesday 18 September 1900), p. 2.

30. The British Newspaper Library, *Sheffield Independent* (Monday 15 March 1897), p. 2.

31. M. E. K. Rundell, *A New System of Domestic Cookery, Formed*

Upon Principles of Economy, and adapted to the use of private families (1840), p. 140.

32. G. Merle, J. Reitch, *The Domestic Dictionary and Housekeeper's Manual* (London, William Strange, 1842), p. 70.

33. E. Ayrton, *English Provincial Cooking* (Mitchell Beazley, London 1980), p. 167.

34. E. Acton, *Modern Cookery, in all its Branches*, second edition, (Longman, Brown, Green and Longmans, London, 1845), p. 230.

9 Empire to Emancipation

1. J. Rowntre, B. Rowntree, *Poverty, a Study of Town Life*, (Macmillan and Co, London, 1900), pp. 104–105.

2. National Archives, Ministry of Food, Report for week ending, Wednesday September 11, 1918

3. H. Walker, (ed), *Oxford Symposium on Food and Cookery 1991: Public Eating: Proceedings*, (Oxford Symposium, 1991), p. 207.

4. *Rearing an Imperial Race*. (London, 1913), pp. 366-390.

5. P. Horn, *The Victorian and Edwardian Schoolchild* (Amberley Publishing, 2013).

6. C. Dyhouse, *Girls Growing Up in Late Victorian and Edwardian England* (Routledge, 2012), p. 94.

7. The British Newspaper Library, *North Devon Journal* (August 3, 1916), p. 6.

8. K. Olsen, *Daily Life in 18 Century England*, (Greenwood Publishing Group, 1999), p. 86.

9. L. H. Yates, *The Model Kitchen* (Longmans, Green and Co., 1905).

10. The Women's Library, Papers of Ethel DM Robson, 1910-1912, Ref No. 7EDR

11. The British Newspaper Library, *Evening Telegraph, Scotland* (06 August, 1903), p. 4.

12. Isle of Wight Record Office, Ref. OG/CC/2271, 21 January 1909.

13. Ministry of Shipping, *A national Settlement With Labour: Memorandum by the Chairman of the National Maritime Board* (1918), p. 6.

14. The British Newspaper Library, *The Graphic* (Saturday May 4, 1872)

15. R. Phillips, *The Servantless House* (Country Life Ltd, 1920), pp. 35–44.

16. A. Maloney, *Life Below Stairs: True Lives of Edwardian Servants* (Michael O'Mara Books, London, 2011).

17. R. Phillips, *The Servantless House* (Country Life Ltd, 1920), pp. 50-53.

18. K. James, *Escoffier: The King of Chefs* (A&C Black, London, 2006), pp. 170–174.

19. The British Newspaper Library, *London Standard* (Wednesday 12 July 1899), p. 3.

20. J. Reekie, *The Ritz London Book of Drinks & Cocktails*, (Random House, 2008), p. 8.

21. E. Denby, *Grand hotels: Reality and illusion* (Reaktion Books, 2002), p. 122.

22. M. C. Rintoul, *Dictionary of Real People and Places in Fiction* (Routledge, 2014), p. 280.

23. National Archives, Ministry of Food. Report for week ending, 23 April 1919, Ref. CAB 4/78/48

24. Ministry of Food, Cabinet Office Papers 3001-3100, Food Production Department, Report for week ending, 18 December, 1917.

25. National Archives, Ministry of Food, Report of week ending Weds June 20, 1917.

26. The British Newspaper Library, *Liverpool Echo* (Friday 11 January 1918), p. 6.

27. The British Newspaper Library, *Cambridge Daily News* (Thursday 19 April 1917), p. 4.

28. The British Newspaper Library, *Morpeth Herald*, (Saturday July 24, 1886), p. 5.

29. The British Newspaper Library, *Sunderland Daily Echo and Shipping Gazette*, (Monday February 08, 1886), p. 3.

30. *Simpson's Cookery, Improved and Modernised, The Complete Modern Cook, Containing a Very Extensive and Original Collection of Recipes in Cookery* (Baldwin and Craddock, 1834), p. 292–293.

31. *The Win-The-War Cookery Book* (Amalgamated Press Ltd, London, 1917), p. 10.

BIBLIOGRAPHY

A Pictorial and Descriptive Guide to London and Its Environs (Ward, Lock & Co., Ltd, London).

Acton, E., *Modern Cookery, in all its Branches*, second edition, (Longman, Brown, Green and Longmans, London, 1845).

Adams, S., Adams, S., *The Complete Servant* (1826) adapted to the use of private families (1840).

Alien immigration: Reports on the volume and effects of recent immigration from Eastern Europe o the United Kingdom, 1894, (Board of Trade, HM Stationery Office, 1894).

Atkinson, G. F., *Curry & Rice, on forty plates, or, The ingredients of social life at "Our Station" in India*, Volume 1 (Day and Son, London, 1860).

Ayrton, E., *English Provincial Cooking* (Mitchell Beazley, London 1980).

Baedeker, K., *Belgium and Holland: Handbook for Travellers*, (Williams and Northgate, London, 1869).

Baedeker, K., *Italy: Handbook for Travellers: third part, Southern Italy, Sicily, the Lipari Islands*,(Williams and Northgate, London).

Baedeker, K., *London and Its Environs*, (London, 1885).

Bailey, T. J., *The Planning and Construction of Board Schools*, (School Board for London1900).

Barr, P., I., *Remember: A Tapestry for Many Voices* (Macmillan, 1970) ...

Basu, S., *Victoria & Abdul: The True story of the Queen's Closest Confidant* (2011).

Beeton, I. M., *The Book of Household Management*, (S. O. Beeton, London, 1862).

Benson, J., Ugolini, L., (ed)., *Cultures of Selling: Perspectives on Consumption and Society Since 1700* (Ashgate Pub Ltd, Hants, 2006).

Bills, M., Knight, V., *William Powell Frith: Painting the Victorian Age* (Yale University Press, 2006).

Board of Trade, *Alien immigration Reports on the volume and effects of recent immigration from Eastern Europe into the United Kingdom*, (HM Stationery Office, 1837).

Board of Trade, *Statistical Abstracts for the Principal and Other Foreign Countries* (HM Stationery Office, 1899).

Boehm, K., *Charles Dickens and the Sciences of Childhood: Popular Medicine, Child Health and Victorian Culture* (, Palgrave Macmillan, 2013).

Booth, M. R., *Theatre in the Victorian Age* (Cambridge University Press, Cambridge, 1991).

Bosanquet, B., *The Standard Life* (Macmillan and Co, London, 1898).

Broomfield, A., *Food and Cooking in Victorian England: A History* (Greenwood Publishing Group, USA., 2007).

Butler, D. A., *The Age of Cunard: A Transatlantic History 1839–2003* (Lighthouse Press, Annapolis, 2004).

Button, M. D., Sheetz-Nguyen, J. A., *Victorians and the Case for Charity* (McFarland, USA, 2013).

Carpenter, M., *Ragged Schools: their principles and modes of operation* (Partridge & Oakey, 1850).

Chadhuri, N., *Memsahibs and their Servants in 19c India* (Kansas State University, 2006).

Chairman of the National Maritime Board (1918).

Charity and Food: Report of the Special Committee of the Charity Organisation Society Upon Soup Kitchens, Children's Breakfasts and Dinners, and Cheap Food Supply (Spotiswoode & Company, 1887).

Clarke, E., *High-class cookery recipes* (H. Allen and Co., London, 1885).

Cobbett, A., *The English Housekeeper: Or, Manual of Domestic Management, Etc.* (London, 1835).

Cole, R. O., Youmans, E. A., King, T., *Lessons in Cookery: Hand-book of the National Training School for Cookery* (Applewood Books, Massachusetts1879).

Collingham, L., *Curry a tale of Cooks and Conquerors* (Oxford University Press, New York, 2006).

Cook and Confectioner (Leary and Getz, Philadelphia, 1849).

Corporation of Salford. *The annual report of the receipts and expenditure of the several committees of the council on account of the township fund ...'* (William Francis Jackson, Salford, 1850).

Coussée, F., Verschelden, G., Williamson, H., (ed)., *The History of Youth Work in Europe: Relevance for Youth Policy Today*, Volume 3 (Council of Europe, Strasbourg, 2012).

Dakin Voolich, E., *A Ring and a Bundle of Letters, an immigrant's story and the family's stories back home: with genealogical information on Eric Helsten's family* (Lulu.com, Somerville, MA, 2013).

Davies, J., *The Victorian Kitchen*, (BBC Books, 1989).

Davies, N., *The Gourmet's Guide to London* (Brentano's, New York, 1914).

Davies, N., *A Gourmet's Paradise in Homes of the Passing Show*, (The Savoy Press, London, 1900).

Davies, N., *Two Restaurants for Kings in Homes of the Passing Show* (The Savoy Press, London, 1900).

Denby, E., *Grand hotels: Reality and illusion* (Reaktion Books, 2002).

Dennis, R., *English Industrial Cities of the Nineteenth Century: A Social Geography* (Cambridge University Press, 1986).

Dickens, C., *Household Words*, Volume 1, 1850).

Drummond, J. C., Wilbraham, A., *The Englishman's Food* (Pimlico, 1939).

Duckworthp, J., *Fagin's Children: Criminal Children in Victorian England*, (A&C Black, 2002).

Dyhouse, C., *Girls Growing Up in Late Victorian and Edwardian England* (Routledge, 2012).

Eden, F. M., *The State of the Poor*, I (London, 1797).

Engels, F., *The Condition of the Working Class in England in 1844*, (George Allen & Unwin Ltd, 1892).

Ferry, G., *A Computer Called LEO: Lyons Tea Shops and the World's First Office Computer* (Harper Collins, 2003).

Fiddes, N., *Meat: A Natural Symbol*, (Routlege, London, 2004).

Fitch, N., Midgeley, A., *The Grand Literary Cafés of Europe* (New Holland Publishers, 2006, London).

Foy, K., *Life in the Victorian Kitchen: Culinary Secrets and Servants' Stories* (Pen and Sword, 2014).

Freeman's Journal, (Monday 13 November, 1837).

French, M., Phillips, J., *Cheated Not Poisoned?: Food Regulation in the United Kingdom, 1875-1938*, (Manchester University Press, Manchester, 2000).

Frost, A., *Death And Disaster In Victorian Telford*, (Amberley Publishing, Gloucestershire, 2013).

Garvette, A., Cook, D., *Traditional Irish Cooking: The Fare of Old Ireland and Its History* (Garnet Publishing Ltd, 2008).

Goodbody, R., *Quakers and the Famine, 18th -19th Century History*, Features (The Famine, Volume 6, 1998, Issue 1).

Gordon, E., *Public Lives: Women, Family, and Society in Victorian Britain* (Yale University Press, 2003).Yale University Press.

Gouffé, J., *The Royal Cookery Book* (Le Livre de Cuisine). (Spottiswode and Co., London, 1869).

Grand Hotel Scarborough. Hotel Information and Charges, etc. (A Guide to Scarborough). (A. Heywood and Son, 1867).

Gray, D. D., *London's Shadows: The Dark Side of the Victorian City*, (Continuum, London, 2010).

Great Britain. Poor Law Commissioners, Report of the Poor Law Commissioners, upon the Relief of the Poor in the Parishes of St Marylebone and St Pancras, (W. Cowes and Sons, London, 1847).

Guilmant, A., *Victorian and Edwardian Kent* (Amberley Publishing Limited, 2013).

Hamilton, J., *Thomas Cook: The Holiday Maker* (The History Press, 2005).

Hardy, S., *The Real Mrs Beeton: The Story of Eliza Acton* (The History Press, Gloucestershire, 2011).

Harrod's Stores, Ltd. Victorian shopping: Harrod's catalogue 1895.

Harvie, C., *Nineteenth-Century Britain: A Very Short Introduction*, (Oxford University Press, Oxford, 2000).

Hatton, H. E., *Largest Amount of Good: Quaker Relief in Ireland, 1654-1921*, (McGill-Queen's University Press, Canada, 1993).

Haw, G., *Workhouse to Westminster. The Life Story of Will Crooks, MP* (1911).

Hayward, F., *Severance, Studies of the Niagara Frontier*, (Heritage Books, USA, 2009).

Hichens, R., *Public Dinners, in 'Homes of the Passing Show,'* (Savoy Press, London, 1900).

Higgs, M., *A Visitor's Guide to Victorian England* (Pen and Sword, Yorkshire, 2014).

Historical Account of Newcastle-Upon-Tyne Including the Borough of Gateshead (Mackenzie and Dent, Newcastle-upon-Tyne, 1827).

Hone, W., *The Every Day Book, Or, A Guide to the Year*, (William Tegg, London 1866).

Horn, P., *Behind the Counter: Shop Lives from Market Stall to Supermarket*, (Amberley Publishing Limited, 2015).

Horn, P., *The Victorian Town Child* (Sutton Publishing, Gloucestershire, 1997).

Horn, P., *Pleasures and Pastimes in Victorian Britain*, (Amberley Publishing, Gloucestershire, 2012).

Horn, P., *The Victorian And Edwardian Schoolchild* (Amberley Publishing, 2013).

Hughes, M., *A London Child of the 1870s* (Persephone Books Ltd, London, 2005).

Hughes, T., *Tom Brown's Schooldays* (Leipzig, 1863).

Isle of Wight Record Office, Ref. OG/CC/2271, 21 January 1909.

Ito, T., *London Zoo and the Victorians, 1828–1859* (Boydell & Brewer ltd, Suffolk, 2014).

J. Gouffe, A. Gouffe, *The Royal Cookery Book. (Le Livre de Cuisine).* (Spottiswoode and Co., London, 1869).

Jalland, P., *Death in the Victorian Family*, (Oxford University Press, Oxford, 1996).

James, K., *Escoffier: The King of Chefs* (A&C Black, London, 2006).

Jennings, J., *Two Thousand Five Hundred Practical Recipes in Family Cookery*, (Sherwood, Gilbert and Piper, London, 1837).

Johnson, J. M., *Food Journal*, Volume 3, (London, 1873).

Journal of the Gypsy Lore Society, (Gypsy Lore Society).

Kay, E., *Dining With The Georgians* (Amberley Publishing, Gloucestershire, 2014).

Kerr, R., *The Gentleman's House: Or, How to Plan English Residences, from the Parsonage to the Palace; with Tables of Accommodation and Cost, and a Series of Selected Plans* (J. Murray, London, 1865).

Killingray, D., *Africans in Britain* (Routledge, 2012).

Kinchin, P., *Taking Tea with Mackintosh: The Story of Miss Cranston's Tea Rooms, Pomegranate*, 1998).

King, A. D., (ed)., *Buildings and Society: Essays on the Social Development of the Built Environment* (Routledge, London, 2003).

Knightsbridge Barracks: The First Barracks, 1792-1877 Survey of London: Volume 45, Knightsbridge. (London County Council, London, 2000).

Kvideland, K., *Sin-Eating* (International Society for Folk Narrative Research, Volume 35, 1984).

Lane, J., *A Right Royal Feast: Menus from Royal Weddings and History's Greatest Banquets* (David & Charles Ltd, Cincinnati, 2011).

Lethbridge, L., *Servants: A Downstairs History of Britain from the Nineteenth Century to Modern times* (W. W. Norton and Company, USA 2013).

Levy, W., *The Picnic: A History* (Rowan and Littlefield, Plymouth, 2013).

Llewelyn Davies, M., (ed)., *The voices of working-class women* (Virago, 1977).

Llewlyn Davies, M., (ed)., *Life as we have known it* (Virago Press Ltd, 1977).

Local Reports on the Sanitary Condition of the Labouring Population in England: In Consequence of an Inquiry Directed to be Made by the Poor Law Commissioners (W. Clowes and Sons, 1842).

Lysack, K., *Come Buy, Come Buy: Shopping and the Culture of Consumption in Victorian Women's Writing* (Ohio University Press, 2008).

MacConIomaire, M., *Public Dining in Dublin: the History and Evolution of Gastronomy and Commercial Dining 1700-1900*, Martin, (Dublin Institute of Technology, 2013).

Macdonald, F., *Victorian Servants, A Very Peculiar History* (Andrews UK Limited, 2012).

Mackenzie, C., *Mackenzie's Ten Thousand Receipts: In All the Useful and Domestic Arts: Constituting a Complete and Practical Library*, (Pennsylvania, 1866).

Macmillan, M., *Women of the Raj*, (Random House, New York, 2007).

Maloney, A., *Life Below Stairs: True Lives of Edwardian Servants* (Michael O'Mara Books, London, 2011).

Manz, S., Beerbühl, M., Davis, J. R., de Gruyter, W. (eds)., *Migration and Transfer from Germany to Britain, 1660–1914* (Verlag, Germany.2007).

Mayhew, H., *London Labour and the London Poor*, Volume 1 (G. Woodfall, London 1851).

McCulloch, G., (ed)., *The Routledge Falmer Reader in the History of Education* (Routledge, London, 2005).

Mennell, S., *All Manners of Food: Eating and Taste in England and France from the Middle Ages to the Present* (Basil Blackwell, Oxford, 1985).

Merle, G, Reitch, J., *The Domestic Dictionary and Housekeeper's Manual* (London, William Strange, 1842).

Miller, R., *Memoirs of George III., Chiefly Illustrative of his Private, Domestic and Christian Virtues.* Second edition, (London, 1820).

Ministry of Food, Cabinet Office Papers 3001-3100, Food Production Department, Report for week ending, 18 December, 1917.

Ministry of Shipping, *A national Settlement With Labour: Memorandum by the Chairman of the National Maritime Board* (1918).

Murray, J., *Murray's handbook for modern London: Modern London or, London as it is* (Peter Cuningham 1851).

Murray, J., London in 1857, (Peter Cuningham, 1857).

National Archives, Ministry of Food, Report for week ending, Wednesday September 11, 1918

National Archives, Ministry of Food, Report of week ending Weds June 20, 1917.

National Archives, Ministry of Food. Report for week ending, 23 April 1919, Ref. CAB 24/78/48

Nostradamus, G., *Consult the Oracle: A Victorian Guide to Folklore and Fortune Telling*

O'Day, R., Englander, D., *Mr Charles Booth's Inquiry: Life and Labour of the People in London Reconsidered* (Hambledon Press, London, 1992).

Olsen, K., *Daily Life in 18 Century England*, (Greenwood Publishing Group, 1999).

Once a Week, Volume 4 (1860).

Partington, C. F., *A Brief historical and descriptive Account of the Royal Gardens, Vauxhall,* (Gye and Balne, London, 1822).

Perkin, J., *Women and Marriage in Nineteenth-Century England*, (Routledge, 1988).

Phillips, R., *The Servantless House* (Country Life Ltd, 1920).

Plover, W., (ed)., *Kilvert's Diary, 1870-1879, Reverend Francis Kilvert* (Jonathan Cape, London, 1944).

Poole, B., *Statistics of British Commerce: Being a Compendium of the Productions, Manufactures, Imports, and Exports, of the United Kingdom* (W. H. Smith & Son, London, 1852).

Poole, B., *Statistics of British Commerce: Being a Compendium of the Productions, Manufactures, Imports, and Exports, of the United Kingdom* (W. H. Smith & Son, London, 1852).

Poole, S., Walker, A., *P&O Cruises: Celebrating 175 Years of Heritage* (Amberley Publishing Limited, 2013).

Prochaska, F. K., *Women and Philanthropy in Nineteenth-Century England* (Oxford University Press, Oxford, 1980).

Punch, Vol XX (London, 1851).

Rappaport, E. D., *Shopping for Pleasure: Women in the Making of London's West End*, (Princeton Uni Press, USA).

Rearing an Imperial Race. (London, 1913).

Redding, C., Taylor, W. C., *An illustrated itinerary of the county of Lancaster*, (How and Parsons, 1842).

Reekie, J., *The Ritz London Book of Drinks & Cocktails*, (Random House, 2008).

Reminiscences of James Holt, (Lancashire Record Office, DDX/978/1/8/9).

Report of the Committee of Council on Education (England and Wales), with Appendix, (HM Stationery Office, 1861).

Reports from Commissioners, House of Commons (1867).

Rintoul, M. C., *Dictionary of Real People and Places in Fiction* (Routledge, 2014).

Roberts, R., *The Classic Slum: Salford Life in the First Quarter of the Century* (Penguin, 1990).

Roberts, J. A. G., *China to Chinatown: Chinese Food in the West* (Reaktion Books, 2004).

Rowntre, J., Rowntree, B., *Poverty, a Study of Town Life*, (Macmillan and Co, London, 1900).

Rundell, M. E. K., *A New System of Domestic Cookery, Formed Upon Principles of Economy, and Adapted to the Use of Private Families* (Thomas Allman, London, 1840).

Russell, D.. *Popular Music in England 1840-1914: A Social History*, (Manchester University Press, 1997).

Sambrook, P., *A Country House at Work: Three Centuries of Dunham Massey* (National Trust Books, 2006).

Sanders, L., *Consuming Fantasies: Labor, Leisure, and the London Shopgirl, 1880-1920* (Ohio State University Press, 2006).

Scott-Keltie, J., (ed.). *The Statesman's Year Book* (Macmillan and Co. Ltd. London, 1899).

Shaw, C., *When I was a Child* (Churnet Valley Books, 1998).

Silby, C., *The Dinner Question or How to Dine Well and Economically* (Warne and Routledge, London, 1860).

Simpson, J., Brand, H. W., *Simpson's Cookery, Improved and Modernised* (Baldwin and Craddock, Lonson, 1834).

Simpson's Cookery, *Improved and Modernised, The Complete Modern Cook, Containing a Very Extensive and Original Collection of Recipes in Cookery* (Baldwin and Craddock, 1834).

Soyer, A., *A Shilling Cookery for the People*, (Routledge and Company, 1854).

Spalding, T. A., Stanley, T, Canney, A. Reay, D., *The Work of the London School Board* (P. S. King & Son, 1900).

Stamper, J., *So Long Ago*, (Chivers, 1960).

Swift, R., *Irish identities in Victorian Britain*, (Routledge, 2013).

Tames, R., *The Victorian Public House* (Osprey Publishing, 2003).

Thackeray, W. M., *Vanity Fair*, (Wordsworth, London, 1992).

The British Newspaper Archive, *Aberdeen Evening Express* (Friday 11 October 1889).

The British Newspaper Archive, *Aberdeen Evening Express* (Friday 19 October 1888).

The British Newspaper Archive, *Aberdeen Evening Express* (Monday 22 January 1894).

The British Newspaper Archive, *Aberdeen Journal* (Friday 26 July 1901).

The British Newspaper Archive, *Aberdeen Journal* (Thursday 4 July 1901).

The British Newspaper Archive, *Arbroath Herald and Advertiser for the Montrose Burghs* (Thursday 21 May 1896).

The British Newspaper Archive, *Bath Chronicle and Weekly Gazette* (Thursday 12 February 1885).

The British Newspaper Archive, *Bedfordshire Times and Independent* (Saturday 8 April 1893).

The British Newspaper Archive, *Belfast Morning News* (Wednesday 14 May 1862).

The British Newspaper Archive, *Burnley Express* (Saturday 16 August 1890).

The British Newspaper Archive, *Cambridge Daily News* (Thursday 19 April 1917).

The British Newspaper Archive, *Cheltenham Chronicle* (Tuesday 30 March 1858).

The British Newspaper Archive, *Dover Express* (Friday 7 November 1890).

The British Newspaper Archive, *Dundee Evening Telegraph* (Monday 17 May 1886).

The British Newspaper Archive, *Dundee Evening Telegraph* (Saturday 04 April 1891).

The British Newspaper Archive, *Dundee Evening Telegraph* (Saturday 17 November 1888).

The British Newspaper Archive, *Dundee Evening Telegraph* (Thursday 20 March 1879).

The British Newspaper Archive, *Dundee Evening Telegraph* (Tuesday 5 December 1893).

The British Newspaper Archive, *Dundee Evening Telegraph* (Wednesday 10 April 1901).

The British Newspaper Archive, *Dundee Evening Telegraph*, (Thursday 20 March 1879).

The British Newspaper Archive, *Edinburgh Evening News* (Friday 1 May 1874).

The British Newspaper Archive, *Edinburgh Evening News* (Tuesday 26 December 1893).

The British Newspaper Archive, *Evening Telegraph, Scotland* (6 August 1903).

The British Newspaper Archive, *Gloucestershire Echo* (Tuesday 15 August 1893).

The British Newspaper Archive, *Grantham Journal* (Saturday 2 March 1895).

The British Newspaper Archive, *Hartlepool Mail* (Friday 12 June 1885).

The British Newspaper Archive, *Hartlepool Mail* (Monday 16 March 1896).

The British Newspaper Archive, *Hull Daily Mail* (Friday 10 May 1889).

The British Newspaper Archive, *Hull Daily Mail* (Tuesday 14 June 1910).

The British Newspaper Archive, *Inverness Courier* (Thursday 23 October 1851).

The British Newspaper Archive, *Leeds Mercury* (Saturday 7 December, 1872).

The British Newspaper Archive, *Liverpool Daily Post* (Tuesday 18 February 1862).

The British Newspaper Archive, *Liverpool Daily Post* (Tuesday 19 November 1867).

The British Newspaper Archive, *Liverpool Echo* (Friday 11 January 1918).

The British Newspaper Archive, *London Daily News* (Tuesday 28 April 1896).

The British Newspaper Archive, *London Standard* (Wednesday 12 July 1899).

The British Newspaper Archive, *Luton Times and Advertiser* (Saturday 11 November 1876).

The British Newspaper Archive, *Manchester Courier and Lancashire General Advertiser* (Saturday 1 February 1902).

The British Newspaper Archive, *Manchester Courier and Lancashire General Advertiser* (Saturday 29 October 1898).

The British Newspaper Archive, *Manchester Guardian* (16 May 1887).

The British Newspaper Archive, *Morning Post* (Monday 10 August 1868).

The British Newspaper Archive, *Morpeth Herald*, (Saturday 24 July 1886).

The British Newspaper Archive, *North Devon Journal* (3 August 1916).

The British Newspaper Archive, *Northampton Mercury*, (Saturday 14 September 1889).

The British Newspaper Archive, *Nottingham Evening Post* (Wednesday 23 September 1891).

The British Newspaper Archive, *Pall Mall Gazette* (Thursday 21 November 1889).

The British Newspaper Archive, *Sheffield Independent* (Monday 15 March 1897).

The British Newspaper Archive, *Southern Reporter and Cork Commercial Courier* (Friday 05 February 1858).

The British Newspaper Archive, *Sunderland Daily Echo and Shipping Gazette*, (Monday 8 February 1886).

The British Newspaper Archive, *The Gloucester Citizen* (Thursday 18 September 1884).

The British Newspaper Archive, *The Graphic* (Saturday 4 May 1872).

The British Newspaper Archive, *The Manchester Courier and Lancashire General Advertiser* (1902).

The British Newspaper Archive, *Western Daily Press* (Saturday 5 January 1889).

The British Newspaper Archive, *Western Daily Press* (Tuesday 25 March, 1873).

The British Newspaper Archive, *Western Daily Press* Thursday 19 September 1895.

The British Newspaper Archive, *Western Gazette* (Friday 20 January 1899).

The British Newspaper Archive, *Whitby Gazette* (Friday 6 April 1917).

The British Newspaper Archive, *Gloucester Citizen* (Thursday 13 September 1900).

The British Newspaper Archive, *Manchester Courier and Lancashire General Advertiser* (Tuesday 26 October 1886).

The British Newspaper Archive, *Sheffield Daily Telegraph* (Saturday 7 August 1880).

The British Newspaper Archive, *Sheffield Daily Telegraph* (Tuesday 16 June 1874).

The British Newspaper Archive, *Sunderland Daily Echo and Shipping Gazette* (Tuesday 18 September 1900).

The British Newspaper Archive, *Taunton Courier, and Western Advertiser* (Saturday 26 November 1938).

The British Newspaper Archive, *Yorkshire Post and Leeds Intelligencer* (Friday 12 March 1937).

The Carlyle Letters online Thomas Carlyle to Alexander Carlyle, 8 December, 1848.

The Church of England Magazine, Vol LXXI (S. D. Ewins and Sons, 1871).

The English note-books of Nathaniel Hawthorne volume I, (Leipzig, 1871).

The Englishwoman in India: information for ladies on their outfit, furniture etc., 1864, by a lady resident, (Smith, Elder and Co., London, 1864).

The Englishwoman in India: information for ladies on their outfit, furniture etc., 1864, by a lady resident, (Smith, Elder and Co., London, 1864).

The Family Oracle of Health, Volume II (1824).

The handbook of dining, based chiefly upon the Physiologie du goût of Brillat-Savarin (Brown, Green, Longmans & Roberts, Longman, London, 1859).

The London City Mission Magazine Vol. XXXIII (Seeley, Jackson and Halliday, London, 1868).

The London Quarterly Review, Volume LVI, (Theodore Foster, New York, 1838).

The Magazine of Domestic Economy, Volume 2 (W. S. Orr & Co, London, 1837).

The Official Guide to the London and North Western Railway : The Royal Mail West Coast Route between England, Scotland, Wales, and Ireland : also between the continents of Europe and America. London (Cassell, 1894).

The Old Bailey, Ref: t18370130-607, James Mason, Theft, simple larceny, 30 January 1837.

The Old Bailey, Ref: t18370403-920 John Rixon, Bridget Rixon, Mary Ann Rixon, miscellaneous, other, 3 April 1837.

The Shorter Novels of Charles Dickens (Wordsworth Editions, Hertfordshire, 2004).

The Steward's Handbook and Guide to Party Catering (Jessup Whitehead, Chicago, 1889).

The Visitor's Guide to Manchester; and Handbook to the Attractions of the City and Suburbs Pub (W. Kent and Co. London, 1857).

The Win-The-War Cookery Book (Amalgamated Press Ltd, London, 1917).

The Women's Library, Papers of Ethel DM Robson, 1910-1912, Ref No. 7EDR

Theodore Hoppen, K., *The Mid-Victorian Generation, 1846-1886* (Oxford University Press, Oxford.2000).

Thiselton Dyer, T. F., *British popular customs, present and past; illustrating the social and domestic manners of the people: arranged according to the calendar of the year* (William Clowes and Sons Ltd., London, 1875).

Timbs, J., *The Mirror of Literature, Amusement, and Instruction*, Volumes 37-38 (Hugh Cunningham, London 1841).

Trubek, A. B., *Haute Cuisine: How the French Invented the Culinary Profession* (University of Pennsylvania Press, 2000).

Verdo, N., *Rural Women Workers in Nineteenth-Century England: Gender, Work and Wages* (Boydell Press, Suffolk, 2002).

Victoria and Albert Museum Survey of London: Volume 38, South Kensington Museums Area. Originally published by (London County Council, London, 1975).

Wagner, J., *A History of Migration from Germany to Canada, 1850–1939* (UBC Press, Canada, 2011).

Walker, H., (ed.), *Oxford Symposium on Food and Cookery 1991: Public Eating : Proceedings*, (Oxford Symposium, 1991).

Ward, J. T., *The Factory Movement, 1830–1855*, (Macmillan, London 1962).

Woodworth, S., (ed.), *The Ladies' Literary Cabinet*, Volume One, (Woodworth and Heustis, 1819).

Woolf, V., *Orlando* (Oxford: Oxford University Press, 1992).

Wydham, H., *The Army School of Cookery*, (1903).

Yates, L. H., *The Model Kitchen* (Longmans, Green and Co., 1905).

Youmans, E. A., (ed)., *Lessons in Cookery, Hand-Book of the National Training School for Cookery*, American edition, (D. Apleton and Company, New York, 1879).

Web Resources

British Library

British Newspaper Archive <http://www.britishnewspaperarchive.co.uk>

Charles Booth, Online Archive http://booth.lse.ac.uk/cgi-bin/do.plsub=search_catalogue_pages&argo=street+seller&arg1=and).

National Archives <www.nationalarchives.gov.uk>

The Carlyle Letters online http://carlyleletters.dukejournals.org/

The Proceedings of the Old Bailey <www.oldbaileyonline.org>

The Women's Library, London School of Economics <http://www.lse.ac.uk/library/collections/featuredCollections/womensLibrary>

INDEX